The Encyclopedia Of One Liners
by
Henny Youngman

Edited by
Ed Shanaphy

Ballymote Books, A Division
of Ballymote Inc.
223 Katonah Avenue, Katonah, NY 10536

Library Of Congress Catalog Card Number: 89-80042

TABLE OF CONTENTS

Take Henny Youngman . . .

Henny Youngman has been a stand-up comic for over sixty years. One of the most popular and best-loved comedians of this century, Mr. Youngman has presented his brand of humor to audiences throughout the world. Dubbed "The King Of The One Liners," by newspaperman Walter Winchell, Henny Youngman never stops testing new lines and jokes to friends, relatives, even people on the street. His collection is vast, and his ability to recall any of his lines is prodigious.

Born in London in 1906, he came to America with his family when he was 6 months old. He eventually began a professional career as a printer in a five and dime store. "But I didn't have any confidence in a business that was run by a guy like me. However, if things went sour in comedy, I could always get a job printing. Or I could be out of two jobs at once! Which meant that I would be twice as broke."

His father started him on the violin. " He wanted me to be a Heifetz." As a band leader of the "Swanee Syncopaters," he used to do some clowning on the fiddle. "One night a comic didn't show up at the nightclub and the boss asked if I could help out. So I went on." Comedian Pat Henry once made this remark about Henny's violin playing: "Henny's the only guy who when he opens his violin case, the audience hopes he's got a machine gun in there."

He was working, sometimes starving, until his big break in 1937, when he was booked on the radio show of Kate Smith. Youngman had been working as social director at a Catskills hotel and performing in synagogues and otherwise gaining experience, when Kate Smith heard him. Her manager Ted Collins (who took 20 percent of the fees paid to all guest performers) booked him on the show and Youngman was a smash. Indeed, he was allowed so much time, the other scheduled guest -- Franchot Tone -- didn't appear at all. Youngman was booked for two years, and he was forced to hire writers to come up with new material.

He employs no writers now. His mental backlog of thousands of jokes (he tells between 200 and 250 in 45 minutes) is sufficient for one-night stands. It was while he was with Kate Smith that his most famous joke evolved; instead of punch-line, it has a punch-word: "Please." Henny was in the writer's room trying to get his act together. His wife entered; she needed eight tickets, which he obtained from friendly ushers ("I used to slip them a couple of bucks to save tickets for me"). Harassed, he blurted, "Take my wife, please." People overheard, and immediately started voicing the phrase to Henny as one of those involuntary gags. Youngman knows what's funny. It didn't take long until the gag was totally voluntary. It was the title of his authorized 1973 biography.

His most famous line, "Take my wife . . . please!" has been included in Bartlett's Book Of Famous Quotations. At 82 years of age he continues to be in constant demand. Still appearing on television, at conventions and sales meetings, even on college campuses where he is being "discovered" by another generation, Henny says, "Just give me a job and I'll play it."

"Call me at any time. Got a phone in my car. Hit a phone booth last week."

. . .Please!

101 of Henny's Favorite Insults

I looked high and low for you, I didn't look low enough.

I don't believe in reincarnation, but what were you when you were alive?

Don't move -- I want to forget you just the way you are.

If they can make penicillin out of moldy bread, surely they can make something out of you.

How can you talk all night without stopping to think?

If you have your life to live over again, don't do it.

Was that suit made to order? "Yes." Where were you at the time?

You have the Midas touch. Everything you touch turns into a muffler.

If you had your life to live over again, -- do it overseas.

He was born at home but when his mother saw him she went to the hospital.

He spends money like water, drip, drip, drip.

I'd put a curse on you, but somebody beat me to it.

I know this man through thick and thick.

Four drunks looked at him, they took the pledge.

He was born on April 2nd -- a day too late.

He's a real good egg, and you know where eggs come from.

Are you naturally stupid or did a Cuban hijack your brain?

I'd like to say we're glad you're here -- I'd like to say it . . .

You look like a talent scout for a cemetery.

Someday you'll go too far, and I hope you'll stay there.

He's hoping for a lucky stroke -- his rich uncle's.

When you get up in the morning, who puts you together?

At least he gives his wife something to live for -- a divorce.

For short people: I've been looking low and low for you.

May we have the pleasure of your absence?

What got you out of the woodwork?

I can't forget the first time I laid eyes on you -- and don't think I haven't tried.

I'm going to name my first ulcer after you.

Why don't you step outside for a few years?

Why don't you go to a window and lean out too far?

I know you have to be somebody -- but why do you have to be you?

I never forget a face, and in your case I'll remember both of them.

You appear to be as happy as if you were in your right mind.

It's good to see you. It means you're not behind my back.

You know, I'd like to send you a Valentine, but I haven't figured out how to wrap lace around a time bomb.

You're the kind of person I would like to have over when I have the measles.

Was the ground cold when you crawled out this morning?

I remember you -- you're a graduate of the Don Rickles Charm School.

Who shines your suits?

Sit down; you make the place look shabby!

I'm paid to make an idiot out of myself. Why do you do it for free?

There's only one thing that keeps me from breaking you in half; I don't want two of you around.

If there's ever a price on your head, take it.

If I were you, I'd return that face to Abbey rents.

Are you naturally stupid or are you waiting for a brain transplant?

He has more crust than a pie factory.

He doesn't get ulcers, he gives them.

He should have been an undertaker -- he has no use for anyone living.

Some people bring happiness wherever they go. You bring happiness whenever you go.

There's a pair of shoes with three heels.

Look at him, sex takes a holiday.

You remind me of some of those new dances, one, two, three Jerk.

If it pays to be ignorant, why are you always broke?

Zsa Zsa Gabor has been married so many times she has rice marks on her face.

Mickey Rooney has been married so many times he has a wash and wear tuxedo.

He had a nightmare last night, he dreamed that Dolly Parton was his Mother and he was a bottle baby.

Let me tell you about our guest of honor. Never has a man been more sworn at -- more spit at -- more maligned -- and rightfully so!

There's one good thing about being bald -- it's neat.

He dresses like an unmade bed!

You're perfect for hot weather. You leave me cold.

He doesn't have an enemy in the world -- he's outlived them all.

I think the world of you -- and you know what condition the world is in today.

There's only one thing wrong with you. You're visible.

I understand you throw yourself into everything you undertake; please go and dig a deep well.

Why don't you sit down and rest your brains?

I'm planning to invite you to my party -- there's always room for one bore.

There's a train leaving in an hour. Be under it!

I'll never forget the first time we met -- but I'm trying.

He was the only man ever kicked out of the army for looking like a one-man slum.

If you'll stop telling lies about me I'll stop telling the truth about you.

I don't know what makes you tick, but I hope it's a time bomb.

Next time you give your clothes away -- stay in them.

Why don't you start neglecting your appearance? Then maybe it'll go away.

I enjoy talking to you. My mind needs a rest.

It's nice hearing from you -- next time send me a post card.

You have a nice personality -- but not for a human being.

Look, I'm not going to engage in a battle of wits with you -- I never attack anyone who is unarmed.

I'd like to introduce you to some friends of mine. I want to break off with them.

Is your family happy? Or do you go home at night?

I wish somebody would kidnap you -- but who would they contact?

Someday you'll find yourself and will you be disappointed.

I like you -- I have no taste, but I like you.

When the grim reaper comes for you he'll have a big smile on his face.

There's a guy who lives alone and looks it.

Do me a favor -- on your way home, make it a point to jaywalk.

I'd like to run into you again -- sometime when you're walking and I'm driving.

His friends don't know what to give him for Christmas. What do you give a guy who's had everybody?

If Moses had known you, there would positively have been another commandment.

The more I think of you the less I think of you.

He lights up a room when he leaves it.

What do you give a guy who has nothing?

Lots of people owe a lot to him -- ulcers, nausea, diarrhea.

Don't sell him short. In college he was a four letter man and they called him bleep.

I love that man -- very few people know this man was born an only twin.

He was a real gentleman. He reminds me of Saint Paul -- one of the dullest towns in America.

The thing he does for his friends can be counted on his little finger.

You have a ready wit. Let me know when it's ready.

If you were alive, you'd be a very sick man.

The last time he was in a hospital, he got get-well cards from all the nurses.

We don't want to make this afternoon too long. Our guest of honor has to get home because this is the night he gets his annual urge -- and his wife gets her annual headache.

10,000
One-Liners
for
Every Occasion

Absence

Absinthe makes the heart glow fonder.

Accidents

The best insurance against car accidents is a Sunday afternoon nap.

Most accidents occur in the home or on the highway; the surest way to be safe is to leave home and sell your car.

With all of today's attractive accident insurance policies, a man can't afford to die a natural death.

A lot of accidents are the result of only looking one way before crossing a one-way street.

A foot on a brake is worth two in the grave.

Accidents will happen. That is why there are so many different kinds of salad.

First impressions are often lasting, especially when they are made by car bumpers.

The only way you can get into a hospital quickly these days is by accident.

An accident is a surprise arranged by nature.

One good way to insure yourself against auto accidents is to take the plane.

I've been in a bad accident--I got hit by a falling stock market.

After you've heard two eyewitness accounts of an auto accident, you begin to worry about history.

Accountants

Show me an accountant, and I'll show you an acrobat who juggles figures and does a balancing act.

Actors

To be an actor and get paid for it is one way of turning conceit into profit.

Adam and Eve

If Eve had lived today she would have looked around for a smaller leaf.

The first woman with a mind of her own was Eve, and look what happened to her.

Adam's experience shows that it's not wise to eat an apple; it should be drunk as cider.

Adam and Eve were a very sociable couple. They were seen in all the best places.

Eve was the first person who ate herself out of house and home.

The only indispensable man was Adam.

Man was made before woman to give him time to think of an answer to her first question.

Adolescence

Adolescence is that period when a young man can show you the best crop of hair he'll ever own.

Adolescence is the awkward age in the life of a youngster. They're too old for an allowance and too young for a credit card.

A child is growing up when he stops asking where he came from and starts refusing to tell you where he's going.

Adolescence is a period of rapid changes. Between the ages of twelve and seventeen, for example, a parent ages as much as twenty years.

Adolescence is the period between hopscotch and real scotch.

Adolescence is when a girl begins to powder and a boy begins to puff.

Adolescence is the period when girls stop making faces at boys and start making eyes.

Adolescence is when your daughter starts to put on lipstick and your son begins wiping it off.

Adults

Adults are really not wiser than children; they're just more cunning.

Advertising

Advertising is like seduction--and some of it is a little less subtle.

Advertising helps raise the standard of living by raising the standard of longing.

Advertising encourages people to live beyond their means, but then, so does marriage.

Advertising has put an end to the power of the most powerful adjectives.

Advertising men can give a favorable image to anything except themselves.

Henny tries out a one-liner on Frank Sinatra and Milton Berle

Advice

Anybody can give advice--the trouble comes in finding someone interested in using it.

When a man asks you for advice you can figure he isn't married.

Both medicine and advice are easy to prescribe but hard to take.

Advice to men over forty: keep an open mind and a closed refrigerator.

Some people give you such good advice that it's hard to reject it without feeling guilty.

If you don't take your lawyer's advice, do you still have to pay him?

Behind every successful man is a woman who didn't bother him with advice.

Advice is like medicine--the correct dosage works wonders, but an overdose can be disastrous.

The best time to give your children advice is while they are still young enough to believe you know what you're talking about.

Most of us find it difficult to take advice from others who need it more than we do.

Advice is wonderful. Take it and you can make the same mistakes everybody else does.

People who give you free advice usually charge too much.

When some people give you a piece of advice, you wonder what's wrong with it.

Age

The best way to tell a woman's age isn't a very good one.

Middle age is when the girl you smile at thinks you are one of her father's friends.

Getting old is merely a matter of feeling your corns more than you feel your oats.

Middle age is when you're just as young as ever, but it takes a lot more effort.

Old age is when you find yourself using one bend-over to pick up two things.

Middle age is when a man is as young as he feels after trying to prove it.

A man has reached middle-age when he is warned to slow down by his doctor, instead of the police.

Some people grow up and spread cheer. Others just grow up and spread.

Middle age is when you start for home about the same time you used to start for somewhere else.

Life begins at forty--but you'll miss a lot of fun if you wait that long.

Adolescence is when you think you'll live forever. Middle age is when you wonder how you've lasted so long.

The difference in the aging process in men and women is that men get sadder and wiser but women get sadder and wider.

An old-timer is one who remembers when we counted our blessings instead of our calories.

Middle-age is when the only thing that can lead you down the garden path is a beautiful seed catalogue.

The most dangerous age for women is poundage.

By the time we learn to watch our step, we're not stepping out very much.

Setting a good example for your children takes all the fun out of middle age.

You're middle-aged when your clothes no longer fit--and it's you who needs the alterations.

My mother-in-law is going to live to a gripe old age.

Maybe it's true that life begins at forty. But everything else starts to wear out, fall out or spread out.

You've reached the difficult age when you're too tired to work and too poor to quit.

The best thing about getting old is that all those things you couldn't have when you were young you no longer want.

Middle age begins when you ask the barber to thicken it a little on the top.

You're getting old when you don't care where your wife goes--just so you don't have to go along.

The best way to tell a woman's age is when she's not around.

As I grow older I find that I don't have to avoid temptation any longer--now temptation avoids me.

Age makes wine worth more and women less.

When a man reaches middle-age, he still has a lot of get up and go--his hair, teeth, and virility all get up and go.

Middle age is when you think your barber charges too much for a haircut.

One of the greatest pleasures of growing old is the freedom you enjoy from life insurance salesmen.

Middle age is the time in life when a woman's curves turn into circles.

Middle age is the one dominated by the middle.

Middle age is when a man has more on his mind, but less on his head.

I've reached the age where if I go all out I end up all in.

The only way a middle-aged woman can hold her school-girl figure is in fond memory.

We call it middle age because that's where it shows first.

The reason some people become old before their time is because they had a time before they got old.

My wife doesn't lie about her age--she just says she's as old as I am, and then lies about my age.

You've reached old age when the gleam in your eye is just the sun on your bifocals.

The best thing to save for old age is yourself.

Middle age is when a man realizes he has to mend his ways if he doesn't want to come apart at the seams.

Middle age is when you get enough exercise just avoiding people who think you should have more.

Whiskey improves with age, but age doesn't improve with whiskey.

A woman has reached middle age when her girdle pinches and the men don't.

People are like plants--some go to seed with age, and others to pot.

Middle age has set in when you become exhausted by your teenager telling you how he spent an evening.

Nothing ages a woman faster than the struggle of trying to remain young.

A man has reached middle age when he meets an old flame and she doesn't seem too hot.

Two things a woman always underestimates are her age, and the time it will take her to get ready.

Air conditioning

The best thing about an air conditioner is that the neighbors can't borrow it.

I gave my girl an air conditioner and she gave me the breeze.

Gracious living is when you have the house air-conditioned, and then load the yard with chairs, lounges and an outdoor oven so you can spend all your time in the hot sun.

A millionaire is a man who travels between his air-conditioned home and his air-conditioned office in an air-conditioned car, and then pays $50 to go over to the steam room at the club and sweat.

Air

The air is about the only remaining thing that's free, and it is becoming dangerous to breathe.

Air pollution is turning Mother Nature prematurely gray.

Airlines

The airlines try, but the best food was on the old railroad day coach when the nice lady in the next seat shared her shoebox full of fried chicken.

Show me an airline stewardess, and I'll show you a plane Jane.

Airline travel is hours of boredom interrupted by moments of stark terror.

Before pollution people used to get airsick only on planes.

It would have helped a lot if the pioneers had located cities closer to airports.

If the average congressman found himself on an airplane about to crash he would take time to appoint a landing committee.

The trouble with traveling by airplane is that you can't walk out on a dull movie.

Alarm Clocks

Some men have alarm clocks; I have my wife's elbow.

Happiness is not setting the alarm clock on Saturday night.

The only thing worse than hearing the alarm clock in the morning is not hearing it.

The trouble with my alarm clock is that it wakes me up just in time to go back to sleep.

Show me an alarm clock, and I'll show you a mechanism used to scare the daylights into you.

Alaska

It's so cold in Alaska that when I was there, a snowman knocked at my door and asked for a hot-water bottle.

Alcoholics

An alcoholic is a man who has worked his way from bottoms up.

Man is the only machine that can be lubricated with alcohol.

You're on the way to becoming an alcoholic if you'll drink with anyone to anyone.

If it wasn't for my neighbor's red nose, bloodshot eyes and stagger--you'd never know he's an alcoholic.

Gasoline and alcohol don't mix--but try drinking them straight.

Alimony

Alimony is a case of wife and debt.

Alimony is the fee you have to pay for name dropping.

Alimony has one advantage. A husband no longer has to bring his paycheck home to his wife--he can mail it to her.

Marriage is always a gamble for a woman because she never knows in advance how much the alimony will be.

Alimony is repossessed love that one must still pay out on the installment plan.

Ever notice that most of the battles of the sexes are over alimony?

Alimony is when husbands who were bounced have to send checks that are good.

It's better to have loved and lost--provided you don't have to pay alimony.

Paying alimony is like paying the installments on a wrecked car.

Alimony is a splitting headache.

Alimony is different from take-home pay; it's leave-home pay.

Some women begin to figure on alimony before the honeymoon is over.

Because of the alimony laws, marriage is the only business that pays money to one of its partners after it fails.

Alimony is when the bride continues to get wedding gifts after the divorce.

Allowances

An allowance is the bribe parents give their children to be able to live with them.

Amateurs

Show me an amateur, and I'll show you a person who is always willing to give you the benefit of his inexperience.

Amateur contests give people with no talent a chance to prove it.

Ambition

Ambition may be all right but it sure can get a fellow into a lot of hard work.

America

America is still the land of opportunity. Where else could you earn enough to owe so much?

Americanism means finding fault with other countries for not solving their problems, while we wait without hope for the Government to solve ours.

America is a land where in the middle of winter women buy spring clothes for summer romances with fall guys.

America is one place where the people have complete control over how they pay their taxes--cash, check, or money order.

Americans are an idealistic people, and we'll make any sacrifice for a cause so long as it won't hurt business.

People in foreign countries are not really rude; they're just trying to imitate American tourists.

Over 40 million Americans move each year. There must be an easier way to get rid of the junk they can't bear to throw away.

Americans don't mind spending their money as long as they know it isn't going for taxes.

Only Americans have mastered the art of being prosperous though broke.

My son is a typical American teenager: he's 34.

Ancestors

The person who boasts about his ancestors believes in going forward by backing up.

Angels

An angel with wings is not as desirable as an angel with arms.

Anger

Swallowing angry words is much easier than having to eat them.

Animals

Nuclear weapons have made man the only animal that man now fears.

Show me a woman who thinks all men are beasts, and I'll show you a woman who would just love to be an animal trainer.

Anniversaries

The biggest surprise the average husband can give his wife on their anniversary is to remember it.

The silver wedding anniversary is the day on which the couple celebrate the fact that the first twenty-five years of their married life is finally over.

An anniversary is the day on which a husband behaves as he always should.

An anniversary is the day a man never remembers and his wife never lets him forget he forgot.

Many a man who misses his anniversary catches it later.

Answers

Answers are what we have for other people's problems.

Antiques

Have you noticed how people who prize an antique for its beauty suddenly find it unsightly when it turns out to be a fake?

I know a fellow in the antique business. To make sure all of his stock is authentic he makes it all himself.

Antiques aren't always as old as they are cracked up to be.

An Antique isn't always as old as it's cracked up to be.

The trouble with most antique shops is that their prices are so modern.

Show me an antique, and I'll show you a dear old thing.

Anxiety

It requires a great deal of inexperience to be beyond the reach of anxiety.

Apartments

The walls in my apartment are so thin that I recently asked a visitor a question and got three answers.

I live in a studio apartment. That's an apartment where, if you are in the living room and want to go into the bedroom, you stay where you are.

Today apartment houses are built with every known convenience, except low rent.

The walls of my apartment are so thin--I asked my wife a question and got three answers.

I finally figured out how to make a landlord paint your apartment--move out.

My apartment is so cold that everytime I open the door the light goes on.

Apathy

One good thing about apathy is you don't have to exert yourself to show you're sincere about it.

Apiary

Show me an apiary, and I'll show you a bee flat.

Apology

Never refuse to accept an apology; you won't be offered more than one in a lifetime, and you can keep it as a rarity.

Appendix

An appendix is what you have taken out before the doctor decides it is your gall bladder.

Appetite

Appetite is a troublesome thing: if you're too rich, you suffer from lack of it; if you're too poor, you suffer from excess of it.

Appointments

The only thing that makes my wife late is an appointment.

Archaeologists

Show me an archaeologist, and I'll show you a man who practices skull duggery.

Archeology is the science that proves you can't keep a good man down.

An architect makes an old house look better just by talking about the cost of a new one.

Argument

When all is said and done makes a dandy time to quit arguing.

When I win an argument with my wife, the argument is not over.

Any man who argues with his wife and wins--loses.

The most difficult part of an argument is not defending one's position, but knowing it.

Anybody who thinks talk is cheap has never argued with a traffic cop.

The worst mistake a man can make in arguing with his wife is arguing with his wife.

After winning an argument with his wife, the wisest thing a man can do is apologize.

There is nothing so annoying as arguing with somebody who knows what he is talking about.

An experienced married man is one who can tell when his wife comes to the end of one argument and begins another.

The quickest way to end an argument between two people is to take sides.

It's a fine thing to be a gentleman, but it's always a handicap in an argument.

Never argue with your doctor--he has inside information.

Armistice

An armistice is proof that truce is stronger than friction.

Army

Show me an army general, and I'll show you an attention getter.

Aspirin

A rule of thumb in the matter of medical advice is to take everything any doctor says with a grain of aspirin.

Aspirin is a miracle drug--a year's supply usually disappears in a month.

Astronauts

Women would never make good astronauts. They'd all refuse to wear the same hat.

An astronaut is a man who qualifies for traveling in outer space without the aid of a clergyman.

I wouldn't want to be an astronaut. As far as I'm concerned, there's no space like home.

An astronaut is a spaceman who finds a place in the sun by reaching for the moon.

Atheists

Now the atheists have an answer to Dial-a-Prayer. When you dial their number, nobody answers.

Bob Newhart, Steve Lawrence, Johnny Carson, Henny, Don Rickles,
Milton Berle at a Friars fest

Show me an atheist, and I'll show you a man who can create his own holidays.

The trouble with atheism is that it has no future.

Athletes

Athletes are not stupid. You have to be pretty smart to get people to pay to see something as boring as sports.

Attic

Nobody who can read is ever successful at cleaning out the attic.

Talk about embarrassing moments--I was rummaging through the attic and I came across my wife's love letters--and they were dated last week.

Auctions

Anyone who thinks that talk is cheap doesn't go to auctions.

Autos

I solved the parking problem, I bought a parked car.

My wife wanted a foreign convertible. I bought her a rickshaw.

If you don't like the way women drive, get off the sidewalk.

The cost of any auto repair is equal to the sum of the parts, your worst fears, and double the mechanic's estimate.

The reason the automobile is so popular today is that you can drive one without owning it.

Automation

Automation has a bright side. Look at all those new jobs which are created to keep track of the ones that are lost.

Automation is a system where electronic devices act just like human beings by doing things without using any intelligence.

Automation has taken over everywhere. The only thing people do with their hands any more is scratch themselves.

Automation is controlling the world: if you get to your job without being hit by a machine, you find that another machine has replaced you.

Automation is man's effort to make work so easy that woman can do it all.

Automation will make more jobs for everyone because fewer people will be able to do all the work.

Average

I don't mind being average, because it means I'm as close to the top as I am to the bottom.

Avon Lady

The Avon lady in my neighborhood is a ding-dong.

Babies

What do you call a Jewish baby who isn't circumsized? A girl!

Babies are such a nice way to start people.

Feeding a baby is one sure way of finding out how badly your suit spots.

A baby born during a hurricane finds out much too early what life is like.

Troubles are a lot like babies--they grow larger if you nurse them.

Today a premature baby is one that's born before its parents are married.

When you think of the government debt the next generation must pay off, it's no wonder a baby yells when it's born.

Our new baby keeps my wife from having an eight-hour day, and me from having an eight-hour night.

I'm convinced that new-born babies can think. Why else do they yell the moment they see the kind of world they're in?

The only time my wife suffers in silence is when she's waiting for me to get up to take care of the baby.

A small town is a place where babies never arrive unexpectedly.

Our baby has stopped being an armful and is fast growing into quite a handful.

Few mistakes can be made by a mother-in-law who is willing to baby-sit.

A family that has no leftover problem probably has a baby sitter.

The most economical time to hire a babysitter is when the refrigerator is about empty.

A baby-sitter is a teen-ager who gets two dollars an hour to eat five dollars' worth of your food.

We have a babysitter who feeds the baby at 10, 12, and 2--and herself at 9, 11, and 1.

A baby sitter is a teenage girl you hire to let your children do whatever they want.

Bachelors

A bachelor doesn't like to hear that phrase "To halve and to hold."

Give a bachelor enough rope and he'll detect the noose.

A bachelor is a man who can keep his foot out of a trap--particularly his own.

Bachelors have no idea what married bliss is--and that's true of a lot of married men, too.

A married man is a bachelor who didn't notice when a girl closed the escape hatch.

There would be more contented bachelors in the world if all the matchmakers worked in match factories.

A smart bachelor stops up his ears when a woman's voice has a ring in it.

Fools rush in where bachelors fear to wed.

Show me a bachelor, and I'll show you guy with bags under his eyes and on his mind.

Bachelors are rightfully taxed more than married people--it's not fair that some men should be happier than others.

Give a bachelor an inch and he'll take alarm.

A bachelor is a guy who thinks planned parenthood is living with your mother.

A bachelor should learn to sew on his own buttons and darn his socks--he may marry some day.

A bachelor always knows how to hold a woman's hand so that she doesn't get a grip on him.

A bachelor is a man who can be miss-led only so far.

A bachelor is a fellow who doesn't think the bonds of matrimony are a good investment.

Show me an altar, and I'll show you a place where a bachelor loses control.

A bachelor is a man who has a cool head and cold feet.

A confirmed bachelor is a guy who thinks that the only justified marriage was the one which produced him.

Next to staying a bachelor, getting married is best.

Show me a bachelor, and I'll show you a man who prefers to cook his own goose.

Show me a confirmed bachelor and I'll show you a knight in shunning armor.

Show me a bachelor, and I'll show you a dame dropper.

A bachelor is a fellow who can take a nap on top of a bedspread.

A bachelor is a man who leans toward a woman--but not far enough to fall.

A bachelor has nobody to share his troubles with--but then, why should a bachelor have any troubles?

Any man who dies a bachelor has never completed his education.

A bachelor is a man who has only his own dishes to do.

To a bachelor, marriage means domain poisoning.

A bachelor is a man who gave up waiting for the right girl and is making the best of the wrong ones.

Show me a bachelor, and I'll show you a man who is footloose and fiancee free.

Give a bachelor an inch and he'll take flight.

Back

The week I got married I developed a back problem. I wished I was back to being a bachelor.

Back Fence

The back fence is the shortest distance between two gossips.

Backache

A backache is man's greatest labor saving device.

Backseat Driver

A backseat driver is generally a woman whose husband drives by ear.

Baking

And then there is the sadistic Chinese baker. He makes misfortune cookies.

Then there was the town that was so weird it held a bakeoff in a crematorium.

Ballet

Part of the popularity of the ballet today is the fact that married men are able to watch a number of ladies who, for over two hours, never say a word.

Bananas

My wife went on a banana and coconut diet. She didn't lose any weight, but she can climb a tree like crazy.

Banks

Banks are peculiar institutions that urge you to save as much as possible of what you earn and urge you to borrow as much as you can spend so you can spend more than you make.

If money doesn't grow on trees, how come banks continue to sprout branches?

Savings banks operate on the principle that everyone should save because spending costs money.

A bank is the place you borrow money from when you can't get it from a friend.

A bank account is a lot like toothpaste: easy to take out but hard to put back.

Bars

I know a fellow with a real drinking problem--his wife insists on accompanying him to the bar.

Many a man goes into a bar for an eye-opener and comes out blind.

There's a bar directly across the street from my brother-in-law's house, so he painted his own crosswalk.

Barbers

If all your barber does is talk your ear off, you've got plenty to be thankful for.

What makes a barber think he can mind two businesses at once?

Any man who argues with his barber should have his head examined.

A good barber and a good tailor can take years off a man's life--but you can't fool a flight of stairs.

As far as barbers are concerned, they can prove that two heads are always better than one.

Bargains

Women may be the weaker sex, but not at a bargain counter.

Some wives are bargain hunters, while others only buy the things they need.

It's easy to tell when you've got a bargain. It doesn't fit.

Today a bargain is anything that is only moderately overpriced.

A bargain today is something so reasonably priced that they won't take it back when you find out what's wrong with it.

A bargain is anything you can buy today at yesterday's prices.

An example of collective bargaining is a man discussing clothes with his wife and teenage daughters.

Bartenders

Show me a bartender's guide and I'll show you a stirring account.

You're getting old when you spend more time talking to your druggist than you do to your bartender.

A bartender is the only psychiatrist who never tells anyone to give up drinking.

Baseball

The cream of a baseball team is either in the pitcher or in the batter.

If you want to see a baseball game in the worst way--take your wife along.

Driving is a lot like baseball--it's the number of times you get home safely that counts.

Bathtub

In winter you can't get the kids into a bathtub, and in summer you can't get them out of a pool.

Why doesn't someone invent a double-deck bathtub for people who like to sing duets?

There is good in everything: if men took baths in the olden days, nobody would have invented perfume.

Bathing Suits

With bathing suits being what they are today, the girls who complain they have nothing to wear are usually wearing it.

The bathing suits on this year's scene must be believed to be seen.

My wife always wants to get the most for her money, except when she buys a bathing suit.

Bathroom

The most frightening horror tales, are those told by bathroom scales.

Time is relative. How long a few minutes are depends on whether you are in the bathroom or out.

Talk about desperation--my neighbor shaves before weighing himself on the bathroom scale.

The importance of time depends largely on which side of the bathroom door you are standing.

Beach

The newest fad with the beachwatching set is imagining the girls with clothes on.

There are more comic strips on the beaches these days than in the newspapers.

While there's nothing new under the sun, on the beach there's a lot more of it showing.

These days on the beach you only have to look half as long to see twice as much.

I spent a weekend at the beach and couldn't decide whether bikinis are getting smaller or girls are getting bigger.

Wouldn't it be nice if it were warm enough to go swimming in the winter when the beaches aren't crowded?

Beauty

A beautiful woman is a blessing to the soul, a paradise to the eyes and a curse to the purse.

Venus de Milo typifies the beauty of women: when they're beautiful, they're probably not all there.

Beauty always comes from within--within jars, tubes and compacts.

A girl who is beautiful to look at is often hard to look after.

Some women have natural beauty along with a special talent for making the worst of it.

Every girl with beautiful eyes should take daily batting practice.

The best beauty aid a woman can have is a nearsighted husband.

A thing of beauty is a joy--unless your wife wants one like it.

A beauty contest is an event where the judges crown the winners and the losers want to crown the judge.

In the beauty parlor my wife patronizes the talk alone is enough to curl one's hair.

A thing of beauty is a great expense.

A beautician is a person who puts a price on a woman's head.

A beauty parlor is a place where men are rare and women well-done.

Bed

I find that I get up on the wrong side of the bed when I don't get into it early enough.

The best time to put the children to bed is when you still can.

If anything makes a child thirstier than going to bed, it's knowing that his parents have gone to bed, too.

Early to bed and early to rise is a sure sign that you're fed up with television.

Early to bed and early to rise makes a man a father.

Every time I see a four-poster bed I figure it's a lot of bunk.

Of all things that are better late than never, going to bed ranks first.

Writing is the only respectable profession where a woman can do her work in bed.

The best night spot is a comfortable bed.

The bedroom is the place where most household accidents occur.

Beer

Beer not only makes you talkative, it also makes you walkative.

I knew I was lost after tramping around in the woods for an hour without seeing a beer can.

Bees

We learn two lessons from the bees: one is not to be idle, and the other is not to get stung.

Betting

Betting is a lot like liquor: you can make it illegal, but you can't make it unpopular.

There are so many foreign cars in Beverly Hills that it has been two years since anyone has been hit above the knees.

Beverly Hills

There's a laundry in Beverly Hills that's so swanky that you have to wash it before they will accept it.

Having a big family around is a good way to make sure there'll always be someone to answer the phone--and forget the message.

Bigamy

Show me a bigamist, and I'll show you a man who makes a second mistake before correcting the first.

If all women are alike, why should any man commit bigamy?

Show me a bigamist, and I'll show you a man who believes that two beds are better than one.

Show me a bigamist, and I'll show you a man whose better half doesn't know how the other half lives.

Bigamy is when two rites make a wrong.

Bigotry

Show me a bigot, and I'll show you a man who is certain of something he knows nothing about.

Did you hear about the Southern bigot who was a bed wetter? He used to go to Klan meetings in a rubber sheet.

A bigot is a narrow-minded man who thinks the straight and narrow path isn't narrow enough.

Bikinis

Statistics are like a bikini bathing suit. What they reveal is suggestive, but what they conceal is vital.

Happiness is finding the owner of a lost bikini.

A bikini never attracts attention until someone puts it on.

The trouble with a bikini is that it shows you off or shows you up.

There is more to the modern girl in a bikini than meets the eye--but not much more.

One way marriage has changed me is that I like to see bikinis worn by all women but my wife.

Bills

Happiness is getting a bill you've already paid, so you can sit down and write a nasty letter.

I never get into an argument with my wife when she runs up big bills--I'd rather have trouble with my creditors than with her.

The only time most of us would want to be president is around the first of the month when we would like to veto a few bills.

After looking at the bill for my operation I understand why they wear masks in the operating room.

Cheer up: birds have bills too, but they keep on singing.

The reason I look run-down is because of the bills my wife runs up.

My wife talks on the phone so much that with last month's bill we got a sample of throat lozenges.

One way the world is sure to beat a path to your front door is if you fail to pay your bills.

One type of bill collector is a bank robber.

Bingo

As I understand it, wife-swapping is a kind of suburban bingo game.

Birds

The early bird has to get his own breakfast.

How can birds flock any other way than together?

Birth

The birth rate would be much lower today if it weren't for three things: early marriages, drive-in theaters and high schools.

Show me a twin birth and I'll show you an infant replay.

Two is company, three is poor birth control.

Most women put candles on their birthday cake to make light of their age.

Birthday

Columbus' birthday -- I forgot to get him a gift.

A man has a choice. He can either consult his wife before buying her a birthday present--or she'll charge it later.

I gave my wife a watch for her birthday. I figure there's no present like the time.

Forget my birthday. It's much kinder not to send me a reminder.

My wife's birthday has become an annual event in our house--every other year or so.

It's surprising that some wives expect their husbands to remember their birthday when they never look a day older.

All my wife wanted for her birthday was not to be reminded of it.

My wife is unpredictable. She doesn't want to be reminded of her birthdays, and is disappointed when I forget them.

Black Eye

A small town is the place where a man with a black eye gives you the true explanation for it.

Blondes

Gentlemen prefer blondes because blondes know what gentlemen prefer.

My idea of the perfect vacation is to rest quietly in the shade of a blonde.

The reason men like blondes is because they get dirty quicker.

Just because men like blondes some women are foolish enough to dye for them.

Blood

The only man who is never criticized when he lies down on the job is a blood donor.

Books

By the time a man can read a woman like a book he needs bifocals.

I bought a book on reducing and in no time at all I realized that what I lost was the price of the book.

A classic is a great book they give you free to join a club that charges a lot for cheap books.

Books make fine gifts for children, but it's hard to find stores that sell battery operated books.

Bores

A yawn is nature's way of giving the person listening to a bore an opportunity to open his mouth.

A bore is a person who talks when you want him to listen.

A bore is the kind of a guy who always attracts inattention.

Boss

I figure that I'm going to remain boss in my house just as long as I do what I'm told.

There would be more successful men if more bosses had marriageable daughters.

I never bring my boss home to dinner--she's already there.

My boss intends to take it with him. He just bought a fireproof money belt.

The real boss of the family is the one who can spend a few dollars without having to say anything about it.

Boxing

Show me a boxing ring and I'll show you a smack bar.

Boys

A boy becomes a man when he wears out the seat of his pants instead of the soles of his shoes.

A good name for a boy born on the first day of the month would be bill.

Remember the good old days when a juvenile delinquent was a boy who played the saxophone too loud?

The footsteps a boy follows in are apt to be those his father thought he'd covered up.

Every boy who has a dog should also have a mother, so the dog can be fed regularly.

Small boys are washable, though most of them shrink from it.

Every boy should have a pet. A cat, for instance, is always a help when it comes to explaining broken cookie jars.

All it takes to separate the men from the boys is girls.

The only time a boy manages to stay off the lawn is when you want him to cut it.

You can't take the boy out of some men--all through life they keep getting into jams.

Just because a boy is quiet does not mean he is up to mischief; he may be asleep.

If anything is as dirty as a small boy, it's probably his bath towel.

The typical American boy would love to go to the moon, but hates to go to the market for his mother.

Show me a small boy and I'll show you an accessory to the grime.

When a small boy has nothing in his pockets, he's probably wearing pajamas.

A boy is a hurry on its way to do nothing.

Bragging

One of the hardest things for most of us to put up with is a braggart who makes good.

Brain

The brain is as strong as its weakest think.

Brains are not a handicap to a girl because a smart girl knows enough to hide them behind a low neckline.

Bravery

A woman's idea of bravery is to walk out of a shoe store in a pair of shoes two sizes too small without showing any signs of pain.

A cad is a fellow who refuses to help his date with the breakfast dishes.

There's only one thing better than a cold shower before breakfast, and that's no cold shower before breakfast.

Brides

Modern brides are wearing their wedding dresses shorter--and oftener.

Judging from some of the specimens they pick, can you blame brides for blushing?

A bride is a girl who quit playing ball with the boys after she made a good catch.

Just because your bride is given away don't think you're getting away cheap.

I know a real loser. The day he got married he carried his bride over the threshold and got a hernia.

The father of the bride should realize he isn't losing a daughter but gaining a bathroom.

Many a bride who is given away turns out to be mighty expensive.

When a young man starts right out complaining about his bride's cooking, one of two things will happen: she'll learn better--or he will.

Today's bridegroom expects some finance company to carry everything over the threshold except the bride.

Where there's smoke, there's probably a bride cooking.

Every bride likes to take her husband with her on her honeymoon.

A wise bride is one who loses her temper--permanently.

Bridge

One way to get a real kick out of bridge is to sit opposite your wife.

Show me a man who beats his wife, and I'll show you a good bridge player.

Show me a bad bridge partner, and I'll show you a person with a one-trick mind.

My wife is so contrary, she won't even do my bidding at a bridge game.

Broke

Being broke isn't all bad: at least it gives you something to think about while watching television.

Bubble Dancer

I went out with a bubble dancer once, but it was no soap.

Budget

A budget is a formula for determining that you need a raise.

A budget is a sort of conscience which doesn't keep you from spending, but makes you feel guilty about it.

A budget is a system of reminding yourself that you can't afford the kind of living you've grown accustomed to.

A budget is something that allows you to live within your means and without almost everything else.

Living on a budget is the same as living beyond your means except that you have a record of it.

Show me a budget deficit, and I'll show you the shy cost of living.

A budget is wonderful; it helps you to learn how much you spend and how little you earn.

Getting by these days is simply a matter of rearranging the budget. By going without lunch and dinner, almost anyone can afford breakfast.

Some housewives carefully go over their budgets each month--others just go over them.

A budget shows some people how much they have to save; unfortunately mine shows me how much I have to borrow.

A family budget is usually made up of a little money and a lot of estimates.

Conservatives are people whose minds become unbalanced just because the budget is.

A budget is what you stay within if you go without.

The only thing that makes electric light bulbs last longer than television is courtship.

Burglars

Say what you will about burglars, they still make house calls.

Just about the only professional still making night calls is the burglar.

The best gift for the man who has everything is a burglar alarm.

The typical burglar loves home cooking.

A siren is a signal used by the police to warn burglars that they are approaching.

Bus

The way things are today it's easier for a woman to get a seat in Congress than in a bus.

People are strange: they want the front of the bus, the back of the church, and the center of attention.

Chivalry may not be dead but it certainly isn't riding on buses these days.

Business

I see where several of our politicians are predicting a return of prosperity as soon as business picks up.

Business is so quiet you can hear the overhead piling up.

To be a success in business you have to make a large part of your income appear as an expense.

Bust

Falsies are the bust that money can buy.

Cheating

A lot of people go through life's revolving door on another person's push.

I'm a man of promise--broken promise.

My credit is so bad, I can't even borrow trouble.

Any time I enter a verbal contract for money, I pay off verbally.

I have a brother who keeps himself busy by looking for someone to do.

Sharp practices have never cured dull times.

Does the button industry subsidize the laundries?

Baking a smaller loaf enables the bakeries to make a larger roll.

It's about all a man can do today to keep from being done.

My brother-in-law's mind is a regular scheme engine.

Always do your best, but not your best friend.

A used car salesman has as much conscience as a fox in a hen house.

You never know whom you can do till you try.

He hasn't been upright for so long, his shadow is crooked.

Some men are always up and doing--up to no good and doing everyone.

When a man pats you on the back, he's figuring where to stick the knife.

Some people will do anything for money--except work for it.

A guy who can take it or leave it--mostly takes it.

The man who is well-to-do is usually hard to do.

When I meet a man of convictions I wonder how many he has served time for.

The thing that smacks most of deceit is when two women kiss.

It's easier to hold an eel by the tail than to pin some men down.

Clothes make the man, and fake the woman.

I got this stoop living up to my ideals.

The last time I moved my landlady actually wept--I owed six months' rent.

The penalty for cheating is the disgrace of dying rich.

To deceive a deceiver is no deceit.

I dislike professional reformers who manage to get the pie out of piety.

Honesty is the best policy, but there are too few policy holders.

I got my principal entirely without principle.

Look out for the woman who takes you in when you take her out.

Never put off till tomorrow what you can put over today.

The only time my brother is on the level is when he's sleeping.

I'm very superstitious. In a fight, I always keep a horseshoe in my glove.

The only thing more deceptive than men's statistics, are women's figures.

Some people change sides more often than a windshield wiper.

There is no fool like the fool who thinks he is fooling you.

Honesty may pay, but it doesn't pay enough to suit some people.

The path of least resistance is what makes rivers crooked--men, too.

I have a sure-fire way to save money. I forget who I borrowed it from.

A con man gets rich quick by finding a victim--who gets poor quick.

I know a stereophonic salesman--he talks out of both sides of his mouth.

If a fool and his money are soon parted, who got yours?

My Dad never lets a day go by without doing someone good.

Sixty percent of the men cheat in America. The rest cheat in Europe.

Some people are polished--in a slippery sort of way.

Cheat me once, you should be ashamed--cheat me twice--I should be.

I'm a very highly suspected person in my community.

After you lend me money, you can charge it up to profit and louse.

My brother has the human touch; it conceals an itching palm.

My wallet is always full of big bills--all unpaid.

Give some men a free hand and they'll stick it right in your pocket.

I used to pin badges on frankfurters and sell them as police dogs.

He's so crooked, when he dies they'll have to screw him into the ground.

When a man lays his cards on the table, it's a good idea to count them.

Children

Everything in today's home is controlled by switches--except the children.

My kid brother was sent from heaven--they must like it quiet up there.

A youthful Henny, in top hat, cane and cigar, hams it up with an early backer, Cy Shore (front right)

Training a young child is always a matter of pot luck.

Parents are the last people on earth who ought to have children.

What is a home without children? Quiet.

I've got two wonderful children--and two out of five isn't too bad.

Know what happens to little boys who tell lies? They travel for half fare.

Most kids are going steady these days before their voices do.

I was such a pure kid that I refused to do improper fractions in class.

There are no problem children--only children with problems.

A kindergarten teacher has to know how to make the little things count.

Show me an illegitimate child, and I'll show you a sinfant.

My mother loved children--she'd have given anything if I'd been one.

As a kid I carried a blackjack in my pencil box.

Even as a boy I had to scrimp and scrape--I saved every cent I stole.

Some kids would rather steal hub caps than third base.

When I was five, my folks helped me to leave home.

Today's kids would be smarter if they smarted oftener.

To most children, the greatest seafood ever is salt-water taffy.

You can lead a boy to water--but you can't make him wash his neck.

I was a tough kid. At six I was chief repaint man for a hot tricycle ring.

My son's report card: His I.Q. is P.U.

My kid is too young to drive--so he steals taxies.

My son is very talented. At ten he's playing the piano and the horses.

Many parents give their children a free hand--but not in the right places.

We lived in a tent when I was a baby--so my head grew to a point.

My youngest is in the "no-it-all" stage.

A careful teen-ager only smokes filter-tipped marijuana.

A boy is a noise with some dirt on it.

For a dad to be a pal takes more than understanding--it takes stamina.

When I was a kid, I was so thin, the teacher kept marking me absent.

Today's accent is on youth--but the stress is on parents.

Children today are just like they've been through the ages--boys and girls.

One thing a child outgrows in a hurry is your pocketbook.

I wasn't like any kid of ten--I was eighteen.

I was raised in a tough neighborhood. I had six notches on my pea shooter.

Vacation time is when kids get out of school and into your hair.

Few children fear water unless soap is added.

Children are a great comfort in your old age--and they help you to reach it.

I grew up to be the kind of kid my mother didn't want me to play with.

I was a bad student--but a whiz at recess.

A really gifted child resembles a wealthy relative.

To train a child properly, start at the bottom.

Most children are descended from a long line their mothers listened to.

As a kid, my father talked me into running away from home.

When I see a child of six in a tantrum, I wonder who'll manage him at thirty.

An allowance is what you pay your child to live with you.

If you think it's easy to take candy away from a baby--you should try it.

Then, one day, I went to school. Couldn't get a table at the poolroom.

I ran away from home--and mother couldn't find me. She didn't even look.

A child is a thing that stands halfway between an adult and a TV set.

I grew up. What other way could I grow?

I was so big, when I was born, the doctor was afraid to slap me.

Never slap a child in the face--remember, there's a place for everything.

Child psychology is what children manage parents with.

Children are a family's ask force.

Child psychology: applying a soft pedal instead of a hard paddle.

Children are the death of marriage.

My neighborhood was so tough, Santa came up from the sewer.

I've had gray hair since I was born. Mother powdered the wrong place.

Children are human gimme pigs.

My parents considered me a bungle from heaven.

Children are often spoiled because you can't spank two grandmothers.

Children are coupons on the bonds of matrimony.

A child is an innocent by-product.

My kid is a stomach entirely surrounded by curiosity.

I was never kept after school. I never went.

Mom! There are only clean towels in the bathroom. Should I start one?

Children are why's guys.

Children--no mother should be without them.

A child is a token of affection.

I was a surprise to my parents--they expected a boy or a girl.

Childbirth is the labor of love.

Here's my report card, Daddy, and one of yours I found in the attic.

Children are unreasonable facsimiles.

He's a fine broth of a boy. Too bad some of his noodles are missing.

A problem child is one who puts two and two together and gets curious.

Children should be seen and not had.

She kept telling me she wanted her children young. Who wants old children?

I played hookey from the fifth grade--so I could cast my first vote.

A child is an accident in the Tunnel of Love.

My kid eats dry toast and washes it down with crackers.

Childhood is when a baby stops wearing its food and starts eating it.

Ma! I managed to miss the school bus!

At six, a kid knows all the questions, and at 16, he knows all the answers.

I always help with the diapers. It's a good way to make a little change.

He must get his brains from his mother. I still have mine.

Mother made me stop kicking the man. I had my new shoes on.

Women should not have children after 35--35 children are enough.

I was born of poor, but unusual, parents--they kept me.

The only things kids wear out faster than shoes are parents and teachers.

Childhood is when nightmares occur only during sleep.

I made Mother jealous--she used to look at other kids and get jealous.

The most annoying thing about children is that they're so childish.

Dad, I'm running away from home. Please call me a taxi.

We need a child labor law to keep them from working their parents to death.

Christmas

If it isn't too cold at Christmas time you have a cool Yule.

Every Christmas she hung up her stockings, but all she ever got was a run.

If postmen had their way, they'd abolish Christmas.

Only Santa is interested in an empty stocking.

Misery is when Christmas has come and gone, but your relatives haven't.

Christmas is when you buy this year's gifts with next year's money.

You should have seen what my child gave me last Christmas: measles!

Dear Santa, I want a plane, a mo-ped, and my violin busted.

The first Christmas was a myrrhy Christmas.

Show me an unemployed Santa, and I'll show you a ho-ho hobo!

*Some comic
"fiddlin' around"
on the Kraft Music
Hall with Morey
Amsterdam, Jack
Benny and
classical musician
Michael Rabin (far
right)*

Christmas comes but once a year, and once a year is enough.

Sign in a big department store: Five Santas, no waiting.

Christmas is a holiday that always comes a month before arriving.

Christmas bills are the real morning after.

All I got for Christmas was my wife's relatives.

This Christmas has added me to the casualty list in the war on poverty.

Christmas is when your wife gives you things that you can't afford.

Christmas dinner: Paunch launcher.

A Christmas shopper's complaint is one of long standing.

On December 26th, Santa is a beat Nick.

If Christmas comes, can bills be far behind?

One thing that's cheaper today than two weeks ago is a Christmas tree.

When Christmas is over, father has more ties than bonds.

Santa is a gardener who likes to hoe, hoe, hoe.

Santa Claus has the right idea: visit people once a year.

I'll tell you what I got for Christmas--bald and fat.

Christmas comes, but once a year is enough.

You might as well do your Christmas hinting early.

Give a man a couple of loud ties and it's Christmas.

The height of irony is to give father a billfold for Christmas.

If you've been saving for a rainy day--Christmas is the monsoon season.

Christmas is when trees, and husbands, get trimmed and lit up.

I gave my wife a pen--and was she surprised! She expected a mink coat.

Christmas is the time when all that matters is the present.

I gave my wife the best piece of jewelry five dollars could buy.

The first thing to turn green in the spring is Christmas jewelry.

By the time I found a place to park, Christmas was over.

At Christmas we wish people didn't come in different sizes.

Every Christmas my wife gets Santa-mental.

Why does Christmas always come when the stores are most crowded?

My wife has me worried. She gave me a gift that I can't afford.

Seen the price of Christmas trees? This year the tree trimmed me.

My girl wants her past forgotten and her present remembered.

I received a lot of wonderful presents I can't wait to exchange.

Christmas shoppers are people with the spirit of brotherly shove.

Christmas Eve is the night that Santa keeps his ho's to the grindstone.

A neatly decorated Christmas tree has a yuletidy appearance.

At Christmas, kids want something that will separate the men from the toys.

The ideal Christmas gift is money, but the trouble is you can't charge it.

Christmas is the day you resolve to shop early next year.

Satan is an anagram for Santa.

Show me a Christmas aura, and I'll show you a holly-daze.

The area under the mistletoe is the scene of many a kiss- understanding.

The month before Christmas is a time when children live for the present.

Christmas is when a lot of others beside Santa find themselves in the red.

Santa's elves have organized. They call their union the A.F. of Elves.

Are Santa's helpers known as subordinate clauses?

Father and Santa Claus, with presents distributed, are left holding the bag.

Christmas is the season when both money and children sprout wings.

The early gift gets the best return.

Holiday drivers are not all they crack-up to be.

Christmas is when father owes best.

Some last-minute shoppers are fit to be Yule-tied.

Show me a Christmas cravat, and I'll show you the tie that blinds.

I avoided the middleman this year. I gave her an exchange certificate.

Christmas is when everyone goes shopping and mangles with the crowd.

By the time the last package has been festively tied--I'm fit to be.

Christmas is when the high cost of giving gets serious attention.

Show me a Yule log, and I'll show you a Christmas list.

I went Christmas shopping and got Santa Claus-trophobia.

Clothing

Some men send old suits to the missions. I send mine to the cleaner.

The short skirt has plenty of legs to stand on.

All that shines is not serge.

Men no longer hide behind women's skirts--neither do women.

Is that a suit you have on, or are you dancing with someone?

My wife wears a hat with delirium trimmins.

All a sweater does for my wife is make her itch.

A cravat is a necktie that sells for $30.

Broadcloth is the cloth used to make girls' dresses.

A fashion show is a clothes-horse show.

Who gave you that tie? Someone angry at you?

Today, when a girl says her evening gown is really nothing, she means it.

Fashion is a racket for selling clothes.

I hand-painted this tie myself. I leaned over a can of wet paint.

A fur coat is a second-hand garment.

I bought a suit with built-in gravy stains.

A woman's garter is a rubber band with glamour.

Clothes make the man; lack of them, the woman.

This kind of suit retains its shapelessness even after dry cleaning.

Show me a girdle, and I'll show you a line tamer.

Clothes make the man, if the right girl is wearing them.

A glove is a shoe for the hand.

A man with buttons missing, should either get married, or divorced.

When a woman is indifferent her reward is a mink coat.

The hardest thing on a woman's clothes is another woman.

Panties are a kind of curtain for the sitting room.

My clothes always fit perfectly--but whom?

A trousseau is what a bride wears for five years after the wedding.

Clothes make the woman, but not the woman who makes her own clothes.

A union suit is a portal-to-portal undergarment.

A brassiere is a device to bring out a girl's best points.

The first costume on record was a hand-me-down from the fig tree.

She should run for office, as the only candidate with nothing to hide.

You don't see a woman with hind-sight wearing slacks.

The girls who model girdles are the ones who don't need them.

Clothes don't make the woman, but often show how she is made.

A girdle makes a woman slimmer on the outside than she is on the inside.

I know why Scotsmen wear kilts--no pockets.

Fashions come and go, but girdles will always be around.

Clothes conceal the body, but more often reveal the soul.

To save money, I cut down my wife's old girdles and make suspenders.

The only exercise my wife gets is struggling in and out of her girdle.

They said this suit would wear like iron--which is why it's getting rusty.

A man shopping for his wife in the lingerie department is a lost soul.

He looks good in his cutaway coat and his torn-away pants.

You should see her in slacks--she's got the end to end all ends.

Women's clothes can show bad taste and good form at the same time.

This suit doesn't do much for me--but then, I don't do much for it.

That's a nice dress. You must wear it sometime.

Hush little hanky, don't you cry--you'll be a sun suit bye and bye.

If women dressed to please their husbands--they'd wear last year's clothes.

The apparel oft proclaims the man--to be what he is not.

My raincoat has a waterproof label--the label is waterproof, but not the coat.

Clothes make the man poor--if he's married.

That's a lovely gownless evening strap you have on.

If seeing is believing, men should have implicit faith in women these days.

I like women's dresses that are cut to see level.

A laundry is a place where clothes are worn out.

If brevity is the soul of wit, women's clothes were never funnier.

I don't like loose dresses. I think tents are for Boy Scouts.

Give some women an inch, and they'll wear it for a dress.

Her sweater was so tight I could hardly breathe.

Many a woman's clothes represent more dollars than sense.

Modern styles are a survival of the faddist.

Is that a very low neckline, or a very high hem?

No wonder they call it high fashion--just look at the prices.

She wore a $200 gown, but her heart wasn't in it.

Clothes make the man--if the right woman is in them.

In choosing clothes, women are practically going all out.

Topless fashions prove how many underprivileged there are.

My wife's clothes fit her--like a convulsion.

Sign in a dress shop: Buy now--our skirts are going up.

My wife insists on wearing too much of not enough.

The girl who makes her own clothes will never die from overwork.

I like Texas dresses--the ones with those wide open spaces.

A girl's hope chest might just as well be called her tulle box.

Even the price of a dress isn't modest any more.

What a howl would ensue if poverty made women wear so few clothes.

Some women reach success by attireless effort.

Women wanted equality--but now they've outstripped us.

She shows more of a lot of woman than a lot of style.

Once, when a girl had nothing to wear, she was out of style.

All her clothes are pressed. She's on the list of the ten best-pressed girls.

Women dress on the theory that nothing succeeds like nothing.

The clothes that make the woman are the ones that break the man.

The apparel off proclaims the woman.

I like those peek-a-bosom type dresses.

I'm convinced that women dress to displease other women.

Fashion has lifted a considerable burden off the clothesline.

In an amber dress with a white collar she looked like a short beer with legs.

Skirt, once a common noun, has become a mere abbreviation.

Some dresses can't even hide a woman's embarrassment.

In short skirts it's not the initial length, it's the up- creep.

Sports clothes are being worn louder and funnier.

No question--the short skirt is having a high old time.

Italian girls are very demanding. Every year they want a new cloth coat.

She has no more on her body than on her mind.

What the well-dressed women will wear this year--is less.

The best-dressed woman usually arrives last with the best.

The clothing that keeps a man looking his best is worn by women.

Most women go to the beach wearing a baiting suit.

If dresses get cut any lower, women will be barefooted.

She's penny-wise and gowned foolish.

Why do women think they are sitting pretty if their knees show?

I've got two changes of clothing--with and without.

Clothes express a woman's interests--most women aren't interested in much.

My wife's wardrobe is in a clash by itself.

This suit was made to order, but the man didn't pick it up, so I took it.

Girls' clothes may go to extremes, but rarely to extremities.

Milliners do a lot for the Go-to-Meeting Church movement.

A stout woman in shorts is an example of a stern reality.

A woman's expensive wardrobe has often started with just a little slip.

A rag is any dress a woman has to wear more than once.

I just bought my wife a tight skirt with a straight jacket.

Nothing is harder on a woman's clothes than another woman.

This is a form-fitting suit, unfortunately I don't have the form it fits.

She's always at the beach trying to outstrip the other girls.

It's not clothes that make men stare--it's clothing that isn't there.

This suit cost me $150--and that was just to have it cleaned.

That dress isn't bad for the shape it's on--I mean in.

"Girdle" is the polite name for an old-fashioned pot holder.

My wife dresses like an unmade bed.

These are my summer clothes. Summer paid for and summer not.

If her dress were any shorter, it would be a collar.

She is as seedy as a raspberry.

To be a live wire, a girl has to wear very little insulation.

I wear convertible underwear. In summer, a screen replaces the back door.

Your gown reminds me of a song: Sweet and Low.

I got my wife a housecoat to wear around the house--it fits either of them.

This suit is made of that ever-durable miracle fiber--wool.

My coat has only one defect. It covers my shoes.

Some of the best comic strips are on the beach.

Never judge a woman by her clothes--there's not enough to go by.

There are two sides to everything--except a bikini.

My new summer suit is so cool, if I wear it all day I catch cold.

I like those dresses that start late and end early.

I caught a very aristocratic moth--he would only eat full dress suits.

She's Vogue on the outside, and vague on the inside.

Modern girls in modern dress, put more and more on less and less.

I like the kind of gown that's more gone than gown.

If men dressed like women, women would turn around and look too.

My wife dresses like she's fleeing from a burning building.

It isn't the initial cost of a strapless gown--it's the upkeep.

She keeps looking for a dress that's both fitting and properl

Her suit looks like a million dollars--all green and wrinkled.

Some women aren't just dressed--they're upholstered.

My interest in a woman's knees--rises and falls with the breeze.

He looks like he got dressed in front of an airplane propeller.

When my wife wears a red dress she looks like a bow-legged fire engine.

I have a suit for every day in the month--it's the one I have on.

Her dress looked pretty good considering the shape it was on.

My wife wears unmentionables--they're nothing to speak of.

My shoes are so tight that I have to unlace them to swallow.

I don't care if women's skirts go up or down. I'm nearsighted.

Actually I'm wearing this suit to pay off an election bet.

Like this suit? I'm thinking of buying it.

Many a maternity dress is not so much a dress as a slip cover.

Some women show a lot of style, and some styles show a lot of woman.

An evening gown should be attractive and distractive.

A dress that makes one girl look slim makes others look 'round.

Nothing lasts as long as a suit you don't like.

Each year my wife pays more and more for less and less.

The way for a man to make a suit last longer is to get married.

I found out what my wife wanted with six dresses--six pairs of shoes.

Clothes make the man, and suits make the lawyer.

I'm still wearing this suit. The Salvation Army refused it.

Henny first met Dinah Shore in a theatrical office and helped her find her first job

Behind every successful man is a woman--who has nothing to wear.

I'd like to see my wife wear her dresses a little longer--about a year longer.

My girl friend is a window dresser--never pulls her shades down.

A really beautiful girl can wear almost anything--or almost nothing.

Yesterday my suit shrank two inches--and it was only a little cloudy.

If a man can't see why you wear a strapless gown, yous houldn't.

African women want American clothes. Africa has the climate for them.

This suit fits me like a glove. See how the sleeves cover my hands?

Nothing is as cold as a woman who has been refused a fur coat.

I'm keeping my coat buttoned up to hide the shirt I'm not wearing.

Today's woman dresses like a lady--Lady Godiva.

My suit isn't inside out. I'm just on the wrong side of it.

She shows a lot of style, and her style shows a lot of woman.

My wife dresses to kill and cooks the same way.

I told my wife her nylons were wrinkled--but she wasn't wearing any.

I got her something for her winter coat--mothballs.

The only thing holding up her dress is a city ordinance.

her last tight girdle convinced my wife that honesty is the best policy.

With that dress I can't tell if she's trying to catch a cold or a man.

When a woman shows up in slacks, she certainly does.

The new necklines are close to where the waistlines ought to be.

She has a dress with a square neck--to go with her head.

She wears tight clothing to squeeze out the last ounce of value.

What would we say if men changed the length of their pants each year?

A girl with hidden talent usually wears clothes that reveal it.

When a man's socks and tie match, he's wearing a present.

A bustle is a covered waggin'.

I wear suspenders and a belt. Why be half safe?

A bustle is an annex in the rear with decorative intent.

A smart husband hides his money in clothes that need mending.

A bustle is a cushion for the sitting room.

Figures don't lie--making tailoring a difficult business.

Some women have ample reason for wearing a low-cut gown.

That's a nice dress you've almost got on.

A bustle is headquarters for the hindquarters.

What would women be without clothes? Cold.

A bustle is a false front in the rear.

My wife doesn't pick my clothes--just the pockets.

Today a girl goes out wearing less than her mother wore in bed.

My brother has so many suits, he keeps one aside, just for the moths.

A bustle is a fender on a bender.

My suit is so shiny, if it ever tears, I'll have seven years of bad luck.

A bustle is a false bottom attached to the rear of the trunk.

The way women dress today, the only thing they conceal is their age.

Women who won't shoulder any responsibility wear strapless gowns.

She looks like she was poured into that dress--and what a pretty stein.

A bustle is a fashion accessory, at present behind the times.

My wife doesn't know which dress she doesn't want until she buys it.

It's easy to meet a man if a girl exposes herself in the right places.

Girls worry a lot about their clothes--much ado about nothing.

A chafing dish is a girl in a tight leotard.

He had a dinner jacket on--with dinner still on it.

Clothing is the material that covers a multitude of sins.

He got a very expensive suit for a ridiculous figure. His!

Decolletage is pearls on the half-shell.

Seeing a girl in a topless bathing suit can be quite a let- down.

Padded bras are hidden persuaders.

Show me a set of falsies, and I'll show you twin bluffs.

A wise man never laughs at his wife's old clothes.

Falsies are used by conniving women to pad their expanses.

The latest thing in men's clothes is women.

Fashion is what a her does to a hem to get a him.

I like a girl to wear a gown that brings out the bust in her.

Fashion forecasts what women's dresses will be up to.

A girdle is the difference between facts and figures.

A sack dress makes a girl look like a kangaroo with the kids home.

My girl friend had an accident--she caught her foot in her neckline .

Lingerie is a kind of gay nighties.

Figures don't lie, but girdles push the truth a little out of position.

Show me a girdle, and I'll show you a waist basket.

Sweaters accentuate the positive, girdles eliminate the negative.

A girdle is a reinforcement for the battle of the bulge.

The evening gown is named after Eve, who didn't wear anything either.

Her stretch pants were so tight I could see the coin in her pocket was tails.

Conscience

Conscience is an inner voice that warns us somebody is looking.

I have a clean conscience, because I've never used it.

Conscience is the still small voice that makes you feel still smaller.

People with a strong conscience need it to carry so much.

Conscience is what makes you tell your wife before someone else does.

Money talks louder when your conscience is asleep.

Conscience is a thing that feels terrible when everything else feels great.

My conscience never troubles me--I have it pretty well trained.

Why do reformers always want their consciences to be your guide?

Conscience tells you not to do something after you have done it.

The world could use an amplifier for the still small voice.

Conscience is a wholesome fear of the police.

Some men are born with a conscience; I married mine.

Conscience is the anticipation of the opinion of others.

Conscience is a guilt-edged knife.

Conscience is a small, still voice that makes minority reports.

Too often, conscience is the fear of being found out.

Conscience: the inner voice that tells you the IRS might check your return.

Conscience gets a lot of credit that belongs to cold feet.

Conscience: the still small voice that yells so loud the morning after.

Conscience is what tells you that instinct is wrong.

Conscience is a mother-in-law whose visit never ends.

Conscience: the voice you wish you could teach not to interrupt you.

I don't listen to my conscience--I get very poor reception.

Conscience is a voice from within that lots of people do without.

Conscience is as good as a thousand witnesses.

Conscience only kicks up a fuss after you've had all the fun.

Most consciences are made with a lever to throw them out of gear.

Conscience is something that no's what's wrong.

Many a man, alone with his conscience, is all by himself.

Conscience is what makes a boy tell his mother, before his sister does.

The best cure for a guilty conscience is success.

I'd listen to my conscience if I could tell it what to say.

A guilty conscience is the mother of invention.

When you battle with your conscience and lose, you win.

Money talks louder when your conscience is asleep.

The conscience is a thinking man's filter.

Let your conscience be your guide and you miss the most exciting places.

Removing a man's conscience is usually just a minor operation.

Anyone with a clear conscience probably has a bad memory.

Conscience is the still small voice that tells us what others should do.

It's only a good person who can have a bad conscience.

Some men are born with a conscience--others marry one.

A well-trained conscience is one that knows when to say nothing.

Silence is not always golden; sometimes it's guilt.

Conscience makes you tell your wife--before somebody else does.

The line is usually busy when conscience wants to speak.

Conversation

Generally speaking, my wife is generally speaking.

No one equals my wife at using more words to say less about nothing.

My wife is a constant source of ear-i-tation.

It takes some people a half-hour just to say "Hello."

Some people's idea of a conversation is a filibuster.

My wife throws her tongue in high gear before her brain starts turning over.

He's a great talker--the best you can ever hope to escape from.

She talks so much her tongue gets tired.

My wife is breathtaking--every few hours she stops talking to take a breath.

My wife can say more in a look than I can in a book.

My wife can talk fifty per cent faster than anyone can listen.

I've never seen my wife's tongue. It moves too fast.

My wife even talks to herself--to be sure of getting in the last word.

Some people tell all they know, others tell a great deal more.

Some people approach every subject with an open mouth.

She talks like a revolving door.

What some people need is a little lockjaw.

When I talk, my wife listens--usually to the stereo or the television.

My wife is always giving everyone a preamble to her constitution.

The only time my wife stops talking is when her mother starts.

Dumb? If anyone said "Hello" to her she would be stuck for an answer.

It's not what a man says that counts, it's what a woman answers.

Then there's the type that holds everyone spielbound.

Her mouth never gets eight hours sleep.

The smaller a man's ideas, the more words he uses to express them.

Never write when you can talk, and never talk when you can listen.

I may be down, but I'm never out-talked.

She has a speech impediment. It's always two hours too long.

My mother-in-law is like a shirt button--always popping off.

The more a chatterbox talks, the less you listen.

Some men take two hours to tell you why they are a man of few words.

We had a power failure in our house. My wife lost her voice.

My wife never has the last word--she never gets to it.

This country needs more good listeners and fewer poor speakers.

He should rent his mouth out as a fly catcher.

Some people would say more if they talked less.

Imagine a woman with a mouth so big, she can whisper in her own ear.

My wife has a long playing tongue.

My wife has a very sad parrot. He's never had a chance.

A good listener is the best talker.

My wife not only has the last word, but the last five hundred.

A woman's word is never done.

She has a small vocabulary, but her turnover is terrific.

She has a tongue that could clip a hedge.

When a woman says "I do!" she usually knows what she's talking about.

Some people are never too busy to talk about how busy they are.

My wife could talk her head off and never miss it.

She has a slight impediment in her speech. She can't say no.

When some women set a trap for a man, they forget to shut it.

I thought talk was cheap until I saw our telephone bill.

I think my wife was raised on tongue sandwiches.

She has a tongue that jaywalks over every conversation.

My wife's laryngitis is the wages of din.

She talks so much, I get hoarse just listening to her.

A real drip is one you can always hear, but can rarely turn off.

If you want your wife to listen, talk to another woman.

Free speech is a right, but not a continuous obligation.

One frog said to another, "I think I have a man in my throat."

A good listener can think of something to say when you can't.

Let's have an intelligent conversation. I'll talk and you listen.

My boss reminds me of a clarinet--a wind instrument.

Think before you speak. Then you won't.

He has to be eschewed if you don't want to be chewed.

He took his time when he spoke. Unfortunately he took ours, too.

Silence is golden, but most people were born on the silver standard.

He was a soothing speaker. He put me right to sleep.

My wife could even have the last word with an echo.

His mouth just opened a new branch of the Bunk of America.

The meaning doesn't matter, if its' only idle chatter.

How can two be happy when only one is talking?

To say the right thing at the right time, keep still most of the time.

My wife has a nice, open face--open day and night.

Tell your wife all about your past, and she'll never run out of conversation.

Wives talk more than husbands because woman's work is never dumb.

It's chatter when much is spoken, but little is said.

You can't get away from a chatterbox, except in the middle of a sentence.

When all is said and done, some people just keep on talking.

Some people won't stop talking until you start walking.

To me, an ideal conversation is one part you and nine parts me.

Conversation is 90 per cent talking and 10 per cent listening.

Repartee is what you think of on the way home.

Conversation is the art of hearing as well as being heard.

My wife has a chronic speech impediment--palpitation of the tongue.

Of two evils, choose the one least likely to be talked about.

Most people feel it's more blessed to be glib than to perceive.

I've tried to argue with my wife, but her words flail me.

When I first met him I liked him a lot, but he soon talked me out of it.

Repartee is a duel fought with the points of jokes.

When I get away from my wife, I feel like a fugitive from a chin gang.

If other people insist on talking, conversation becomes impossible.

Money talks, and that's the conversation I'm most interested in.

Some people are too busy discussing new books to find time to read them.

Each morning my wife brushes her teeth and sharpens her tongue.

It's not what she says that hurts--it's the number of times she says it.

Of course, there's a lot to be said in her favor, but it's not as interesting.

Talk about others, you're a gossip; talk about yourself, you're a bore.

The only time my wife suffers in silence is when the phone is out of order.

Last night, my wife was so tired, she could hardly keep her mouth open.

Some things go without saying--like my mother-in-law's tongue.

Cosmetics

My wife makes up her face more easily than her mind.

Nothing makes a woman blush like the drugstore.

It's impossible to call the complexion of a girl today a straight flush.

To keep lipstick from smearing, eat a lot of garlic.

Cosmetics are only skin dope.

Most women aren't as pretty as they are painted.

She got her good looks from her mother, who owns a beauty parlor.

Cosmetics are the proof that women have the skin they love to retouch.

Ladies, if nature hasn't been kind to you--make up for it.

A decided blonde is a brunette who decided to dye her hair.

Her hair is titian; imi-titian.

Many women mistake make-up for the fountain of youth.

She's a fictitious character. Fictitious means made-up.

Women never have hard faces--it's not the face, it's the finish that's hard.

The beauty parlor is where your wife is driven by the cosmetic urge.

Any girl can be as pretty as a picture, provided she's well-painted.

Beauty comes from within--within jars, tubes, and compacts.

Without make-up, a girl can have a winning smile, but a losing face.

One reason women kiss and make up is that cosmetics wear off.

A woman is as old as she looks until she puts her face on.

Some powder goes off with a bang; some goes on with a puff.

Some women look healthy on only one side of their face.

Every beautician knows that woman's face is her fortune.

Laugh and the world laughs with you--cry and you streak your mascara.

Make-up keeps men from reading between the lines.

Those bottles on the dresser are my wife preservers.

Make-up is a disguise used to make a woman look like her portrait.

Make-up makes a woman look old-fashioned when she doesn't use any.

A change of lipstick, now and then, is relished by the best of men.

Any man with lipstick on his forehead is slipping.

When a woman makes up her lips, it is usually to a man's taste.

The trouble with lipstick is that it doesn't.

Kissing a girl always leaves its mark on a man.

Don't envy a good complexion--buy one!

A woman's real complexion usually travels under false colors.

My wife is as beautiful as when we first met--only now it takes her longer.

Now there's a Bourbon lipstick. It's kissproof, smearproof, and 100 proof.

Women paint what they used to be.

A shining example of old-fashioned simplicity is an unpowdered nose.

Courtship

She's my peach, I'm her plum; we're a pair. Hm-m, fruit salad.

I got a real kick out of kissing her. Her husband caught me.

I ran after one chicken only to find it was a wild goose chase.

He's a father? They must have lowered the requirements.

Courting is the past tense of the word "caught."

A spinster is a "yes-girl" who never had a chance to talk.

In courting, forbidden fruit can get you in a bad jam.

She sent me a stinging letter. There were two bees in it.

Courting makes the heart light and the parlor dark.

We argue a lot. She doesn't like the way I feel about her.

A love letter is a missive calculated to speed up the males.

Like medicine, she used to cure my blues--now she's a drug on the market.

Love is like war; easy to begin, but very hard to stop.

Just think, we don't have to pull the shades down any more. We're married.

I like a girl who can stand on her own two feet--especially while dancing.

Love is what makes you lose your head to win a hand.

Only the brave desert the fair.

Courtship is when you pretend you like the girl more than the kiss.

She never said "Good-bye"--that's a nice how-dee-do.

A girl knows when the right man comes along--he notices her.

She's lonesome for me--especially when I'm not with her.

It's difficult to finish with a girl with whom it was easy to begin.

I've been in love four times, and married three times.

He who courts and runs away, lives to court another day.

When we got engaged she said: "It won't be wrong now."

Faint heart ne'er won fair lady--without lots of help on her part.

How can I live without her? Cheaper.

If a woman doesn't chase a man a little, she doesn't love him.

I want a girl, just like the girl, that Dad had on the side.

Until he's married, a man goes with a girl; after that, he's taken.

My word is as good as my blonde.

Courtship is an animated introduction to a wearisome play.

A diamond is a woman's idea of a stepping stone to success.

To fall in love you must have an open mind--a hole in the head.

Today, the only sign of toil on a girl's hand is an engagement ring.

She's always drunk--that's why I love her. They say that love is blind.

She's such a hot kisser, she melts the gold in a man's mouth.

Love is a three-ring circus. Engagement ring, wedding ring, and suffer-ring.

I have terrible luck--last week my chauffeur ran off without my wife.

She wanted a gift to go with her looks--so I bought her a set of horse shoes.

There was something dove-like about her--she was pigeon-toed.

She had a heart of gold--and teeth to match.

Happiness is the only thing that multiplies by division.

Know how I met my wife? I whistled for a cab--she got there first.

We thought we were stuck on each other--but we were only plastered.

You can't tell how a girl will turn out until her family turns in.

A good girl is good but a bad girl is better.

Lots of little things have been started by a kiss.

My wife is on a greens diet. Takes nothing but tens, twenties, and fifties.

I like my girl friend because she doesn't "no" much.

I take her everywhere, but it's no use. She always finds her way back.

Then she showed her true colors. She ran out of make-up.

I met her just twenty check stubs ago.

Speaking of girls--and I usually am.

A man is weakest when a girl is telling him how strong he is.

She found my kisses intoxicating--until she caught me mixing my drinks.

I learned about romance at the movies--I never let the picture distract me.

Courtship is love's sweet dream--it's followed by marriage, the alarm clock.

Some girls string a guy along only to see if he's fit to be tied.

Love is a condition of the mind when the mind is out of condition.

Courtship is a state of perpetual anesthesia.

The word love consists of two vowels, two consonants, and two fools.

In courting, two people associate for the benefit of one.

Love is an ocean of emotion, complete with gulls and buoys.

Love is the triumph of imagination over intelligence.

Courting is a passion fancy.

Love is the triumph of the reflexes over reflection.

For me, love turned out to be sentimental measles.

Love is a delightful feeling--the hitch occurs when the knot is tied.

When courting, remember that a love letter is a noose paper.

Cowards

I wouldn't even open an oyster without first knocking on the shell.

His final decision seldom tallies with the one immediately following it.

They have an apt nickname for him: Old Man Quiver.

He's as spineless as spaghetti.

He's a regular Rock of Jello.

Real courage is marrying a three-times-widowed woman.

When a fight starts, I always do my best--one hundred yards in ten seconds.

He's as nervous as a diner watching the chef read a racing form.

Once I make up my mind, I'm full of indecision.

Cowardice is the surest protection against temptation.

Some people do everything the herd way.

Courage is often just ignorance of the facts.

At the first sign of trouble--I think with my legs.

He's such a lightweight, he could tap-dance on a chocolate eclair.

I'm not a "Yes" man. When the boss says "No"--I say "No."

It takes real courage to walk naked through a cannibal village.

I have a sure-fire way of handling temptation--I yield to it.

His big trouble is that he never no's his own mind.

To me, necessity is the mother of tension.

He always stoops to concur.

I need an anesthetic just to sit in my dentist's waiting room.

Don't cry out for help at night--you might wake up the neighbors.

I've never been married--I'm a self-made mouse.

The bitter part of discretion is valor.

His trouble is too much bone in the head and not enough in the back.

Cowards always tell you that discretion is the better part of valor.

I'd commit suicide, if I could do it without killing myself.

Nothing frightens me more than people who are scared.

I'm living in the present--tense.

A man with a reputation for being energetic may merely be nervous.

He bits his nails so much, his stomach needs a manicure.

You have reached middle age when all you exercise is caution.

I'm so tense, my office furniture is overwrought iron.

It often takes less courage to die for a woman than to live with her.

In his spinal column, all the bone is in a lump at the top.

In me it's caution; in someone else, it's cowardice.

My boss calls me the "Caterpillar"--I keep my job only by crawling.

Any girl afraid to stay home alone at night should not get married.

You can break some people easier than a biscuit.

When a woman says she's "high strung," it means she's out of tune.

I'm as nervous as a cat up a tree.

A man has to have a lot of courage to admit he hasn't any.

No contact lenses for me. What would I put on in case a fight started?

Marriage doth make cowards of us all.

I have as much guts as a skeleton.

A woman is the only thing I'm afraid of that I know won't hurt me.

Some people crumble up like an old ruin under responsibility.

A man is old when girls get on his nerves instead of his lap.

They call me "Jigsaw." When faced with a problem, I go to pieces.

If you have cold feet have sense enough to stay out of hot water.

My motto is: "It isn't who you know, but who you `Yes'."

Cold feet are usually the result of burnt fingers.

I'm a man of conviction--after I know what my wife thinks.

Do right, and fear no man; don't write, and fear no woman.

Some people fall for everything, and stand for nothing.

Some men are so cautious they look both ways crossing a one-way street.

He's always on the fence to avoid giving offense.

Silence isn't always golden: sometimes it is just plain yellow.

I once had a job that took lots of guts--I strung tennis racquets.

A good scare can be worth more to a person than good advice.

He bows and scrapes like a windshield wiper.

Always watch your step--even when you're not going anywhere.

You don't get ulcers from what you eat, but from what's eating you.

Look before you leap, but look ahead, not behind.

He reminds me of a weathercock that turns with every wind.

A confirmed coward carries two rabbit's feet--at the end of his legs.

Imagine a man who asks permission to ask permission!

A coward is an inveterate invertebrate.

I'm so indecisive, I have a five-year-old son I haven't named yet.

I'm such a coward even my own shadow is afraid of me.

I never take tranquilizers--if I'm not tense, I'm nervous.

I have a bad back--it has no bone.

I'm the decisive type--I'll always give you a definite maybe.

I never run away from a fight. I just back up for a good running start.

It's better to have courage than a wife; a man can't have both.

What he needs more than his intercom system is an inner calm system.

He has a lot of courage--to bear the misfortunes of others.

In an emergency, he's as helpless as the owner of a sick goldfish.

Brave? He'll go into the morgue and offer to lick any man in the house.

He gives his conscience a lot of credit that belongs to his cold feet.

He wouldn't say "Boo" to a goose.

Then there is the willing minion to mass opinion!

I even say "Thank you" when the automatic door opens for me.

He's so nervous, he twangs in a high wind.

Imagine a man more nervous than a turkey in November.

Crime

My wife tried to poison me, but I've eaten out so often it wouldn't take.

Crime doesn't pay, but only if you get caught.

Give a criminal enough rope and he'll tie up a cashier.

A jail is the only place where they won't raise your rent.

I met a hold-up man--he sells suspenders.

Crime doesn't pay--at least, not on television.

When I was a cop I pinched many a killer--one was a girl.

My brother is very popular in jail. He's the lifer of the party.

At ten, I ran away with a circus--but the cops made me bring it back.

Crime doesn't pay, except for the writers of detective stories.

Worse than a crime is a blunder.

The judge gave my brother 200 years. It's lucky he didn't get life.

An arch criminal is one who robs shoe stores.

The only people who still make house calls are the burglars.

These days there doesn't seem to be any arrest for the wicked.

Crime is getting so bad in some big cities--even the muggers travel in pairs.

Things are so tough in Chicago, one gangster had to let two cops go.

Crime doesn't pay. Nice hours though.

Crime, too, has its permanent wave.

A burglar is a man seeking an opening in the better stores.

I know a guy who is so crooked, he raised a check on himself.

Crime may not pay, but hardly anything else does either.

It's beginning to look at if the underworld has gotten on top.

Policeman's Union: Amalgamated Copper.

Pickpocket's motto: Every crowd has a silver lining.

Either crime is subsiding or people are getting used to it.

Gangsters seem to get everything, except what is coming to them.

An arsonist is a person who sets the world on fire--in a small way.

Tidy hold-up man: "--and let me have it all in new bills, please."

A criminal is one who hasn't enough money to hire expensive lawyers.

A criminal is one who gets caught.

Murder is a form of retroactive birth control.

I'm a police reporter--once a month I report to the police.

Murder is a form of glorified assault.

Crime doesn't pay--but policemen don't earn much either.

A murderer is a man who takes life too easily.

A counterfeiter is a man who wants money bad.

Robbery is a way to earn a living by doing unwanted work.

A convict is a person who is doing time for others.

These are trying days for everyone except the criminals.

One thing that never works properly after it is fixed is a jury.

A courageous man never needs weapons, but he may need bail.

A grand jury is one that says to the defendant: "Not guilty."

In America, we're willing to try anything once--except the criminals.

Today a murderer is asumed innocent until proven insane.

He's so crooked he'd steal two left shoes.

A clue is what the police boast about when they can't find the criminal.

A counterfeiter gets into trouble by following a good example.

The Doctors of Law don't seem to be able to effect a cure.

He'd steal a hot stove and come back for the smoke.

The way of the criminal is hard, but then, so is any other well-beaten path.

Living is getting cheaper. So is life.

The way of the criminal is a get-away.

Be careful, and you will save many men from the sin of robbing you.

When crime stops paying, gansters and politicians will do something else.

The F.B.I. has the most magnificent collection of clues in existence.

An alibi is a kind of slip cover.

Arson is a sure-fire proposition.

Drunk driver's alibi: I didn't know I was loaded.

A pleasant murderer is one who takes life cheerfully.

Apparently the underworld has finally gotten on top.

Jail is the place where they keep the litter of the law.

The wages of sin are the high cost of low living.

The true story of crime cannot be told in sentences.

Shoplifting is a private-enterprise attempt to curtail the profit system.

A crook is a business competitor who is doing well.

A rustler is the shepherd's crook.

A department store detective is a counter spy.

A rapist is a neurotic who takes things into his own hands.

A forger is a man who made a name for himself.

Rape is a hit and run romance.

A forger is a person who gives a check a bad name.

Rape: seduction without a sales talk.

Capital punishment: spending the summer in Washington, D.C.

Rape is assault with intent to please.

Outlaws may be a menace to society, but in-laws are worse.

Racketeering is big business on a small scale.

Crime doesn't pay, but the hours are optional.

The auto is a great moral force. It stopped horse stealing.

A crime wave is the only permanent wave that's permanent.

My wife got caught stealing a girdle and got sent up for a two-way stretch.

I'd be willing to earn my money honestly if it didn't take so long.

This town has some of the best cops money can buy.

It takes all sorts of people to make the underworld.

A crooked path is the shortest way to the penitentiary.

We can't seem to stop crime--so let's legalize it and tax it out of business.

I can't say that he picked pockets--he took them as they came.

Bluebeard had a way with women, and then did away with them.

I hate burglar alarms. They interfere with my work.

The husband of a policewoman often takes the law into his own hands.

I learned to steal so that I could follow in my father's fingerprints.

In every racket, the overhead is less important than the underhand.

Officer, where do I apologize for shooting my husband?

Burglar: one who feels that he isn't as rich as he ought to be.

Many a checkered career ends in a striped suit.

Poverty isn't a crime, but it counts against you if you commit one.

Give a convict enough rope and he'll skip.

A TV mystery is a detective story where the sponsor gets away with murder.

Highway patrolmen are cops specially trained to examine drivers' licenses.

A racketeer may go away for a rest, but more often to avoid arrest.

Many a man is saved from being a thief by finding everything locked up.

There would be even more crime if some people had more nerve.

If crime doesn't pay, how come it's one of the biggest businesses?

A burglar is a person who tries to live within another man's means.

Crime doesn't pay--or wouldn't if the government ran it.

A successful burglar can afford to stop making house calls.

In most murder cases there is no clue to the whereabouts of the police.

Crime doesn't pay, but at least you are your own boss.

What the police department doesn't know would fill a jail.

The way of the transgressor is hard--for the police to find out.

A thief believes that heaven helps those who help themselves.

Crime doesn't pay, unless, of course, you do it well.

Crime doesn't pay--sooner or later every thief gets a parking ticket.

With some safecrackers the safest safes are unsafe.

the story of crime and punishment is not to be told in short sentences.

Society prefers self-made men to self-made widows.

Criticism

Two things are bad for the heart--running upstairs and running down people.

The show had two strikes against it--the seats faced the stage.

To avoid criticism say nothing, do nothing, and be nothing.

For the first time in my life I envied my feet. They were asleep.

Of a singer, all her high notes are promissory.

They say every day in Europe is Pan America Day.

Most of today's movies should be pitied, rather than censored.

A critic is a man who knows the way, but can't drive the car.

Its impact was like the banging together of two dish cloths.

This country also needs lighter whines.

The scenery was beautiful, but the actors got in front of it.

The critics arrived after the world was created.

Critics are venomous snakes that delight in hissing.

It is a short step from critical to hypocritical.

A critic is a wet blanket that soaks everything it touches.

I like criticism, just so long as it's unqualified praise.

I came in late--but I wish I had missed it from the beginning.

Criticism wouldn't be so hard to take if it weren't so often right.

A critic is a person who finds a little bad in the best of things.

The worst fault of many people is telling other people theirs.

Critic: one who is quick on the flaw.

The cast was well-balanced--they were all rotten.

Everyone finds fault with a man who finds fault with everyone.

This show has a message, which is: Know your nearest exit.

A critic is a wet blanket that soaks everything it touches.

All the world's a stage, with most of us playing the critic's role.

Never judge women or gifts by what they are wrapped up in.

This show has a new look, but still keeps the same old smell.

I don't stay quiet when my friends are being criticised--I join right in.

A man is judged by his peers, a critic by his cheers, jeers, and sneers.

A man needs a wife because he can't blame everything on the government.

This show is a riot of off-color.

No man ever rises so high that he is above reproach.

Why can't our neighbors do as we do, and close their eyes to our faults?

A critic is a legless man who teaches running.

The play had a happy ending. Everybody was glad it was over.

A critic is a man who writes about things he doesn't like.

Never judge a man by his purse, but by his personality.

One critic may not be an ass, but two are bound to be bi-assed.

Finding fault is the most common type of unskilled labor.

The best way to look at a woman's faults is to shut your eyes.

A critic has no faults, but everyone he writes about has.

A critic is a stowaway on the flight of someone else's imagination.

The snap judgments of impulsive people are easily unfastened.

A man is judged by his deeds, a woman by her misdeeds.

We judge others by their actions; we judge ourselves by our motives.

If you have occasion to criticize a mule, do it to his face.

It is easier to look over a person's faults than to overlook them.

When a man has only himself to blame, he is probably a bachelor.

What a critic lacks in appreciation, he makes up in depreciation.

If a critic's work were done by a woman, it would be called nagging.

Relatives are inherited critics.

A man will often admit to a dozen faults in order to hide one.

A ham actor is the drama critic's meat.

Gold is the only thing that critics haven't panned.

A bachelor is the only man who never finds out how many faults he has.

Never question your wife's judgment--remember, she married you.

Don't be critical: the man everyone likes usually likes everyone.

Any man can prove he has good judgment by saying you have.

Dance

In dancing, women know the steps--men know the holds.

Only an old-timer can remember when dancing was done with the feet.

My girl friend is light on her feet, but not on mine.

Hula dancer: a shake in the grass.

I used to dance with Arthur Murray, but I found out I liked girls better.

In Hawaii, the hula girls just twiddle their tums.

The greatest sound I ever heard was a flamenco dancer with false teeth!

I have a built-in obstacle course--my feet.

Rhumba: a fox trot with the backfield in motion.

I don't care if a girl can dance, if she can intermission well.

I learned to dance by turning over a bee hive.

The hula is a dance with a lot of waist motion.

I took my girl to a barn dance, and she gave me the same old stall.

When disco dancing you exercise everything but discretion.

In disco dancing no one can tell when you make a mistake.

A girl is something you look very silly dancing without.

Some dance floors are so crowded you can't tell who your partner is.

Is a man who dances with a wallflower a lemon squeezer?

The advantage of dancing with a fat partner is that your toes are safe.

Some men are all feet when they dance, and all hands when they stop.

My daughter wanted to be a bubble dancer, but I said: "No soap!"

A poor dancer makes you feel more danced against than with.

I went to a square dance and ended up dancing with a square.

Waltz a little faster, dear, they're playing a rhumba.

A striptease dancer is a girl who has everything and shows it.

There's always room for a good man, except on a crowded dance floor.

I do a terrific cha-cha, no matter what the band is playing.

The square dance has developed by leaps and bounds.

It's hard to tell today if your partner is a good dancer, or if he's just drunk.

My girl friend is a toe dancer--she dances all over my toes.

I went to the country to see a barn dance.

If a girl can't dance it may be because she is all bustle bound.

Hula dancers have no future--it's such a shaky business.

A girl who can't dance well often makes up for it during intermission.

This place was so old-fashioned, the couples were dancing together.

It's no feat to dance on feet, unless they're your own.

My girl friend dances like popcorn over a hot fire.

The waiter dropped a tray of dishes and six couples got up to dance.

My wife only dances with me so she can stamp on my toes.

Some girls love to dance, while others dance to love.

Talk about troubles--pity the poor fan dancer who is ticklish.

Disco dancing is like trying to get on a merry-go-round after it has started.

Dancing is like wrestling, except that no holds are barred.

The dance floor was so crowded, I couldn't tell who my partner was.

I asked one girl to dance, and she was on my feet in a second.

Some people grow old gracefully; others go to discos.

He who dances must pay the piper--also the waiter and the hat-check girl.

Either I learn some new dances, or I remain a waltz flower.

On the dance floor I never know what to do with my mind.

I was bewitched by a fan dancer--I was hip-notized.

I could dance like this all night--if they'd allow it.

Death

When relatives are glad a man has died they say: "He's better off."

If you hang yourself, you die of your own free will and accord.

Life is great! Without it you'd be dead.

Killing time isn't murder--it's suicide.

He left a loudspeaker to the church--in memory of his wife.

More people commit suicide with a fork than with a gun.

The last thing a man wants to do is the last thing he does--he dies.

Everyone wants to go to Heaven, but nobody wants to die.

There is one thing in favor of suicide: it never becomes a habit.

He could never lead a procession unless he were dead.

Be guided by an undertaker and he'll put you in a hole.

I want to die with my boots on--I've got a hole in my socks.

Death frees us from the thought of death.

You can see by the obituary column that people die in alphabetical order.

The good die young because only the young die good.

Time and tide take man for a ride.

The last lap of a joy ride is usually made in a hearse.

I never wish anyone dead, but I read some obituaries with pleasure.

He looks as if an undertaker started on him and was called away.

He was such a bore: died at twenty--buried at sixty.

Everything comes to him who waits, including the hearse.

Dead men tell no tales, but their obituaries often do.

My sister dated an undertaker but he just wanted her body.

The only bad publicity is an obituary notice.

Death is nature's way of telling a man to slow down.

Debt

When you buy a car you don't run into debt; you ride into it.

Nowadays you need a credit card to pay cash.

Cheer up! Birds have bills too, but they keep on singing.

My wife sure gets a charge out of my credit cards.

The wages of war is debt.

My wife just had plastic surgery--I cut up her credit cards.

Never call a man a fool; borrow money from him instead.

My credit is so bad, they won't even take my cash.

The national debt has reached the braking point.

What this country needs is a credit card for taxpayers.

A deadbeat is always short of funds, but long on promises.

I lost my appeal to women--I couldn't find my credit cards.

A debtor is one who has enough money to make the down payment.

Credit cards help you live within your income and beyond your means.

Too many of us are dolling up on a dollar down.

My car has something that will last a lifetime--monthly payments.

The best possible thing to do with a debt is to pay it.

Credit cards: Due unto others.

The world owes each man a living--the kind he earns.

I'm poor today because my credit card was good yesterday.

Debts make wars and wars make debts--and there you are.

Credit card: Instant debt.

A rubber check can give the writer a long bounce.

The sum total of our national debt is some total.

I'd be a rich man if I was paid all the money I owe.

The customer is always right--until his bill is overdue.

More people want me to live than any man alive--my creditors.

If at first you don't succeed, try borrowing from another friend.

I'd have A-1 credit if I could borrow on my debts.

A deadbeat doesn't care whose means he lives beyond.

Give a man credit for anything today, and he'll take it.

A man who is long in debt is usually short in money.

You can get everything on credit today--except money.

Credit cards make buying easier, but paying harder.

One thing that doesn't get smaller when it is contracted is a debt.

Here's to our bills--and may we some day meet 'em.

"The King of the One-Liners" impersonating "The King of Country Music," Willie Nelson

My ambition is to owe money to as many people as I don't owe money to.

Credit card slogan: An unpaid balance in every American home.

The "b" in debt is silent--it was stuck there to supply the sting.

Buying on credit isn't bad. It's the paying that hurts.

Loan sharks attack those who go out beyond their financial depth.

If only my car would go as fast as the payments come due.

What you don't owe won't hurt you.

A credit card is a plastic I.O.U.

My wife brings more bills into the house than a Congressman.

Debt is a buy-product.

Every business loses money on bad bills, except one--the counterfeiter.

Nobody who can borrow money easily ever wants it badly.

Some men are known by their deeds; others by their mortgages.

A deadbeat never pays as he goes, but goes anyway.

The faster you run into debt the more you get behind.

To teach your kids the value of money, borrow from them.

Some of the hardest things to keep up are the easy payments.

People who run into debt usually try to crawl out of it.

The difficulty is not in buying on time--it's paying on time.

Debt is the only thing that expands as it is contracted.

Debts are the certain outcome of an uncertain income.

There's one bill none of us escape--the mosquito's.

Most of us are like the letter "b"--in debt when there's no need of it.

Always borrow from a pessimist--he never expects it back.

There is nothing as short as a short-term debt.

About the only thing a man can acquire without money is debt.

Today, anyone who isn't in debt is probably underprivileged.

Time is money, especially for a person who buys on time.

The first thing a man runs into when he buys a new care is--debt.

In the midst of life, we are in debt.

Spend money like water and you'll never liquidate your debts.

If you want to borrow $50 from a friend, ask for a hundred.

Nowadays people go into debt for things they don't need.

The man who squares his debt will probably be around again.

There are bigger things in life than money--bills, for example.

Dieting

A diet is something that helps--no end.

I'd go on a diet, but I'm a poor loser.

Sandwich spread is what you get from eating between meals.

To diet you stop eating food and start eating calories.

I'm allowed to eat all I want of anything I don't like.

Women diet to keep their girlish figures, or their boyish husbands.

Losing weight is a triumph of mind over platter.

One thing many people get fed up with is a reducing diet.

Dieting is a way of starving to death so you can live longer.

If at first you don't recede, diet and diet again.

I'm on a garlic diet. So far I've lost 5 pounds and 12 friends.

Today dieting is more widespread than the women who follow it.

The best way for a woman to watch her calories is from a distance.

One new diet food comes in cans. You open one and there's nothing in it.

The one thing harder than sticking to a diet is keeping quiet about it.

I've been on a diet for three weeks and all I've taken off is my shoes.

The best thing for a person on a diet to eat is--less.

No wonder my wife is fat. She says eating makes her hungry.

If you have to diet, you are better off when you are on it.

Dieting is the art of letting the hips fall where they may.

Eat, drink and be merry, for tomorrow ye shall diet.

Each time my wife goes on a diet, all she loses is her sense of humor.

A reducing diet will take the starch out of you.

My wife went on a banana diet. Now she looks like one.

A diet is what you keep putting off while you keep putting on.

When dieting the hours get longer and the portions get shorter.

Diets make other people lose weight.

On one diet you watch your food. You don't taste it, you just watch it.

The day I went on a diet, my stock went down and my weight went up.

You have to keep your diet up in order to keep your weight down.

My wife won't eat anything that starts with the letter "Z."

My wife is always on a diet--but she's just a wishful shrinker.

My wife takes her reducing pill in a chocolate malted.

More diets start in dress shops than in doctors' offices.

Diets are for people who are thick and tired of it.

Dieting is less a matter of health than it is a matter of form.

Dieting is the new national pastime.

What this country needs is a five-course 500-calorie dinner.

I just lost ten pounds. I'm on a low salary diet.

My wife diets religiously--one day a week.

Dieting is breaking the pound barrier.

A diet is a strait jacket for the appetite.

To reduce you've got to keep your mouth and your refrigerator shut.

Another of the world's grueling tasks is dieting.

The second day of a diet is easier than the first--by then you're off the diet.

My wife keeps young by dieting, jogging, and lying about her age.

To diet is to do without the dishes your doctor doesn't like.

I went horseback riding to lose weight. It worked! The horse lost 20 pounds.

You can't tell which women count their calories--only those who don't.

It took a lot of will-power, but I finally gave up trying to diet.

Everytime I go on a diet, the first thing I lose is my temper.

There's a new weight-watchers spaghetti. It comes in an unopenable can.

One easy way to diet is to only eat what you can afford.

Remember, what's on the table eventually ends up on the chair.

There's a new reducing salon called: Thinner Sanctum.

To lose weight my wife went to a diet doctor. In one week she lost $100.

The best place for the bathroom scale is in front of your refrigerator.

Sandwich spread is what you get from eating between meals.

Calories don't count--they multiply!

The best way to diet is to "No" thyself.

I've got an easy diet. I never eat when my wife is talking.

Either my wife goes on a diet or we'll have to let out the couch.

If you cheat on a diet you gain in the end.

Skipping can help you lose weight--skipping lunch, skipping supper.

Give a woman an inch--and immediately the entire family is on a diet.

An onion a day gives your diet away.

Then there's the cannibal who is on a diet--he only eats midgets.

In dieting, the first thing to remember is to forget seconds.

Henny lays on one-liners 'til Al Jolson cries "Mammy"

Why can't two weeks on vacation seem as long as two weeks on a diet?

My sister was on a diet so long, she disappeared.

I went on a champagne diet and took off $75.

If you don't worry about your diet, everything may go to pot.

The older you get, the wider you get.

My wife doesn't count calories--and she has the figure to prove it.

Show me a woman with a beautiful body, and I'll show you a hungry girl.

I lost over 100 pounds in one week--my wife left me!

No matter how much she reduces, my wife will never become a bargain.

Not only has my wife kept her girlish figure--she's doubled it.

I want on a 14-day diet, but all I lost was two weeks.

You can't eat your cake and diet too.

My diet calls for less food, but my appetite calls for more.

You should watch your diet--not eat it!

You follow a reducing diet for days, but talk about it for months

I'm on a new tranqulizer diet--I haven't lost an ounce, but I don't care.

Divorce

They're called divorce suits because nothing but a divorce seems to suit.

The two chief causes of divorce are matrimony and alimony.

Divorce is the price people pay for playing with matches.

Cupid loves courting, but draws the line at a jury.

About the only way to stop divorce is to stop marriage.

Divorce is the result of his losing his capital, and her losing her interest.

A divorce suit always costs more than a wedding gown.

All that's needed for a divorce today is a wedding.

A starlet is a young actress who has been married only once.

Marriage slogan: Cheer up! Divorce is yet to come.

If divorce didn't separate some couples the police would have to.

With today's divorce rate, most of the courting comes after the wedding.

Many a divorce suit is of the two-pants variety.

Divorce results when a husband decides he's too good to be true.

Divorce is a marital dissolution that follows a mutual disillusion.

To hear the evidence, divorces are made in heaven, too.

How do movie stars spend their time between husbands?

June is the month of brides. The other 11 are devoted to divorces.

Truth is more of an estranger than fiction.

My wife and I got remarried. Our divorce didn't work out.

What I want most to get out of my marriage is to get out.

In my divorce, I got custody of the kids--she got custody of the money.

Some women take a man for better or for worse, but not for good.

She's so thrilled with her first marriage, she can hardly wait for the next.

For the woman that has everything--a divorce.

Love is the shortest distance between two marriages.

Divorce is the past tense of marriage.

Two's company and three's a divorce.

Divorce is a hash made of domestic scraps.

The wife who always has the last word often gets it as the divorcee.

A divorcee is a woman who gets richer by decrees.

Divorce has done more to promote peace than the United Nations.

Divorce: flying out of the little hate-nest.

Hell hath no fury like the lawyer of a woman scorned.

Desertion is the poor man's method of divorce.

Judging by the divorce rate, many who said "I do," don't.

After a divorce, a woman feels like a new man.

They're having trouble getting a divorce--neither one wants the children.

Divorce: going through a change of wife.

A divorce costs much more than a marriage, but it's worth it.

Reno: residence of the bitter half.

Divorces are caused where the blind have led the blind.

Divorce is so common that some couples stay married just to be different.

Reno is where the cream of society goes to be separated.

She lost the marriage, but she won the divorce.

My sister's been to Reno so ofteh she's a little swap-worn.

There is only one quick relief from cold misery--a divorce.

The proper time for divorce is during courtship.

We got divorced because of illness--we got sick of each other.

My neighbors couldn't afford a divorce, so she shot him.

Love at first sight ends with divorce at first slight.

Divorce: the banked fires of the flame of love.

Divorce suits are always pressed with the seamy side out.

We found out we weren't fit to be tied.

For years I suffered from a pain in the neck, so I'm finally divorcing her.

Divorce is a legal formula that follows "I do" with "Adieu."

In France divorce is called "French Leave."

Actually we were mis-pronounced man and wife.

I'm divorcing my wife, and naming her mirror as correspondent.

Divorce is the result of a transition from a duet to a duel.

Divorce is a parting word.

Divorce is when lovers become leavers.

My wife divorced me for being more interested in spice than spouse.

Couples divorce when the marriage tie becomes a forget-me-knot.

Divorce is the result of holy wedlock turned into any unholy deadlock.

Divorce is a severance of the ties that bind.

Divorce is the transition from co-existence to go-existence.

Divorce is the aspirin tablet for marital headaches.

Divorce is the result of compatibility turning into combatibility.

We were determined to prove that love can find a way--out.

Give a man enough rope, and he'll skip.

Divorce is a judicial solution for injudicious people.

We got divorced when we found we weren't fit to be tied.

Divorce is matrimony's Great Divide.

Divorce is the proof that one man's mate is another man's poison.

Divorce is the proof that truce is stranger than fiction.

Our marriage gave out because there wasn't enough giving in.

Divorce is what happens when couples stop toasting and start roasting.

Our "I do" turned out to be much "I do" about nothing.

Our divorce was the result of unpleasant relations--such as her parents.

Our marriage went from duet to a duel.

Divorce cocktail: Marriage on the Rocks.

The grave of our love was excavated with little digs.

Divorces are made in heaven.

My wife's in Reno, the land of the free and the grave of the home.

Only the brave desert the fair.

A divorcee is always looking for fresh he-quipment.

She was the light of my life. I put her out ten years ago.

Our married life was tense, now our divorce is past tense.

My wife has given me something to live for--a divorce.

We're incompatible. I want a divorce and she doesn't.

I'm celebrating my anniversary tonight. I've been divorced for five years.

Our marriage was a three-act drama: Announced, Denounced, Renounced.

I owe my success to my wife. She divorced me.

I just bought a pain-reliever--a divorce.

My wife sued for divorce because of a little miss-understanding.

I got divorced because my wife was tried and found wanton.

I'd divorce my wife, but I'll be darned if I make her that happy.

In 25 years of marriage I never once thought about divorce--murder, yes!

It's called "grounds for divorce" because of the dirt.

She didn't marry me for my money--she divorced me for it.

Divorce is so prevalent lately that it's hard to tell who's whose.

The surest sign that a man is in love is when he divorces his wife.

To help the Women's Lib Movement--I divorced my wife.

Doctors

My doctor put his hand on my wallet and asked me to cough.

A guy says to a doctor, "My foot hurts, what will I do for it?" "Limp!"

I was so ugly when I was born, the doctor slapped my mother.

A doctor gave me a flu shot, and I got it.

After my medical exam I asked, "Doc, how do I stand?" He said: "That's what puzzles me."

My doctor has performed over 400 operations--and never cut himself once.

Before you operate, show me your operator's license.

Never argue with a doctor. He has inside information.

My doctor put me back on my feet. To pay his bill, I had to sell my car.

He's a bone specialist. He carries his own dice.

I know a surgeon whose card reads: "May I cut in?"

Now they have a doctor doll: you wind it up and it operates on batteries.

I couldn't afford surgery, so my doctor retouched my x-rays.

I wonder what she meant when she told the doctor to cut it out?

A specialist is a doctor who diagnoses your case by feeling your wallet.

When I swallowed a dime the doctor made me cough up twenty dollars.

The only appendix safe from a doctor is the one in a book.

My son is thinking of becoming a doctor. He has the handwriting for it.

It's double jeopardy when your doctor calls in a consultant.

Weight reduction doctors live off the fat of the land.

Would you call a patient's complaints to his doctor an "organ recital?"

Doctors get round-shouldered from looking at people in bed.

An osteopath is a doctor who works his fingers to your bones.

Hello, Doc. Make any grave mistakes today?"

An osteopath makes no bones about his profession.

A surgeon is a large fish.

Doctors often think a patient cured who has simply quit in disgust.

A doctor is a man who is always out for his cut.

A doctor is the only man without a cure for a cold.

He's a specialist--an ear, nose, and threat man.

A doctor is a man who tells you if you don't cut something out, he will.

The doctor felt the patient's purse and decided there was no hope.

Doctors prevent people from dying natural deaths.

A minor operation is one performed on someone else.

Show me an unethical doctor, and I'll show you a dirty quack.

My son is a born doctor. He can't write anything anybody can read.

Show me a hypodermic needle, and I'll show you a sick shooter.

Doctors are those to whom we entrust our lives--and our fortunes.

Then there was the panhandler who worked in the hospital.

My mother-in-law has a lousy doctor. The quack saved her life.

Cure: what a doctor does to a disease while killing the patient.

A specialist is a doctor whose patients can only be sick during office hours.

It's the doctor who suffers from good health.

A doctor kills you today to prevent you from dying tomorrow.

A doctor acts like a humanitarian and charges like a plumber.

An obstetrician makes his money on the stork market.

My doctor calls his suburban estate: "Bedside Manor."

A maternity hospital is an heirport.

A specialist is a doctor with a smaller practice, but a bigger home.

A doctor is a man who has his tonsils, adenoids, and appendix.

My brother drowned while taking acupuncture treatments on a waterbed.

A doctor is a healthy man who can't keep away from sick people.

A specialist is a man who is ignorant on all subjects but one.

Medical care is expensive. So, when you bit the bullet, don't swallow it.

One doctor who doesn't cultivate a bedside manner is the veterinarian.

Doctors should let the well enough alone.

Never leave the hospital until you are strong enough to face the cashier.

I was at death's door--and my doctor was trying to pull me through.

The things the average drug store carries today are apt to make you sick.

When sick go to a specialist and he will do you good--and plenty.

I know a surgeon who takes out tonsils, appendixes, and nurses.

The new miracle drugs can keep a patient alive until he pays his bill.

The only doctor who never sends his patients a bill is the veterinarian.

Doctors get by--they have inside information.

The only way to get a doctor to make a housecall is to marry him.

One person who always knows what to do till the doctor comes is his wife.

A doctor's fees are ill-gotten gains.

When I got my bill I understood why the surgeon wore a mask.

My doctor says I need a complete change--so I'm changing my doctor.

Before treating my nose and ear, my doctor asked me for an arm and a leg.

My doctor charges $25 a visit--more if you're sick.

My doctor told me to watch my food. Where I eat, I have to watch my coat.

I'm trying to find a doctor whose patients are not all sick.

My doctor divorced his wife. She started giving him an apple every day.

My doctor discovered a cure for which there is no disease.

When my doctor found out what I had, he relieved me of most of it.

My doctor has more degrees than a themometer.

My doctor is so busy, while in his waiting room I caught another disease.

My doctor is mean. He keeps his stethoscope in the freezer.

My doctor has the flu. Now he's getting a taste of his own medicine.

My doctor has magic hands. Each time he touches me $50 disappears.

My doctor's prescriptions are hard to read, but his bills are legible.

There is one advantage to being poor--a doctor will cure you faster.

Dogs

I call my dog "Bulova." He's a watch dog.

Some dogs are pointers. Mine's a nudger. He's too polite to point.

My dog is sort of a cockeyed spaniel.

My dog is a real poetry lover. He's mad for Trees.

He was a fire dog. He helped locate hydrants.

I got this dog for my wife. I'd like to make a trade like that every day.

He may not look it, but he's a police dog. You see, he's in the C.I.A.

He's a genuine Mexican Hairless--in fact, he shaves every day.

He's supposed to be a bird dog, but I never heard him sing a note.

A dog fills an empty place in a man's life--especially a hot dog.

My dog even helps me in the office. He's a kind of secret-terrier.

Dogs don't have fleas--that's silly. Dogs have puppies.

I know he's not a bloodhound. I cut my hand the other day and he fainted.

The noblest of all dogs is the hot dog. It feeds the hand that bites it.

And now a message to puppies all over the world: On the paper!

The right time for gathering apples is when the dog is tied up.

Every dog has his day--but the nights are reserved for the cats.

I know a man who went to the dogs--chasing chickens.

Every dog isn't a growler, and every growler isn't a dog.

There is only one smartest dog in the world, and every boy has it.

A dog is a man's best friend, and vice versa.

If a dog could talk, he wouldn't be man's best friend for long.

When some men go to the dogs, it's pretty tough on the dogs.

The perfect dog food would be one that tastes like a postman.

Play it safe: let sleeping dogs lie, and let lying dogs sleep.

The fate of the flea is that all his children will eventually go to the dogs.

My favorite dog is a St. Bernard--I like a dog that can hold its liquor.

I had to get rid of my lap dog. Every time I sat on his lap he bit me.

He made his dog sit in the sun. He wanted to get a hot dog.

I call my dog "Photographer"--he's always snapping at people.

I have to get my dog a present, or he'll bite my wife again.

I was the teacher's pet. She couldn't afford a dog.

When a man bites a dog, it's his wife's pet chow.

No, no! A dogma is not a mama dog!

A dog is the only friend you can buy for money.

When my dog visited a flea circus he stole the show.

One K-9 dog in the army asked to be transferred to a new post.

Drinking

This guy gets so loaded with liquor, they make him take the freight elevator.

If there's a nip in the air, he tries to drink it.

I just redecorated my bar. I put new drunks around it.

I read about the evils of drinking, so I gave up reading.

I'm not a steady drinker. My hands shake too much.

The modern girl no longer comes out--she's carried out.

They make such a dry martini you have to use a spoon.

My brother-in-law has a new position--he's standing up.

I never drink unless I'm with someone or alone.

I found five dollars in the street. Smell my breath if you don't believe me.

The best way to hold your whiskey is in a glass.

A drink in time is fine.

Liquor may be slow poison, but I'm not in a hurry.

Drinking doesn't drown your troubles--it just irrigates them.

If you drink to forget, forget it!

Orange juice is great for breakfast. It makes a wonderful chaser.

I don't drink to my wife--I drink because of her.

My wife can't drink. She gets high on Scotch tape.

We played house. I was the walls and got plastered.

I better stop drinking--I can't remember what I'm trying to forget.

Every morning I get up tight and early.

If you drink like a fish--swim--don't drive.

I'm on the wagon half-way. I cut out chasers.

I'm suffering from bottle fatigue.

Alcohol was first distilled in Arabia, which may explain the nights.

People say I'm never sober. Why, I've been sober four times today.

I never do anything by halves--always by liters.

I drink to make other people interesting.

He breathed on the back of her neck and bleached her hair.

A good year for whiskey is the year you drink it.

I distill Bullfrog Gin. Drink a little--hop a little--and croak.

Problem drinkers are those who never buy.

He's leaned on so many bars his clothes have padded elbows.

With the price of liquor today--beggars can't be boozers.

She wasn't born--she was squeezed out of a bar rag.

Hangover: the wrath of grapes.

I'm going out tonight--but not completely.

He's not shot if you can still see the whites of his eyes.

New drink advertised in air terminals: Traveler's Aid.

The man who gets loaded too often will eventually get fired.

Dad never gets his suits cleaned--he has them distilled.

Now they have a low-cal bourbon for fat drunks.

We're not responsible for guests left over thirty days.

He's so wet, everytime you blow on him, he ripples.

Some people have glowing personalities only when lit up.

Each evening I have a shot glass of water--that takes care of the chasers.

He was last seen in a bottle of bourbon.

I hold my liquor--especially when it's in a girl.

My red eyes don't mean that I'm drunk--I might be a white rabbit.

And to pass the time away, we all took Mickeys.

He has cheeks like roses, and a nose to match.

The cost of living is like bad booze--you have to fight to keep it down.

Miniature cocktail: Drink one, and in a miniature out.

This club has curb service. Get drunk and they put you on the curb.

To get rid of a red nose from drinking, drink more--then it'll turn purple.

I don't hit the bottle any more. Hit it? I can't even see it.

He's not shot if you can still see the whites of his eyes.

Dad drinks something awful. I know, I tasted it.

Not only do I like to drink Zombies--I married one.

I'm a very light sleeper; I always wake up at the crack of the ice.

When you get loaded too often you eventually get fired.

My father spends a staggering amount of money on liquor.

I had one rye after another. I must have had ten slices.

He drinks so much that he's got bonded ulcers.

I either have to give up drinking, or get my knees half-soled.

It only takes one drink to make me drunk--usually the fifth.

He can empty a bottle as quick as a flask.

He doesn't really drink. He just gargles gin. Sometimes it slips.

Blessed are the pure in spirit, for nothing is worse than a mixed drink.

He drinks to forget, and the thing he forgets is when to stop.

Nothing makes me drink the way I do--I'm a volunteer.

Alcohol preserves everything except secrets.

I left a bar and keeled over from fresh-air poisoning.

I'm suffering from bottle fatigue.

Shot: that which, if you have more than one, you are half.

Let him who is without gin cast the first moan.

I'm so anemic that when I get drunk only one eye gets bloodshot.

When you drink doubles, you see the same way.

My girl friend is cold up to a pint.

You can ruin your health drinking to everyone else's.

He was dispossessed. They were repairing the gutter.

Get the best of liquor or it will get the best of you.

You'll never have a hangover--if you stay drunk.

My favorite drink is the next one.

A little blurred tells me when I've had enough.

Who says I'm a hard drinker? I do that easier than anything.

I only put on weight in certain places--like in bars.

To me, every day is an alcohol-iday.

If a mosquito bit him, it would die of alcohol-poisoning.

You're drunk when you feel sophisticated and can't pronounce it.

I hate to be beaten to the punch, especially if it's spiked with gin.

I'm working my way down from bottoms up.

He's so high, if you smell his breath you get a nosebleed.

My wife is sticking to me through thick and gin.

My wife has a sobering effect on me--she hides the bottle.

The only thing stronger than Mother's love is father's breath.

Laugh and the world laughs with you. Cry and they say you're drunk.

I enjoy cocktail parties where drinks mix people.

People who get gassed shouldn't light matches.

My idea of a corking good time is uncorking.

No wonder he looks so pale--all the blood is in his eyes.

An alcoholic is someone you don't like who drinks as much as you do.

When a girl drinks too much she gets weak in the nays.

I can always beer up under misfortune.

Strange, the more oiled a man is, the noisier he becomes.

The Bigamy Cocktail: they serve you doubles and you see single.

I do not drink like a fish. No fish drinks what I drink.

He not only drinks--he drinks between drinks.

Actually, I only drink on occasion. Just any occasion.

Two Scotsmen are ruining me: Haig & Haig.

How can anybody be that blind without a white cane?

I don't like to see a woman get drunk. I don't approve of tight skirts.

He was so loaded they made him use the freight elevator.

I only go to parties where there's rum for one more.

I'm not saying he drinks, but everybody calls him a "ham on rye."

There's hardly a morning when he doesn't get up with a toot-ache.

Four drinks and my girl friend goes hug-wild.

I once went to a party incognito--stone sober.

Sophistication is the art of getting drunk with the right people.

I only drink until liquor mortis sets in.

High noon: three martinis before lunch.

I'm a man of high-fidelity--I stagger home to my wife every night.

I put vitamins in my gin--to build me up while I'm tearing myself down.

If I've got to go, I want to be killed by a flask of lightning.

Two drunks looked at my wife and took the pledge.

I'd be the nicest guy on two feet, if I could only stay there.

I want to send my brother-in-law a gift. How do you wrap up a saloon?

I've never cultivated the fine art of nixing drinks.

A bartender is a kind of plasterer.

If it wasn't for the olives in the Martinis, he'd starve to death.

This club has the nicest tables I've ever been under.

Dad's gone on the wagon--the paddy wagon for being drunk.

I'm proud to be this bar's unsteadiest customer.

I may drink a lot, but I always know the way to go home: drunk.

I was out with a Wick last night--Wick, that's a lit up WAC.

My doctor is worried--I have too little blood in my alcohol stream.

The wages of gin is breath.

I do other things besides drink--I also hiccup.

If I throw a pretzel in my mouth and it splashes, I've had enough.

I do a great magic trick. I walk down the street and turn into a saloon.

Each man kills the thing he loves--let's open another bottle of Scotch.

I can sit at a bar for hours--I pay when I glow.

They say whiskey and gasoline don't mix. They do, but they taste lousy.

He has Saloon Arthritis--every night he's stiff in another joint.

I'm also a flyer. I'm a test pilot for Seagram's.

The Blood Bank rejected my blood--my plasma had an olive in it.

I studied for the bar, but I flunked in Dry Martinis.

There was a nip in the air--so I tried to drink it.

He's a C.P.A.--a Certified Public Alcoholic.

He's an alcoholic intellectual--a fried egghead.

Drinking gives you patriotic eyes. Blue, with red whites.

I've been unsteadily employed here for the past ten years.

I took a blood test and the doctor offered me $50 a case.

He's an outstanding candidate for the Alcohol of Fame.

Hangover advice: wear swim trunks to bed, in case your icebag leaks.

I believe in a balanced diet--a drink in each hand.

It's not a real hangover unless you can't stand the fizz of an Alka-Seltzer.

The only thing my health means to me is something to drink to.

My Dad is as straight and as tall as a rifle, and just as loaded.

There's a new drink called "Old Maid"--it has no chaser.

Quiz Cocktail: have one and you don't know the answer to anything.

I never stand up while the room is in motion.

The Bar Exam is a test to determine just how much you can hold.

The only time I go to the refrigerator is when I need ice cubes.

I've been on the wagon about a year now--since last Monday.

I got so high yesterday that I had to drink with a net under me.

Alcohol is the social lubricant.

I'd go on the wagon if I could find one with a bar.

Glasses don't always improve vision--particularly whiskey glasses.

I fix a lot of things around the house--Martinis, Manhattans.

Looking at your troubles through the bottom of a glass magnifies them.

You can't make both ends meet, if you make one end drink.

Alcohol is an anesthetic against reality.

Liquor is a form of instant courage.

The Blood Bank uses my blood to sterilize the instruments.

Another name for liquor is "totter sauce."

I drink to steady my nerves. Sometimes I get so steady, I can't even more.

Never drink on an empty wallet.

I'm going to be starred in a movie called "The Unquenchables."

A problem drinker is one who never buys.

Drinking makes some people lose their inhibitions and give exhibitions.

A Mickey Finn is a liquid blackjack.

I'm having my eyebrows furrowed, so they won't slip off a wet bar.

I know my capacity, but I keep getting drunk before I reach it.

They knew I was delirious in the hospital--I kept asking for water.

The only thing that keeps bars in business is customers.

I went on the Drinking Man's Diet--and now I'm a thin lush.

Where moonshine comes from is a mystery still.

Hiccups are merely messages from departed spirits.

We don't serve women at the bar--you have to bring your own.

Want a drunk to take notice of you? Pretend you're a bartender.

A man who can stand drinking can usually drink standing.

The one for the road may be two for the cemetery.

Nothing can be more frequent than an occasional drink.

I drink to forget the woman who is driving me to drink.

Whiskey is a magician that can make a monkey out of an ass.

Drinking to drown your misery is like putting a fire out with oil.

Never drink from your finger bowl--it only contains water.

Some contemptible scoundrel stole the cork from my lunch.

To modernize an old-fashioned girl, feed her lots of Old Fashioneds.

Man ages whiskey, and whiskey ages man.

Some men are driven to drink, but most walk to a bar.

An alcoholic is a person who puts thirst things first.

When I have a problem, I drop in a bar and drink it over.

If drinking is a disease, why isn't it covered by Blue Cross?

Some men can take a drink or leave it alone--for a few hours.

A bar is a counter that separates drinkers from their money.

Absinthe makes the heart grow fonder, and the breath grow stronger.

The barmaid is what the boys in the backroom will have.

Of all the remedies that won't cure a cold, I like whiskey the best.

Champagne is the wine of least resistance.

Alcohol is like success: both are all right until they go to your head.

A bartender is a contact man for Bacchus.

An alcoholic is anyone, who will drink with anyone, to anyone.

A cocktail lounge is a half-lit room full of half-lit people.

Two can live as cheaply as one can drink.

You could call a cocktail glass a "hic cup."

Don't drink and drive; it's hard enough to hit a pedestrian when you're sober.

A bar is where drinks mix people.

In the Caribbean, all roads lead to rum.

Cocktail parties are where mixed drunks drink mixed drinks.

Liquor is legal, but some people think it's compulsory.

At a cocktail party you meet old friends you never knew before.

An alcoholic is the only sponge that never fills up on water.

I never put off till tomorrow the drinking I can do today.

Some people drink to success, others to excess.

I only drink to forget I drink.

Liquor should not be given to any man who is given to liquor.

Anyone who orders a soft drink has no kick coming.

Whiskey drowns some troubles, but floats a lot more.

Talk about boozing! Every time he passes a liquor store his nose lights up.

The higher I feel in the evening, the lower I feel in the morning.

I don't spend all my money on booze. I save some for luxuries.

Men always make passes at girls who drain glasses.

I was taking shots for my cold, but my wife took the bottle away.

With me it was love at first drink.

I gave up drinking. Now I have nothing to live on but food and water.

Love makes the world go 'round, and so does a good stiff drink.

You're never drunk as long as you can lie on the floor without holding on.

When I don't feel well, I drink; and when I drink, I don't feel well.

Show me a drunk with false teeth, and I'll show you a gummy rummy.

I never drink when I'm driving--only when my wife is driving.

I prefer drink to food because it interferes less with conversation.

I'm not a big drinker--I just put away a lot of little ones.

Card Table Cocktail: One drink and your legs fold up.

Sign at bar: If you're drinking to forget--please pay in advance.

Now there's a Tax Cocktail--two of them and you've withheld nothing.

His idea of frozen food is Scotch on the rocks.

We didn't know Dad was a lush--until one day he came home sober.

One more for the road and I'll need a road map to get to my car.

I don't like to drink--it's just something to do while I get drunk.

I feel terrible. Even a hangover would be an improvement.

I promised I'd stop drinking, but I didn't promise I'd stop lying.

A drunk put a dime in a parking meter and said, "My God--I weigh an hour!"

I never drink before noon--luckily it happens to be noon in Paris right now.

Mom never drinks anything stronger than pop--and Pop will drink anything.

Dumb

He has a brain, but it hasn't reached his head.

Man is the only animal that speaks, except when he talks like an ass.

She has a soft heart, and she's let it go to her head.

The closest some people ever come to a brainstorm is a light drizzle.

He was born stupid, and lately he's had a relapse.

She has a pretty little head. For a head, it's pretty little.

He has a one-track mind, and the traffic on it is very light.

If you want a thing to be well done, don't do it youself.

He's brighter than he looks--but then, he'd just have to be.

A man may be dumb and not know it, but not if he is married.

He doesn't know his own mind--and he hasn't missed much.

My problem is having too much confidence in my own inability.

Being full of brotherly love, he never lets anyone beat a jackass.

What some people lack in intelligence they often make up for in stupidity.

If he ever gets a bright idea it'll be beginner's luck.

They've named a town after him: Marblehead, Massachusetts.

Many doctors have examined his head, but they can't find anything.

Our car needs a new muffler--so my wife has started to knit one.

Dieting won't help her--no diet will reduce a fat head.

He isn't scatterbrained. He hasn't any brains to scatter.

The only way she can make up her mind is to powder her forehead.

My wife's going in for a minor operation--they're putting a brain in.

He'd have to step out of his mind to get an idea.

He has a strange growth on his neck--his head.

Everything about her is open--an open mind with a vacant stare.

His train of thought is just a string of empties.

No wonder he looked upset--he was holding the mirror upside down.

Ignorance is bliss, but not when you're a dropout.

He's afraid to be lost in thought--he's a total stranger there.

He's so dumb, the mind reader only charged him half-price.

She thinks a can opener is the key to the john.

When people become prosperous, they often become preposterous.

She is so dumb--she thinks Band-Aid is a charity for musicians.

Henny "makes time" with three of Hollywood's great ladies, Lana Turner, Judy Garland and Patrice Munsel

My wife is always doing things around the house that she can't.

He's studying to be a moron.

My girl friend has no more on her mind than anywhere else.

He's so stupid he can't spell LSD.

She's recovering from an accident--a thought recently struck her.

This idiot took the screens off her windows to let the flies out.

You never know how dumb you can be until life gives you the chance.

They say it pays to be ignorant--so how come I'm broke?

There is no more terrible sight than ignorance in action.

I finally had to move from Massachusetts. I couldn't spell it.

It takes my wife an hour to cook Minute rice.

If ignorance is bliss, why aren't more people happy?

There's no fool like an old fool, except an older fool.

The only thing my mother-in-law ever read was an eye-chart.

If she said what she thought, she'd be speechless.

Talk about dumb! He took his girl to her apartment, and then left her flat.

It's all right to be dumb, but he's making a career of it.

Wisdom often comes with age, but with him age came alone.

I asked her to pass the plate and she asked: "Upper or lower?"

My brother would have to climb Mt. Everest to reach a deep thought.

My wife bought a cheap dictionary--it's not in alphabetical order.

A fool and his money are soon parted, but rarely by another fool.

She thinks intercourse is the time spent between classes.

I never shave in front of a mirror--I can't stand the sight of me.

She thinks statutory rape means doing it standing up.

He lost his mind when a butterfly kicked him in the head.

She's so dumb, she takes off her sweater to count to two.

When he gets an idea into his head, he has the whole thing in a nutshell.

She thinks blood vessels are some kind of ship.

There's no fool like an old fool--unless he's got money.

She thinks a Peeping Tom is a night watchman.

The world is full of fools, and there's always one more than you think.

Imagine a guy who needed a tutor to pass recess.

My mother-in-law is an M.D.--Mentally Deficient.

She squeezed a can of soup to see if it was fresh.

The chip on his shoulder is a splinter from the wood above it.

She spent two days in a revolving door looking for a doorknob.

I never shot billiards--they have as much right to live as anybody else.

She was 16 years old before she could wave goodbye.

Every so often you meet a man whose ignorance is encyclopedic.

When our gas pipe was leaking she put a pan under it.

Some husbands are very versatile--they can't do anything.

They had to keep her in summer school all winter.

Nothing can give man a sense of the infinite like human stupidity.

When she worked for a tea company she asked for a coffee break.

A demitasse would fit his head like a sombrero.

My boss has one of those mighty minds--mighty empty.

She wrote a post card and said: "Check enclosed."

Ignorance is when you don't know something, and somebody finds out.

He walked through a screen door and strained himself.

Too bad they don't sell toupees with brains in them.

He wore a blindfold so he could go on a blind date.

No one is perfect except a man who makes a perfect fool of himself.

He took a ruler to bed with him to see how long he slept.

When money talks, it doesn't always know what it's talking about.

He runs around his bed trying to catch some sleep.

He goes to a podiatrist for psychoanalysis--his brains are in his feet.

Many a man thinks he has an open mind, when it's merely vacant.

He should study to be a bone specialist. He has the head for it.

I didn't know the meaning of fear--until I looked it up.

Generally, a man who doesn't know his own mind hasn't missed much.

What you don't know doesn't hurt you, but it amuses a lot of people.

A cold in the head is at least something.

His brain is like a politician's speech--mostly empty.

If my girl friend said what she thought--she'd be speechless.

He's always putting off decisions--he's waiting for a brainy day.

You can't underestimate the ignorance of some people.

They put better heads than his on umbrellas.

Just when we discover that ignorance is bliss, it isn't.

I changed my mind, but it didn't work any better than my old one.

He's the kind of guy to use for a blueprint--if you are building an idiot.

What fools these mortals think other mortals be!

He manages to keep his head above water--but that's because wood floats.

There's no fool like an old fool--you just can't beat experience.

I like to walk. I seldom take a step without walking.

Ears

My ear is ringing. Pardon me, while I answer it.

Being deaf is not as bad as having to listen to some people.

The husband who learns to listen, rarely listens to learn.

My early struggles started when my Mother tried to wash my ears.

My wife will do anything I say except listen to me.

Blessed are the deaf, for they shall miss much idle gossip.

If you believe what you hear, you're probably eavesdropping.

My son has sensitive ears. He screams every time I pull them.

A woman likes a strong silent man because she thinks he's listening.

Money talks, but it's hard of hearing when you call it.

A first-class listener is a woman's best friend.

My wife has an ear like a shovel--always picking up dirt.

The trouble with some people is that they listen with their mouths.

Hearing is one thing, and listening is another.

Be wary of any man who lets you do all the talking.

My brother is a big ear doctor--he only looks at big ears.

He can swat flies with his ears.

What you hear never sounds as important as what you overhear.

A good listener is usually thinking about something else.

Talk about big ears! From the front he looks like a loving cup.

"Doctor, I have a ringing in my ear." "Don't answer it."

One of the best hearing aids a man can have is an attentive wife.

A rumor is something that goes in one ear, and in another.

The only time my son washes his ears is when he eats watermelon.

Any woman who never hears any gossip needs a hearing aid.

If you want to hear everything, keep both eyes open.

Only a teen-ager talks on the phone long enough to have to change ears.

Egotism

Egotism is just a case of mistaken non-entity.

When a man is wrapped up in himself, he makes a very small package.

If he ever changes his faith, it'll be because he no longer thinks he's God.

An egotist is a man who thinks he is everything you think you are.

He has gone the way of all flash.

An egotist is a self-made man who worships his creator.

A high brow is a person educated beyond his own intelligence.

The man who is in love with himself seldom has any cause for jealousy.

She thinks she's a siren, but she looks more like a false alarm.

He shaves with cold water, because hot water steams up his mirror.

His head is getting too big for his toupee.

I know an actor who is so conceited, he had his x-rays retouched.

An egotist is an "I" specialist.

Nothing gets you all up in the air quicker than an inflated ego.

Every time he opens his mouth, he puts his feats in.

When two egotists meet, it's a case of an I for an I.

He has an alarm clock and a phone--neither rings--they applaud.

One thing that grows without nourishment is an ego.

Egotism is a drug which enables some people to live with themselves.

My girl friend is so ritzy, she has alligator bags under her eyes.

He'd need a hole in the ground to shrink to his normal proportions.

She had to go to a plastic surgeon to have her nose lowered.

Egotism is the art of seeing qualities in yourself which others can't see.

Conceit is God's gift to little men.

Someone should press the "down" button on his elevator shoes.

I dine with the upper set--I use my lowers, too.

He keeps getting carried away by the sound of his own mouth.

I know one woman who was born with her face lifted.

Her body has gone to her head.

I just applied to the Post Office for an unlisted Zip Code number.

He thinks it's a halo, but it's only a swelled head.

They hired an upstairs maid--and they live in a ranch house.

He thinks that if he hadn't been born, people would wonder why.

The way she acts, you'd think it was her duty to be snooty.

If his halo falls one more inch, it will be a noose.

My ancestors didn't come over on the Mayflower--they had their own boat.

The hardest opinion she's ever had to keep is her opinion of herself.

The upper crust is just a lot of crumbs sticking together.

Egotists don't go around talking about other people.

I can trace my family tree back to the time when my family lived in it.

Success is going to his head, but it's bound to be a short visit.

My mother-in-law is as stuck-up as a billboard.

He's so big-headed, he can't get an aspirin to fit him.

My wife insists that we use monogrammed tea bags.

He'd be more attractive if his I's weren't so close together.

I wear a riding habit just to pitch horseshoes.

He stands high in his own mind, but he's still a long way from the top.

Our home is in a nice location--just on the outskirts of our income.

Every time he looks in the mirror, he takes a bow.

A man can be listed in Who's Who, and still not know what's what.

Success turned his head, and it left him facing in the wrong direction.

My mother-in-law belongs to the uppish classes.

He's carrying on a great love affair--unassisted.

His trouble is that he's always me-deep in conversation.

She has two nose specialists--one for each nostril.

I'm not really conceited, but every time I hear thunder, I do take a bow.

All I need to boost my ego is a swivel chair.

She's as overbearing as a woman giving birth to quintuplets.

My wife worships me--and so do I.

Some people feel snubbed if an epidemic overlooks them.

Take care when speaking about me--you're speaking of the man I love.

His bathroom ceiling has a mirror, so he can watch himself gargle.

I know when an idea is good--when it's one of mine.

I always hire people who like what I like--me.

He's always letting off esteem.

I'm studying geometry to learn how to move in the best circles.

One day he'll fracture his pride and fall over his own bluff.

Remember, if you're not talking about me, I'm not listening.

He's the type who talks big and performs small.

I'm a problem to my psychiatrist--I'm too big for the couch.

His conceit is the tribute of a fool.

I'm the greatest admirer of my wife's husband.

Her head's like a weather vane: easily turned by the slightest wind.

Then there are those women who snoop and snub.

He's a fellow of real high-hat-itude.

Most tourists come home brag and baggage.

Money has brought him everything except sense and humility.

His dream is to go from the cash register to the social register.

He didn't just grow with responsibility--he bloated.

It's not true that vanity is a sin. Sometimes it's a mistake.

He thinks he's worth a lot of money just because he has it.

He sees qualities in himself that other people can't see.

You could make a fortune renting his head out as a balloon.

Vanity is caused by too much Vitamin "I" in the system.

Success turned his head. Too bad it didn't wring his neck.

Conceit may puff a man up, but it can never prop him up.

Success hasn't changed him. He's still the same louse he always was.

Love is blind, but self-love is full of I's.

He thinks he's a big shot just because he explodes.

The girl with a jutting exterior isn't always her sister's superior.

He can pat himself on the back better than a contortionist.

Vanity is what makes the man in a rut, think he's in the groove.

He's as pompous as an undertaker at a $10,000 funeral.

His trouble is that he let his father's success go to his head.

Self-made men cause me to wonder who interrupted them.

Egotism is a disease--it makes everyone sick except the person who has it.

A really self-made man has no one to blame but himself.

Egotism is the ability to think you're a whale, when you're really an eel.

Egotism makes a man's mind shrink while it makes his head swell.

I'm easily entertained. All you have to do is just listen.

If a man can't marry himself, how can he ever marry his first love?

I don't mind criticism as long as it's out-and-out approval.

He's suffering from infantuation.

Success has not only gone to his head, but to his mouth, too.

He's going through life with his horn stuck.

An egotist thinks first of himself, and then thinks of himself, second.

A man is never more serious than when he praises himself.

Every man thinks he's smarter than others, but only the egotist says so.

The course of true love never runs smooth, except when it's self-love.

Being egotistical is the only satisfaction some men find in life.

Love is full of faith, but no love is so faithful as self-love.

Etiquette

The test of good manners is to be able to put up pleasantly with bad ones.

He had the manners of a gentleman. I knew they didn't belong to him.

My Dad is a 100% gentleman--he even tips his hat when passing tomatoes.

Always say "pistachios." It's impolite to say "nuts."

We expect our children to learn good table manners without ever seeing any.

His coffee has been poured, saucered, and blown.

I don't like the way they treat visitors to New York. They threw me out.

Etiquette is the art of knowing the right way to do a wrong thing.

Uncouth means lacking in couth.

A refined man never takes his undershirt off in the presence of ladies.

I'm not uncouth--I'm as couth as anyone.

A hostess should not wear a T-shirt to serve tea.

A bird in the hand is bad table manners.

Never break your bread or roll in your soup.

A gentleman is one who never insults anyone intentionally.

Only chew tobacco when you wear a brown suit.

A polite man offers a lady a seat when he gets off the bus.

Girls like a man to be gentle, but not necessarily a gentleman.

If you don't go to a friend's funeral, don't expect him to come to yours.

Never take a gentleman's hat and coat--while he is looking.

When playing the part of a thoroughbred--make sure what part.

I never pick up a girl's handkerchief--I use Kleenex.

Chaos is defined as four women with one luncheon check.

Always fold your napkin--to make it fit your pocket.

Nowadays chivalry on a bus is a standing joke.

Never mind which side the bread is buttered on--eat both sides.

In olden days men stood up for women, but there were no buses then.

The less a man knows about you, the politer he is.

Cultivate good manners, and you'll be mistaken for a doorman.

Profanity saves a gentleman from a nervous breakdown.

Breeding isn't everything, but it's lots of fun.

Never add cream and sugar to your coffee after it's in the saucer.

Never treat a guest like a member of the family--treat him with courtesy.

When visiting, never spit haphazardly--the floor may leak.

The keynote of good breeding is B natural.

My fiancee likes flowers. So I sent her a packet of seeds.

I almost died of thirst on my vacation. The hotel didn't have any saucers.

The only thing ever lost by politeness is a seat on a crowded bus.

My wife is very proper. She won't even look at things with a naked eye.

Courtesy is contagious--let's start an epidemic.

Some people eat with their fingers and talk with their fork.

Don't bite your nails, especially if you are a carpenter.

My brother-in-law is as refined as a cabbage.

Never eat mashed potatoes with your hand. Use a knife.

The greatest points of interest in his life are 7 and 11.

Don't spit. Remember the Johnstown flood.

Tourists all have the same slogan: "Stop, Look, and Litter."

Never drink on an empty wallet.

My brother-in-law is a contact man--all con and no tact.

Never slap a man while he is chewing tobacco.

My mother-in-law has dirty fingernails, and a mind to match.

Some people have tact--others tell the truth.

She has one of those mighty minds--mighty dirty.

A well-bred man steps on his cigarette before it can burn the carpet.

I hate those salesmen who have an approach like a dentist's drill.

For years I ate with the wrong fingers.

He's only tidy at a bar--he drinks his whiskey neat.

My wife is so modest, she blindfolds herself while taking a bath.

The only uplifted thing about my sister is her bust.

Etiquette is yawning with your mouth closed.

In polite society, whispering is not aloud.

Dipping your bread in gravy is bad manners--but it's good taste.

To keep your dishes clean, eat out of the pot.

Women should be handled with kid gloves--and nylon negligees.

To keep a kitchen spotless, don't use it.

If you get sparks out of your knife and fork, you're eating too fast.

There is no man so bad that a woman cannot make him worse.

My mother-in-law is so refined. She drinks her booze with a spoon.

My family acquired polish by drinking it.

Toothpicks give people something to do after dinner.

I kiss your hand, madam--a second choice, of course.

Never stand between a lamppost and a dog.

Experience

Experience teaches best because it gives you individual instruction.

You can get experience on the easy-payment plan.

Experience is what's left after you've lost everything else.

Experience is a teacher that demands, and gets, its own price.

Experience is always a best seller--everyone is continually buying it.

Experience is knowledge acquired when it is too late.

The class pin of the school of experience is the safety pin.

Experience either makes a person better, or bitter.

Experience is cheapest when you buy it secondhand.

Experience is an expensive teacher. The rest are underpaid.

Experience is what you get while you are looking for something else.

To tell your grade in the school of experience, you have to count the scars.

Experience is a good school, but it never lets you have a vacation.

There's a new course in the school of experience, every time you graduate.

You get experienced by being inexperienced.

Experience seldom teaches a subject that interests us.

You acquire experience in one of two ways: by doing, or by being done.

Experience is made up of the mistakes we like to remember.

Experience enables you to recognize a mistake when you make it again.

Experience is one teacher that gets paid if not obeyed.

Experience is the classification where most of us file our mistakes.

Considering our national debt, experience is a dear teacher.

Experience is a good teacher, but no students bring her any apples.

We learn from experience that we never learn from experience.

There are no free scholarships to the school of experience.

Experience is the only thing most people get out of life.

The trouble with experience is that so few of us are born with it.

Experience is something you get whether you want it or not.

Learn by experience--if at all possible, by other people's.

Experience is like drawing without an eraser.

Experience is a matter of knowing how much is too much.

Experience is the best teacher, but the tuition is too high.

Unfortunately we never have experience until after we need it.

Experience is what is bound to happen in everyone's experience.

Experience, unfortuntely, gives the test first and the lesson later.

You become experienced by watching what happens to you when you're not.

Experience is what happens to you while you are making other plans.

Eyes

Carrots must be good for the eyes. You never see a rabbit wearing glasses.

Some people are born with black eyes--others have to fight for them.

When your sight begins to blur, use stronger glasses and weaker drinks.

She's got patriotic eyes--blue, with red whites.

Keep your eyes wide open before marriage and half-closed afterwards.

Love is blind, and marriage is the eye-opener.

Some girls close their eyes when you kiss them, but others close yours.

She has two beautiful eyes. Too bad they're not mates.

The way she keeps her eyebrows takes a lot of pluck.

When she cries, the tears from her right eye fall on her left cheek.

I'm as nearsighted as a mole.

He must sleep very comfortably--he has such big pillows under his eyes.

I'm so nearsighted, I once lost a bass fiddle in a one-room apartment.

Drink to me only with thine eyes--it's cheaper that way.

Some people sleep with one eye open; others are awake with both eyes shut.

A bright eye indicates curiosity; a black eye, too much curiosity.

In life, actions speak louder than words, but in love, the eyes do.

If you marry a girl taller than you are you'll never see eye to eye.

It's the eyes of a woman that disturb the ease of a man.

When a man stops looking at pretty girls, he probably needs bifocals.

An oculist is the doctor you go to see when you can't see.

A man doesn't need 20/20 eyesight to appreciate a 36-24-36 vision.

Hindsight is good, foresight is better, but insight is the best of all.

Often a case of love at first sight involves a near-sighted man.

Chicago is so windy that it's possible to spit in your own eye.

Her eyes are so bad, she has to wear contact lenses to see her glasses.

I lost my glasses and can't look for them until I find them.

My eyes were never good and I have a wife to prove it.

My mother-in-law has social circles under her eyes.

I had bad eyesight until I was eight. Then I got a haircut.

My eyes have never been checked. They've always been brown.

Her eyes intoxicate me. I think it's the eyeballs.

I'm so nearsighted, I can't even see my contact lenses.

Failure

Failure is the line of least persistence.

The only time you mustn't fail is the last time you try.

I always take my salary to the bank. It's too little to go alone.

There's a lot less to some people than meets the eye.

If at first you don't succeed--forget it.

He's not working up a steam; he's generating a fog.

I just made the list of the nation's Ten Best Nobodies.

I got ulcers without being a success.

I never made Who's Who, but I'm listed in Who's Through.

A has-been is the proof that nothing recedes like success.

Half-doing has been my undoing.

A has-been is anybody who was formerly somebody and is now nobody.

Like a fence, some people run around a lot without getting anywhere.

I had an itch to succeed, but got loused up just thinking about it.

At least a failure has succeeded in failing.

He had the world by the tail--too bad he couldn't swing it.

I had a forward spring--and an early fall.

Failure is not falling down; it is remaining there when you've fallen.

He never has ups and downs--he always goes around in circles.

I was once an unknown failure--now I'm a known failure.

I had the right aim in life, but I ran out of ammunition.

My brother wanted to be a lawyer badly, but he became a bad lawyer.

It's better to be a has-been than a never-was.

I'm money-mad. I never had any--that's why I'm mad.

To be a failure, go through life pushing doors marked "Pull."

He puts up a big bluff and always stumbles over it.

If at first you don't succeed, blame it on your wife.

Most marriage failures are caused by failures marrying.

My brother-in-law is so seedy he won't go near a canary.

One sure way to fail is to plant both feet firmly in the air.

Talk about a failure! My uncle robbed a bank just to feel wanted.

In high school I was elected most likely to go to seed.

Success goes to your head, failure to your heart.

My luck! The last time I turned over a new leaf, it was poison ivy.

I rose from obscurity and am now headed for oblivion.

Bankruptcy proves that a business with a slow turnover will overturn fast.

I know of a jack-of-all-trades who is out of work in all of them.

One thing that I have got is that certain nothing.

I finally started selling furniture for a living--my own.

I've been up against the wall so long, the handwriting is on me.

I thought I was on the right track until I got run over sitting there.

If you always watch the clock you'll end up as one of the hands.

Are you a success, or do you still lie to your wife?

The only way I'll ever get up in the world is in an airplane.

My aptitude test shows that my one aptitude is for taking aptitude tests.

Many a short cut to success turns out to be a trap door to failure.

Hatching ideas isn't enough--you've got to hitch them.

The only one with successful pipe dreams is an organist.

I'm very responsible. No matter what goes wrong--I'm responsible.

My boss says I'm giving failure a bad name.

Nothing succeeds like success, and nothing fails like failure.

As soon as success turns a man's head, he's facing failure.

Yesterday's formula for success is tomorrow's recipe for failure.

Success comes in cans, failure in can'ts.

The secret of success is: don't fail.

Just when you think you have it in the bag, the bag breaks.

Success is only a matter of luck--ask any man who has failed.

Dad wasn't affected by the crash of '29. He went broke in '28.

Pawnbrokers live off the flat of the land.

I turned black and blue from overeating. I ate more than I could pay for.

We had a sinking fund. It just went down for the third time.

I've got what no millionaire has got. I've got no money.

More rabbits than people have made their million.

Gold is a basic metal--without it you can't get to first basic.

I stretched a million dollars into a shoestring.

I walk in the middle of the street. I owe people on both sides.

Not even the Missing Persons Bureau could help him find himself.

I'm so fond of hard luck I run halfway to meet it.

If I started selling lamps, the sun would stop setting.

You can't undertake vast projects with half-vast ideas.

You can always count on him to hit the nail squarely on the thumb.

He was born with a silver spoon in his mouth, but never made a stir with it.

I was too busy learning the tricks of the trade to learn the trade.

The way he manages his money--well, confidentially, it shrinks.

Care isn't killing him--it's don't care.

I had something to fall back on, and then, one day, I landed on it.

Family

There were three kids in my family--one of each sex.

A family is the thing most needed, nowadays, in the home.

Mom's yearning capacity is greater than Dad's earning capacity.

A traffic-court judge has more relatives than anybody else.

I'm bothered by flat feet. They keep giving me parking tickets.

A big family is proof that married folks love children--or something.

I'm going to learn a trade--so I'll know what kind of work I'm out of.

There is no such thing as a distant relative.

Dad's with the F.B.I. now--they caught him in Los Angeles.

Rich relatives are the kin we love to touch.

Pauper: the man who married Mama.

Hot words passed between us--she threw hot alphabet soup at me.

Family life is a case of perpetual commotion.

Relatives always wonder how you manage to be so well off.

We make breakfast together. She makes the toast, and I scrape it.

My home is so quiet that you can hear a pin drop--a rolling pin.

Every family tree always produces some nuts.

Home is the family's filling station.

We have six girls and five boys--I'm the scorekeeper.

Dad is very popular in prison. He's the lifer of the party.

A family jar is no good for preserving the peace.

Every family tree has some sap in it.

My wife comes from such an old family--it's been condemned.

I would have been two years older, but my father stuttered badly.

When you marry you replace the money in your wallet with snapshots.

Home is where you can trust the hash.

My uncle was very high strung. He got caught stealing a horse.

I was born behind the 8-ball. My mother liked to shoot pool.

No man believes genius is hereditary until he has a son.

Speaking of trade relations, almost everyone would like to.

I've got all the girls eating out of my hand--I'm a waiter.

Mother drinks to forget that she drinks.

A person's pride in his ancestors increases in proportion to the distance.

I would rather start a family than finish one.

One night I put the cat out and my mother-in-law with it.

I think there's insanity in my family. They keep writing me for money.

Forgive me for speaking so long--I've got my wife's teeth in.

The first thing a social climber wants is a family tree.

Don't criticize your wife's relatives; remember, you chose them.

Once, large families were the rule, not the exemptions.

Dad was a wonderful baseball player. I was his first error.

I was an only child. Dad knew when he was licked.

Some men are born lucky; others have large families.

Money doesn't grow on trees, but it grows on many family trees.

Blood will tell: no one criticizes your faults quicker than your relatives.

Dad is a joiner by trade. If anyone orders a drink, he joins them.

My mother-in-law has a nice open face--open day and night.

The way of the transgressor is hard--on his family.

The family that stays together probably has only one car.

I miss my wife's cooking--every chance I get.

My father can carry more brandy than a St. Bernard.

A close relative is one you see occasionally between family funerals.

Money talks. In my family it keeps up a running conversation.

My uncle is a cannibal--he's been living on us for twenty years.

I come from a family of swimmers. I lost one brother in a dive in Chicago.

Money talks. In my family it keeps up a running conversation.

Children keep a family together, especially if you can't find a baby-sitter.

Would you say your wife is your bitter half?

I've got some very close relatives--so close they won't lend me a dine.

A wife and kids can be a great handicap, especially if you're not married.

I have an uncle who has so much money, I never see him at all.

My son writes home for money on a typewriter--it's the touch system.

I hate my brother-in-law's guts--they're ful of my food.

To bring your family closer together, buy a small car.

Don't judge a man by his family--Cain belonged to a good one.

My daughter doesn't live at home--she's not married yet.

His idea of thinking is to go to the poolroom and rack his brains.

It's a wise child that resembles a rich relative.

Never judge a man until you've spoken to his wife's relatives.

I call my mother-in-law "Iodine" because she's a drug on the market.

Mother broke a leg--so father can't work--it was his leg she broke.

The best way to find a missing relative is to become very rich.

Even after a man loses his last friend he still has his relatives.

My brother is so high strung he joined a circus.

If a man doesn't like his aunt, is he anti-aunty?

In my marriage the problems are all relative.

My family has more trouble than a soap opera.

Of all my relations, I like sex best.

My marriage is a give and take proposition. I give and she takes.

My monthly salary runs into three figures. My wife and two children.

We have a lazy susan in the middle of our living room: my sister-in-law.

I'm very lucky. I've got a wife and a cigarette lighter--and they both work.

I'm a pedestrian--my wife beats me to the garage in the morning.

I cured my wife's nervousness. I told her it was caused by advancing age.

I come from a wealthy family. My brother is worth $50,000--dead or alive.

All the world loves a lover--except her husband.

I admit that I married my wife for her money--and boy, do I earn it.

My daughter gained 150 pounds last spring. She finally found a husband.

My wife didn't come from a big family. She was sent.

This is my fourth wife. I believe in parlays.

As an inducement to hard work nothing beats a big family.

Please don't yell at me. I'm not your mother.

My wife didn't nag me last night. I wonder if there's someone else.

Relatives are people who are satisfied to live within your means.

A rich relative is a wealthy ex-husband.

They are a perfect pair. She's a hypochondriac and he's a pill.

Cary Grant and Henny enjoy the festivities at a birthday party for Sammy Cahn at the Frontier Hotel in Las Vegas

For a mother, the son always shines.

Things are so tough in Hollywood, even the relatives are leaving.

A distant relative is one who recently borrowed money from you.

My wife didn't come from a big family--she brought most of them with her.

I'm descended from a long line--that my mother fell for.

A relative is a natural enemy.

A family is a spending unit.

Why is it that the people who live the longest are rich relatives?

My mother got up at 5:00 every morning--no matter what time it was.

Families are wonderful things--especially if everybody is related.

Economy is anything your wife wants to spend money on.

My wife opens nothing more, by mistake, than her mouth.

A genius is a stupid kid with very happy grandparents.

We had ten kids in my family. I never slept alone, until I got married.

Adam must have been a happy man. He didn't have a mother-in-law.

Food

When you go in a restaurant always ask for a table near a waiter.

It isn't travel that's broadening--it's all that rich foreign food.

To hide the smell of fish on pots and pans, rub them with garlic.

My wife is such a bad cook, she blushes after every meal.

My wife can boil the softest hard-boiled egg you've ever seen.

A glutton is a person who likes to diet on all kinds of food.

The only thing digestible about a doughnut is the hole.

Home cooking is what a man misses when his wife isn't.

I never ask my wife "What's cooking?" I ask her "What's thawing?"

My wife will go anywhere for dinner, except to the kitchen.

When a lobster comes ashore it risks getting into hot water.

Our kitchen never has cooking odors--my wife refuses to cook.

My girl friend may not know how to cook, but she knows what's cooking.

Meat prices have gotten my family into a perpetual stew.

An oyster never gets stewed, except during the "R" months.

All my girl friend knows about cooking is how to bring me to a quick boil.

A cookbook is a book with a lot of stirring chapters.

The proof of the pie is in the amount of the crust that is eaten.

Some recipes are so fancy, they sound almost good enough to eat.

Too many cooks spoil the figure.

My wife enjoys cooking--especially when it's done in a restaurant.

A woman is like a salad--everything depends on the dressing.

A poor man eats potato soup--a rich man, vichyssoise.

When my wife makes Jello, I get a lump in my throat.

My boss wanted me for dinner, but I didn't fit into his oven.

To an Englishman, the only thing lukewarm in America is tea.

Early to bed and early to rise makes a man get his own breakfast.

My idea of a seven-course dinner is a hot dog and a six-pack.

Then I ordered dinner for a party of 18--and could she eat!

Good coffee keeps more people awake than a bad conscience.

Home cooking is something that most wives are not.

I asked my wife what we were having for dinner. She said her family.

To avoid doing the supper dishes, I take my wife out to dinner.

Where there's smoke there's fire, except when it's a barbeque.

Two can live as cheaply as one--if one doesn't eat.

What this country needs is a nine to five coffee break.

Leftovers is food that is here today, and here tomorrow.

Garlic is good for flavoring food, but what is good for garlic?

A glutton's greedy sense of taste, shows little sense, but lots of waist.

Every morning I make coffee in my pajamas--some day I'll try a pot.

No home is complete without a man, but every kitchen is.

The more lobster you eat, the more you leave on your plate.

One thing about my wife's coffee--it's not habit-forming.

One man's meat is another man's high cost of living.

A Sunday picnic with the kids is no picnic.

When you don't know what kind of pie it is, it's mince.

My wife's coffee won't keep you awake--unless you drink it.

Pie isn't fattening--not the way most restaurants cut it.

Once you taste English coffee, you know whey they drink tea.

I've got my wife trained--she makes her own breakfast.

To get a good cup of coffee in the morning--wake your wife first.

What my wife doesn't know about cooking would fill a book--a cookbook.

Why does a neighbor's barbecue always smell better than ours tastes?

I almost went blind drinking coffee--I left the spoon in the cup.

The reason I eat with my knife is that my fork leaks.

We drink blended coffee at my house--today's and yesterday's.

The only food that doesn't go up in price is food for thought.

One thing that is stronger than a mother's love is garlic breath.

Don't laugh at our coffee. You, too, may be old and weak some day.

Some stout people would sooner die than diet.

No woman is as old as she looks before breakfast.

I've heard of weak coffee--but this is helpless.

Even though my wife cooks on an electric stove, I still get gas pains.

Half of what you eat keeps you alive--the other half kills you.

The trouble with espresso is that a week later you're sleepy again.

The ideal way to serve leftovers is to someone else.

Some people eat as if they're fattening themselves up for market.

I drink several cups of water a day--my wife calls it coffee.

The perfect place for a picnic is somewhere else.

To make the sun shine, just call off a picnic.

My wife's coffee is so weak it can't even hold the sugar.

The only way I get breakfast in bed is if I'm in the hospital.

When my wife's away I do wonderful things with leftovers--I throw them out.

The thing I like most about gravy is that it has no bones.

The caffeine doesn't keep you awake any more--now it's the price.

There I was eating fish--and I can't swim a stroke.

A cannibal sometimes has his friends for dinner.

Mama won Papa with her cooking. Sort of a girl meats boy.

My wife cooks just the way I had better like it.

People who bolt their food shoud eat nuts afterward.

Brussel sprouts: a cabbage that never made good.

The only thing my wife and I save for a rainy day is a picnic.

Our steaks are so tender I don't see how the cow holds together.

The caviar here is terrible. It has a fishy taste.

The one thing my wife knows how to cook is my goose.

Appetizers: the little bits you eat until you lose your appetite.

Vegetable soup is the same as hash, only looser.

The best place to stop for a picnic is a little further on.

A hamburger by any other name always costs more.

Watermelon is a fruit you can eat, drink, and wash your face in.

My wife needs a full day to make a cup of instant coffee.

I feel that the nicest way to serve spinach is to somebody else.

Any girl who knows how to cook can find a man who knows how to eat.

I once broke a tooth on my wife's gravy.

Canapes are a sandwich cut into 24 pieces.

Let's go to the Automat and get a couple of sandwiches out of prison.

My wife makes strong coffee. Drink a cup at dinner and you perk all night.

My daughter made lunch today: cotton candy with pastrami sandwiches.

I've eaten so much sea food, my stomach rises and falls with the tide.

I try not to have coffee in the morning. It keeps me awake all day.

I've got a wife that dresses to kill, and cooks that way, too.

I had a submarine sandwich before coming here--and it's starting to surface.

My wife can't cook. Last night she burned the potato salad.

In the morning, my wife and the coffee start to boil at the same time.

Indigestion is the failure to adjust a square meal to a round stomach.

My idea of interior decoration is a square meal.

A spectacular career always ends up in stomach trouble.

The reason I don't dunk is that my fingers blister too easily.

When my wife eats soup, couples get up and start dancing.

A picnic is a shoe box filled with indigestion.

The steak was tough--evidently the part that rubs against the shafts.

In Alaska, it gets so cold they serve soup in sieves.

Breakfast in bed is the hardest meal for a mother to get.

Catsup is a disguise for steaks.

The proof of the pudding is sometimes in the obituary notices.

You may eat your cake and have it too, by making two cakes.

Celery is a vegetable which should be seen and not heard.

Cheese is milk's leap toward immortality.

If the bravest are the tenderest, this steak came from a coward.

A pinch of salt tastes much better when sprinkled on a two-inch steak.

For years I thought that cheese was rancid butter.

A cracker is the last resort of an anchovy.

I miss my wife's cooking--every chance I get.

A doughnut is a fried halo.

Cranberries are grapes with high blood pressure.

Crepes suzettes are four-alarm pancakes.

You can't have your cake and someone else's cookie too.

In the army, food is a sad snack.

A cruller is a doughnut that has become psychotic.

A gherkin is a pretty pickle.

Grapefruit is a kind of eyewash.

This world could use a grapefruit that can yell, "Fore!"

Leek is the poor man's asparagus.

Some restaurants are institutions for the distribution of indigestion.

I go to a restaurant when I want to rest and rant.

A lunch counter is a filling station for humans.

Mealtime is when the children sit down to continue eating.

Where there's smoke--there's toast.

Most wives would learn to cook if they weren't so busy trying to get meals.

The menu is the list of dishes the restaurant has just run out of.

In the armed forces, mess call is the battle cry of feed 'em.

Bologna is a sausage known in Bologna as mortadella.

Cheese is milk plus microbes.

A nut is a fruit built like an oyster.

A chef's idea of decor is parsley.

A pear is a banana with its girdle off.

Chili sauce: catsup with seeds.

Cream is the flower of milk.

A drumstick is chicken-on-the-cob.

All too often a picnic turns out to be an ant's lunch.

Pineapple is the porcupine of the palm family.

An eggplant is an apoplectic squash.

A gooseberry is a sour grape.

A hot dog is a poached pooch.

Minced pie is the stuff that dreams are made of.

To me, pie is an advance agent of indigestion.

A prune is a plum that didn't take care of itself.

Popcorn is the corn the audience eats.

A potato is an Irish avocado.

An artichoke is a strip tease with mayonnaise.

Bacon is a hog-caller's visiting card.

A Baked Alaska is a sultry Good Humor.

Borscht is beet soup with high blood pressure.

To settle my wife's hash, I take bicarbonate.

A pretzel is a biscuit on a bender.

A prune is a plum that has seen better days.

A raisin is a prune that has been whipped down to a nub.

Rhubarb is a form of bloodshot celery.

Only one thing is bigger than my wife's appetite: her stomach.

Remember, an egg is a whole day's work for a chicken.

I boiled an egg for twenty minutes, but it never got soft.

A sandwich is two slices of bread trying to get together.

A club sandwich is one that fights back.

A sardine is a herring's pup.

I don't eat breakfast. I don't like to eat on an empty stomach.

The best thing to put in a homemade pie is your teeth.

I don't mind my wife serving TV dinners, but now she's serving re-runs.

Snacks are the best weight lifters.

Soup is the food that people eat at the top of their voices.

She has the only kitchen in the world where flies commit suicide.

In a restaurant, my favorite dish is a clean one.

A typical American snack is pizza, chow mein, and blintzes.

A stuffed pepper is a hamburger with a girdle.

Tapioca is proletarian caviar.

A tart is a cutie pie.

I think my wife has been getting her recipes out of Popular Mechanics.

Her cooking is so bad, our garbage can got ulcers.

What a cook! Pygmies come to dip their poison darts in her soup.

She fed a stray dog, and it never left--it couldn't move.

When my wife makes ladyfingers, they turn out all thumbs.

Zwieback is sponge cake that has lived.

Zwieback is bread with backbone.

One man's meat is another man's cholesterol.

Hamburger is a steak that didn't pass its physical.

The last time I had a hot meal was when a candle fell in my TV dinner.

Some people can't boil water. My wife can. She calls it soup.

Our dining room table has a garbage disposal for a centerpiece.

We keep Alka-Seltzer on tap.

My mother was an awful cook. She raised me on radio dinners.

My wife has a great way to keep food costs down--her cooking.

When my wife makes coffee it's grounds for divorce.

Remember: a fly in your soup is better than no meat at all.

Last night my wife served a real swill dinner.

Her food is like a good man--you can't keep it down.

My wife's food can cure you of anything, including life.

Her grub tastes like one.

Her food is for thought--it's certainly not for eating.

Cooks are often decorated in France. I feel like crowning some of ours.

Jam is the stuff you see on toast, neckties, and piano keys.

He who indulges, bulges.

To eat is human; to digest, divine.

Green peas haven't missed a banquet in fifty years.

Breakfast is the only meal to which no one is ever invited.

Beware of the girl who likes to eat her cake and have yours, too.

Many a man dawdles away an hour over a cup of instant coffee.

Too many cooks spoil the broth--far too many.

Many foods that are well done are not done well.

A barbeque often cooks steaks rare and fingers well-done.

I broke our dog from begging for food from the table. I let him taste it.

The proof of the pudding is not in the eating, but in the digesting.

A buffet dinner is one where the guests outnumber the chairs.

The reason pediatricians eat so well is that children don't.

A cannibal is a guy who loves his fellow man--with gravy.

On our honeymoon my wife burned the toast--so I wouldn't notice the coffee.

Friends

One way to keep your friends is not to give them away.

A friend who is not in need is a friend indeed.

Some friends are a habit, others are a luxury.

The fastest way to wipe out a friendship is to sponge on it.

A true friend knows all about you and loves you just the same.

A true friend walks in when the rest of the world walks out.

A friend is a person having the same enemies as you have.

To make an enemy out of a friend, talk to him as only a friend should.

To keep a friendship from breaking, don't drop it.

Be kind to your friends. Without them you'd be a total stranger.

A friend in need is the only kind of friend a person has these days.

A man's best friend is rarely his neighbor.

When it comes to helping a friend some people will stop at nothing.

You can have your close friends--give me generous ones.

A real friend remains a friend even when you don't deserve a friend.

A friend in need is a friend to avoid.

The closer a man is the more distant his friends are.

I have trouble keeping friends, but no trouble keeping enemies.

When you have to buy a friend, you get an enemy free.

Friends aren't made--they're recognized.

It's surprising how many friends you have until you need one.

If at first you don't succeed, you'll have a lot more friends.

You never know your worst faults until you quarrel with your best friend.

When a man needs a friend he often makes a mistake and gets a wife.

It's not possible to use your friends and have them too.

The best time to make friends is before you need them.

Nothing is more wearing than sitting up with a thick friend.

I have no enemies--all my friends hate me.

We were friends until debt did us part.

A man's best friend is his dog, and his worst enemy is his dogma.

Any friend of yours is--a friend of yours.

Time and money separate the best of friends--and don't forget marriage.

I only like you if you dislike the same people that I dislike.

I dislike the kind of friend who is hard to find and harder to lose.

Friendship between two women is always a plot against each other.

A friend is always happy about your success--if it doesn't surpass his own.

With some kinds of friends, who needs enemies?

He hasn't an enemy in the world and none of his friends like him.

A friend in need is a friend who has been playing the horses.

Money can't buy friends--but it certainly can rent them.

A friend in need is a drain on your bank account.

I pick my friends--to pieces.

I'll share your lot with you--if it's a good-sized one.

My best friend ran away without my wife. My luck!

If you lend a friend money, and you never see him again, it was worth it.

It's best to test new ideas on old friends.

I have a lot of close friends--but not one generous one.

Happiness is having a friend who is not too close.

Want to lose a friend? Tell him something for his own good.

The only use some people have for a friend is to use him.

Some friends remember what they give and forget what they get.

To be friendly is a vice only in a watchdog.

I hate a friend who is always around--when he needs you.

The only way some people can get a friend is to buy a dog.

Every time you win an argument, you lose a friend.

I never forget a friend, especially if he owes me money.

You can always depend on some friends--to depend on you.

I always do my best--including my best friends.

A man can always depend on 3 friends: an old wife, an old dog, and cash.

It's easy to make friends fast, but difficult to make fast friends.

A lawyer comes in handy when a felon needs a friend.

The way to be sure of a man's friendship is not to put it to the test.

I have friends I haven't even used yet.

Friendships and bank accounts require making deposits.

A fair-weather friend will only lend you an umbrella on a sunny day.

Friends excuse you when you make a fool of yourself.

When your ship comes in you'll find your friends on the dock.

There is nothing more wearing than sitting up with a thick friend.

Some friends are close to you until you try to touch them.

The closer a man is the more distant his friends are.

A friend forgives your defects--a real friend doesn't see any.

A friend is a speaking acquaintance who also listens.

I had a really fine friend--he stabbed me in the front.

A real friend will listen to your troubles without telling his.

Gambling

I have property in Las Vegas. Cesar's Palace has my luggage.

All I ever got from hot tips were some nasty burns.

I've got the worst luck. Even when I cheat I can't win.

A card room is where men are men and spades are double.

And so it came to pass, as the gambler would say.

A kibitzer will bet your shirt on someone else's hand.

I picked up two girls at the track--it was my daily double.

He may not be a crook, but when playing cards, he shuffles his sleeve.

If the dice weren't loaded, how come they left skid marks?

The most dangerous wheel of chance is the steering wheel.

The most deceptive mistress of all is Lady Luck.

Gambling is a way of getting nothing for something.

The safest bet is the one you didn't make.

A bookie is a pickpocket who lets you use your hands.

No wife likes a gambling husband unless he's a steady winner.

The best throw of the dice is to throw them away.

Las Vegas is the land of the spree, and the home of the knave.

A lot of people who wouldn't bet on a horse turn around and get married.

The less you bet, the more you lose, when you win.

In Las Vegas the odds are you won't get even.

You can't beat the climate in Las Vegas--or the slot machines.

Las Vegas isn't a city--it's a garbage disposal for money.

We all love a poor loser--if we don't have any bets on him.

When I play bridge is when I get good poker hands.

Two can live as cheaply as one can gamble.

Las Vegas is where you find the best entertainers and the worst gamblers.

One sure way to learn how to pray is to play poker.

A gentleman never cheats at cards--unless it's absolutely necessary.

Life is a game played with cards: playing, post, greeting, and credit.

In life, money can be lost in more ways than won.

I went to Reno to get away from it all, but Reno got it all away from me.

If you lose at poker and keep on playing, you'll always have friends.

An ace in the hand is worth two in the deck.

Many women go through life never remembering what trump is.

Marriage is a gambol--spelled g-a-m-b-l-e.

Las Vegas has two main sources of income: seven and eleven.

Poker is a card game that makes a poor player poorer.

Two can live as cheaply as one can play gin rummy.

Never trust a man who cheats himself while playing solitaire.

The only person who can afford to gamble is a man who is broke.

There's safety in numbers, except when you're in Las Vegas.

The best way to conceal your hand in poker is with your face.

In playing cards, a good deal depends on a good deal.

The most popular game of chance in America is marriage.

If you win in poker, it's good judgment; if you lose, it's bad luck.

Ladies! To keep your husband from gambling--spend it first.

Always sympathize with the underdog, but never bet on him.

My favorite game is solitaire--that way I meet a better class of people.

I love to go to Las Vegas--to be near my money.

In poker it's darkest just before you've drawn.

'm really unlucky. In Las Vegas, I even lost $10 on the stamp machine.

I gambled away the rent money. It was a moving experience.

A rolling bone gathers no gross.

Las Vegas is always crowded because no one has the fare to leave.

I hope they have more luck with my money than I did.

Las Vegas is a strip of lights surrounded by slot machines.

Show me a chronic gambler, and I'll show you one who doesn't miss a bet.

To a gambler the largest diamond is the ace.

I got in my daily dozen--twelve games of pool.

My idea of royalty is a pair of jacks or better.

The abolition of bingo should be done away with.

Gardening

A garden is something men prefer to turn over in their minds.

By the time your back gets used to gardening, your enthusiasm is gone.

Old gardeners never die--they just spade away.

About all the relief a gardener can expect is some liniment.

Plant a better lawn, and the world will beat a path across it to your door.

To tell the vegetables from the weeds, watch your neighbor's chickens.

One thing I've discovered is that trees grow on money.

You don't get much service out of a spade by merely calling one.

My dad ran a farm with less equipment than I need to keep my lawn.

The man who makes his own flower bed usually has to lie about it.

Next year I plant weeds--maybe the flowers will choke them out.

My bulbs seem to think they're buried instead of planted.

In gardening, a thing of beauty is a job forever.

My garden dies if I don't water it, and rots if I do.

Gardening is man's effort to improve his lot.

My family ate my entire vegetable garden at one meal.

Grass wilts in the yard and flourishes in the garden.

I was lucky with my garden this year--not a thing came up.

A good gardener is a handy man, with a sense of humus.

About all I've been able to grow in my garden is tired.

Cauliflower is a cabbage with a college education.

I get a good deal of pleasure out of my garden--mostly out of it.

Gardening is a painstaking endeavor, especially in the small of the back.

I mow the lawn when my neighbor's kid practices the piano.

Work well done never needs redoing, unless it's weeding.

To raise a successful garden you should use trowel and error.

Don't plant a big garden if your wife tires easily.

Each spring I look at my lawn and hope the plot will thicken.

I never met a gardener who didn't know better than other gardeners.

The only thing I've been able to grow is round-shouldered.

I'll let anybody borrow my lawn mower as long as they keep it in my yard.

If you don't grow your own vegetables, praise your neighbor's garden.

About all I got for my pains was liniment.

Gardening is good for the waistline, but even better for the appetite.

Each spring my wife puts me under her green thumb.

My wife is all thumbs--but at least they're green.

A gardener is a woman who loves flowers, or a man who hates weeds.

In the fall, my family rakes together and aches together.

Gardening is one of the first symptoms of lumbago.

I had great luck with my garden this year--nothing came up.

The man who makes his own flower bed usually has to lie about it.

Girls

Girls have been known to raise their hems to get their hims.

I treat my girl like a dog--a lap dog.

I don't know much about girls--only what I pick up.

Girls are so knowing these days that birds and bees study them.

I didn't meet my new girl friend--she overtook me.

She's a home-loving girl, but she does some loving in the car, too.

Do you know where bad little girls go? Almost everywhere.

Any girl with shapely legs proclaims it from the hose-tops.

Getting a girl is easy--losing her is the real job.

Girls who look good in the best places usually get taken there.

At 16, a girl's voice starts changing from "No" to "Yes."

A girl's baby stares are for men to trip on.

One day I found the girl of my dreams, but I was already married.

Girls don't look upon men as the problem, but the solution.

A girl with a lot of nerve is worth her weight in gall.

She's a home girl--she doesn't care whose.

My girl is so bashful, she goes into the closet to change her mind.

These days it's difficult for a girl to look as young as her mother.

Here's to girls, God bless 'em, no matter how they dress 'em.

She's a lover of the outdoors. Does pretty well indoors, too.

A green girl, in the pink of condition, can give a man the blues.

Opposites attract. Poor girls are always looking for rich husbands.

She showed him her new Fall Line--and he fell for it.

Today's girl may have little weaknesses, but she isn't effeminate.

A good girl may be good, but a bad girl is better.

Beautiful girls don't bother me--and that's my problem.

She leads a conventional life--she shows up at all the conventions.

A teen-age girl will outgrow it in 20 years, when she is 25.

Even when I can't read a girl like a book I enjoy thumbing the pages.

The most expensive thing I know is a girl who is free for the evening.

My girl friend has given me the best weekends of her life.

She's leading a delightful sexistence.

A girl's maiden aim is to change her maiden name.

Sympathy is what one girl offers another in exchange for details.

Her conscience never no's what's wrong.

She leads a simple, natural life. Her won't's are few.

If a girl is smart, she doesn't have to have any brains.

The girls in the typing pool are a bunch of copycats.

My girl can't cook, but she knows what's cooking.

Good girls are born, but girls like her are made.

Show me a telephone operator, and I'll show you a call girl.

The girls in the secretarial pool are typecast.

Her kiss speaks volumes--but it's far from a first edition.

"Always flirting" describes some girls to a tease.

A call girl never gives a busy signal.

A virgin is a girl who wears hot pants but never takes them off.

My girl's idea of a romantic setting is one with a diamond in it.

Some girls keep the wolf from the door by inviting him in.

Any girl with a "D" cup is a big bust.

Lots of girls in this town look good enough to eat--and they do eat.

My girl can't dance, but she certainly can intermission.

Henny with "tell you what I'm gonna' do" Sid Stone from the Milton Berle show

I don't like a girl to have a faminine look.

A lot of girls who smoke aren't even lukewarm.

My girl is sports-minded. Passing out twice an evening is par for her.

All a sweater does for some girls is make them itch.

I don't go for girls that are straight and narrow.

A wise girl is determined to mate good.

Most girls today have a keen sense of rumor.

Almost any girl can talk rings around a jewelry store.

My girl can't swim a stroke, but she knows every dive in town.

"Girls" are what women over 45 call each other.

It's amazing how many mere striplings know how to strip.

My girl friend is skinny, so I don't get around much.

Funny, when a girl is old enough to go out alone, she doesn't.

My girl has a low-cut atom bomb dress--30% fall out.

Today's modern miss doesn't miss much.

A girl can't be a bonnie lassie if she's got a bony chassis.

She's the picture of her father, and the sound track of her mother.

I won't say she was ugly--but it was love at first fright.

My girl friend is a well-reared girl.

If she's the shy, demure type, you have to whistle twice.

Today's girl doesn't know how to cook, but she knows what's cooking.

Today's version: little girls should be seen and not hard.

The story of her popularity can be summed up in one word: "Yes."

Girls with hidden charms do their best not to hide them.

What a hairdo! It's like a floor mop in a high wind.

A smart girl holds a man at arm's length, but doesn't lose her grip on him.

Any girl can make a good impression on a boy--with lipstick.

Men make passes at girls who drain glasses.

Show me a beauty contest, and I'll show you a lass roundup.

My girl's the type to take home to Mother--when Mother isn't home.

My girl friend looks like a million--every year of it.

The only sign of toil on her hand is her engagement ring.

A coed would rather be well-formed than well informed.

My girl likes to whsper sweet nothing-doings in my ear.

A bathing beauty is a girl worth wading for.

My girl is a vision--a real sight.

The biggest worry of a doting father is a dating daughter.

A girl flirting is wishful winking.

In Hawaii, the men make passes at girls who wear grasses.

She turned my head with her charm, and my stomach with her cooking.

Any girl who has been overlooked, has been looked over.

The only time some girls say "Stop" is in a telegram.

The child is father to the man, except when the child is a girl.

A heroine is a girl who is game, but not everybody's.

Where do mothers learn all the things they tell their daughters not to do?

A miss in your car is better than a miss in your carburetor.

Mother knows best--until daughter becomes a teen-ager.

Girls are the reason that even love sometimes needs refinancing.

A career girl would rather bring home the bacon than fry it.

If you don't think girls are explosive, try dropping one.

What mother used to call "sin," daughter now calls "experience."

I never expect to find the perfect girl--but it's great fun searching.

Some girls use an old flame to burn up a new boy friend.

My girl let her shoulder-strap slip. It was her first undoing.

Any girl who is easy to get is usually hard to take.

I'm partial to the kind of girl who rides home from a walk.

A girl with a million-dollar figure can really draw interest.

I'm going with a well-bred girl, so I keep her buttered up.

A girl needs horse sense to know when to say "Neigh."

A pretty girl is more to be petted than censured.

My girl isn't complex--anyone can grasp her.

It takes a lot of soft soap to make some girls slip.

My girl looks good in everything--but a mirror.

Any girl who skates on thin ice ends up in hot water.

With a negative type girl you never know what's going to develop.

The girl who goes out on a lark can end up in some bird's nest.

A working girl is one who quit her job to get married.

Her telephone has a private number--every private has it.

A girl who pursues the wrong policy needs accident insurance.

Girls! It's okay to be bitten by the lovebug, but not by a louse.

A brainless beauty is a toy forever.

It's a dumb girl who doesn't turn a deaf ear to a blind date.

A girl's maiden aim is to change her maiden name.

I know a girl whose grammar is awful--she can't decline.

A girl can brighten things up for a man by sitting in the dark with him.

Every time I take a girl out, I try to take her in.

Every girl wants a clear white skin--especially if it's ermine.

My girl is a vision in the evening and a sight in the morning.

Girlhood is sixty pounds ago.

Girls are the ones that dance backward.

Golf

I'm not a golfer.I can't tell one end of the caddie from the other.

In golf, the ball always lies poorly; and the player well.

I played Civil War golf. I went out in 61 and came back in 65.

I've either got to sell my golf clubs or get a divorce.

There are two times to address a ball--before and after swinging.

A golfer know how to express his thoughts to a tee.

Golf is about the only thing that depreciates above par.

You can't keep a good golfer downtown.

I play golf to relax, when I'm too tired to mow the lawn.

The course of true golf never did run smooth.

Golf keeps you on the green, in the pink, and in the red.

You play golf with your own worst enemy--yourself.

To me it's life, liberty, and the pursuit of golf balls.

Golf is an ideal hobby, but a ruinous disease.

A golfer is a gardener digging up someone else's lawn.

A golf bag is an elderly female golfer.

When playing golf nothing counts like your opponent.

Some men play golf religiously, every Sunday.

All is fair in love and golf.

Golf isn't a rich man's game--there are plenty of poor players.

I almost made a hole-in-one today--just missed by three strokes.

Of course, one of golf's birdies is the chipping sparrow.

A duffer is one who constantly passes the cup.

I only play golf to aggravate myself.

A caddie is a lie-detector.

The way I play golf, the greens flags should be at half-mast.

My wife told me, either I sell my golf clubs, or we get a divorce.

Water hazard: take tee and see.

You chase a golf ball when you are too old to chase anything else.

My golf is improving. Now I miss the ball much closer than I used to.

I shoot golf in the low 70s. When it gets any colder, I quit.

May our stocks go up, and our game go down--to par.

His friends call it madness, but he calls it golf.

If you drink, don't drive--putt!

I'm so used to cheating that when I made a hole-in-one, I put down zero.

By the time a man can afford to lose a ball, he can't hit that far.

Even Samson couldn't break away from the links.

A golf ball is a golf ball--no matter how you putt it.

My golf is improving. Yesterday I hit the ball in one.

Golf is a long walk punctuated with disappointments.

Golf is nothing but pool played out of doors.

I used to play golf, but then I lost my ball. The string broke.

Par is attained with a soft pencil and a softer conscience.

On a public golf course, you hit a ball, and a picnic runs out and grabs it.

Golf is the most popular way of beating around the bush.

You can judge a man by the golf score he keeps.

The way I see it, golf is just an expensive way to play marbles.

The way some Sunday golfers play--they'd be better off in church.

One thing you can say about golf is that it isn't compulsory.

I prefer a golf cart to a caddy--they don't count, criticize, or laugh.

Only a remarkable man can live down a hole in one.

As soon as a businessman takes up golf, he becomes an executive.

A handicapped golfer is one who plays with his boss.

Gossip

Gossip is a way of putting one and one together to make talk.

I detest gossip--but only when it's about me.

Her tongue should be declared a lethal weapon.

I don't know her to speak to--only about.

My wife can keep a secret--with telling effect.

My mother-in-law is always the knife of the party.

Don't talk about yourself--it'll be done when you leave.

Nothing is more useless than gossip that isn't worth repeating.

Her tongue hangs out like a pump handle.

A gossip is a professional athlete--of the tongue.

A gossip is a person who suffers from acute indiscretion.

A gossip's tongue, 3 inches long, can kill a man 6 feet tall.

My wife's gossip is enough to make me she-sick.

I seldom repeat gossip--the way I hear it.

People, like cats, lick themselves with their tongues.

In any verbal duel, my mother-in-law's choice of weapons is mud.

When it comes to running down people, she never runs down.

She doesn't spread rumors--she shovels them.

My wife is a good conver-sensationalist.

It's easy for folks to make monkeys of themselves just by carrying tales.

When you are in deep water, it's a good idea to keep your mouth shut.

A closed mouth gathers no foot.

What we hear is never as exciting as what we overhear.

What a gossip! When you wind her up, she runs someone down.

It's easier to float a rumor than to sink one.

A gossip can turn an earful into a mouthful.

A flying rumor never has any trouble in making a landing.

The breath of scandal is an ill wind.

My wife suffers from acute indiscretion.

She's as inquisitive as an x-ray.

With her it's never too early to tell--or too bad.

Gossip? Everyone she talks to leaves with a rundown feeling.

Accustomed as I am to public peeking...

Half the evil in the world is gossip started by good people.

Her tongue is like a reckless driver--it's always running people down.

You can never tell about people, unless you're a gossip.

A gossip is anybody who is not too busy to be a busybody.

Gossip is a form of malicious talk indulged in by other people.

Gossips are the spies of life.

Gossip, unlike river water, flows both ways.

A gossip is one with a mouthful eager to give others an earful.

I never put off till tomorrow the gossip I can spread today.

Tell some people a secret and they chin and bare it.

A gossip put two and two together--whether they are or not.

Some gossip is too good to be true.

A little gossip goes a long way.

A gossip listens in haste and repeats at leisure.

Some people can sling dirt faster than a gravedigger.

There is no fun in listening to gossip unless you believe it.

Gossip is like spinach: it all boils down to very little.

I dislike repeating gossip, but what else can you do with it?

A gossip is always letting the chat out of the bag.

Some people like to be first with the worst.

I never repeat gossip, so please listen carefuly the first time.

Some things go without saying, but gossip isn't one of them.

A gossip takes people at their deface value.

Women don't only engage in conversation--they syndicate it.

My wife is a slight-of-tongue artist.

"They say" is the biggest gossip in the land.

Gossip is an ill wind that blows nobody good.

A gossip always gives you the benefit of the dirt.

She weighs her friends; faults with her thumbs on the scale.

A gossip burns her scandals at both ends.

In a beauty parlor, the gossip alone can curl your hair.

Nothing makes gossip grow like a grain of truth.

Gossip is the only sound that travels faster than sound.

My wife is on spiking terms with everyone.

A gossip's business is what's none of his business.

A sewing circle is the ideal place to needle everyone.

Groundless gossip covers ground rapidly.

My mother-in-law's tongue is like a pink dart.

I never tell a lie--if truth will do more damage.

His chief delight is giving the low-down on the higher-ups.

A gossip can make a mountain out of a little dirt.

In the business world a gossip is known as a "meddle"-man.

A gossip has the words of a saint and the claws of a cat.

Her problem is that she can't leave bad enough alone.

A gossip whitewashes himself by blackening others.

Anything you tell my wife goes in one ear and over the back fence.

My mother-in-law has a tongue that could clip a hedge.

The discriminating gossip picks her friends--to pieces.

To a gossip the worst scandal is the best.

Not every woman repeats gossip--someone has to start it.

One woman's past is another woman's pastime.

My wife's gossip is strictly her-say.

Nasty rumors are usually spread over the sour grape-vine.

A gossip is an expert in hint-imation.

Some gossips have more inside information than a surgeon.

A gossip puts who and who together and gets--whew!

A woman who doesn't gossip has no friends to speak of.

A gossip likes to discuss the events of the day, friend by friend.

Her tongue is her sword, and she never lets it get rusty.

Time never tells on a woman's friends as much as she does.

To spread news fast you can telephone, telegraph, or tell-her.

Then there's the eavesdropper who gets in your hear.

Even when a gossip doesn't believe it all, she tells it all.

I can keep a secret--the reason is I forget them.

Sooner or later every gossip gets caught in her own mouth-trap.

Gossips talk about things that make them speechless.

A gossip can give you all the details without knowing any of the facts.

A gossip can keep a secret going.

Nothing is more useless than gossip that isn't worth repeating.

The vacuum-cleaner type gossip purrs and takes in the dirt.

She cultivates friendships like a garden--with continuous digs.

Cars don't run down as many people as my wife does.

When she's in a train of thought someone is about to get run down.

A gossip is a person with a narrow mind and a wide mouth.

If you want a rumor to be believed--whisper it.

Gossip is like a grapefruit, to be really good, it has to be juicy.

A gossip is a newscaster without a sponsor.

My wife tells everything she can get her ears on.

She'd rather listen to dirt than sweep it.

A sly gossip knows exactly how much to leave out of a story.

Most women cluck like hens over grains of gossip.

Gossip is what you hear; news is what you tell.

Hair

My barber says my hair is getting thin. So who wants fat hair?

Hair today--gone tomorrow.

Now there's a wig to wear to the supermarket. It has curlers in it.

When lawyers split hairs, for sure it's someone else's hairs.

My wife has dyed by her own hand.

She's a cross between a brunette and a drugstore.

I went out with a girl who looked like a doll. Her hair was pasted on.

To a bald man dandruff is a thrill.

He was so bald--he looked like a part with ears.

Every cloud has a silver lining. My mother-in-law has gray hair.

All her gray matter is outside her head.

Her hair looks as though she dyed.

Now they sell imitation dandruff for people who wear wigs.

I regard a blonde as a golden opportunity.

Many a dumb blonde is really a smart brunette.

At the movies, they have to ask my wife to take off her hair.

My optometrist gave me a prescription for my bad eyesight: Get a haircut.

Straight hair is beautiful on a woman, provided she has legs to match.

I call my wife "Kitty" because she has dyed nine times.

May I have a lock of your hair? You see, I'm stuffing a mattress.

My wife is an established bleach-head.

She has one of those new hair tints, the ones where you hue-it-yourself.

My wife has dyed her hair so often, she's got technicolored dandruff.

The only cure for dandruff is a French invention--called the guillotine.

After two days you wonder where an upsweep hair-do was swept up from.

A man is usually bald four or five years before he notices it.

Everything comes to the man who waits, including a beard.

Love is more often blonde than blind.

When a woman starts stroking your hair, she's probably after your scalp.

I don't know why, but after I get a haircut, I hear better.

A man is as young as he feels--until he buys a toupee.

A bald spot is not an asset, but it's better than no head at all.

Look at that beard--he looks like an armpit.

Of two evils, most men choose the blonde.

Gentlemen prefer blondes because where there's light there's heat.

Look at this guy's hair--he looks like a chrysanthemum.

The only thing that can stop falling hair is a floor.

Today's toupees really fool people, but only those people who wear them.

I inherited one thing from my father--a bald head.

If the truth were told about some blondes, it would be off-color.

To keep your hair from falling out, knot it on the inside.

Everyone has hair problems: with women it's tint, with men 'tain't.

I think my wife's hairdo was arranged in front of an electric fan.

One advantage of a wig is that it doesn't have dandruff.

A bald barber is always the one who has a cure for baldness.

A woman's head is turned by flattery, or by tinting.

A hair in the head is worth two in the brush.

My dad is 70 years old and he hasn't got a single gray hair in his toupee.

He bought an expensive wig on credit. He's in debt over his ears.

The best way to avoid falling hair is to jump out of the way.

As long as you can count your gray hairs, they don't count.

The more natural a toupee, the less you can tell it from a wig.

A baldheaded man is one who came out on top and still lost.

He isn't bald; he just has a tall face.

Hair is the only thing that prevents baldness.

Her hair color changes so often, she has a convertible top.

Nothing keeps a girl's hair so neat as a bashful boyfriend.

Happiness

Another form of endurance test is the pursuit of happiness.

Happiness is often the result of not knowing any better.

Show me an optimist, and I'll show you a happy-chondriac.

The happiest people are those who are too busy to notice.

A poor man can be happy; but a happy man isn't poor.

The bluebird brings happiness, but the stork brings tax-exemptions.

Happiness has to be cranked up; trouble is a self-starter.

A woman is unhappy until she finds a way to use her brains.

If a man is happy everyone thinks he is doing something wrong.

A hearty laugh is worth a hundred groans in any market.

School days are life's happiest days--once your kid is old enough to go.

Smile and the world smiles with you; snore and you sleep alone.

Happiness is a form of courage.

Happiness is no laughing matter.

To be happy, be satisfied with what you've got--and what you haven't got.

Happiness is the one thing that doesn't go up in price during inflation.

Happiness is four feet on a fireplace fender.

Happiness is good health, and a poor memory.

Happiness is the way station between too little and too much.

Be content with what you have, not with what you are.

Never put off happiness, because there's no time like the pleasant.

What a terrible time people have trying to be happy.

The only really happy people are married women and single men.

The happiest man on earth is the one who never knows it.

Happiness is the best of all riches--and it's not taxed.

Many people never seem to enjoy life until it's too late.

If ignorance is bliss, why isn't the world happier?

You'll be happier if you stop worrying because you're not.

Most of us won't be happy with our lot until it's a lot more.

A man is usually as happy as he wishes his acquaintances to be.

Happiness is better than money, but only if you have both.

A happy man is never poor; an unhappy man is never rich.

Money can't buy happiness--but it can help you look for it in more places.

Money can't buy happiness--but it makes shopping more fun.

We lived happily until the day we got married.

I've had a very happy marriage--now and then.

My wife is happy I'm not perfect--she likes to nag.

For twenty years my wife and I were happy--then we met.

You want to make someone happy today? Mind your own business.

A man is never happy until a girl comes along and makes him miserable.

What good is happiness? It can't buy you money.

Happiness is when an old man marries a frigid woman.

Every man has a key to happiness--be sure you pick out the right lock.

Happiness is when your girl sees you out with your wife--and forgives you.

Health

I'm full of the joy of almost living.

A hypochondriac can't leave being well-enough alone.

I'm on drugs that haven't even been written up in Reader's Digest.

I won't even talk on the phone to anyone who has a cold.

I always carry a thermometer. I even stir my drinks with it.

My wife's life is a bed of neuroses.

Money can't buy health, but it can buy a car for the doctor's wife.

Medicine is a science; acquiring a medical practice is an art.

Convalescence is the period when you are still sick, after you get well.

I get most of my exercise watching the sports programs on television.

Like a bus straphanger I have complaints of long standing.

My wife is unhappy when she has no troubles to speak of.

My wife's ailment is not so much chronic as chronicle.

Youth thinks nothing of health, and age thinks of nothing else.

No one feels worse than the man who gets sick on his day off.

If you don't find time to exercise you'll have to find time for illness.

My wife has had every ailment and disease shown on television.

I never take tranquilizers. I get very agitated if I'm not high-strung.

I'm so afraid of surgery I won't even read the opening pages of a book.

A hypochondriac is one who goes to a drive-in movie in an ambulance.

My wife wants to have her ache and treat it too.

My doctor always looks like a cheerleader for the morgue.

My wife has a talent for organ recitals--about her operations.

Some people call a doctor when all they want is an audience.

I left instructions in my will to be buried alongside of a doctor.

Sometimes I think I was created for the benefit of doctors.

To be the picture of health you must have a happy frame of mind.

A hypochondriac is always sure to have some ailment in mind.

I don't know much about medicine, but I know what I like.

The fault I find with exercising is that it makes me tired.

My wife is always on pills and needles.

One tourniquet that stops circulation is a wedding ring.

I got up at the crack of dawn, stuffed up the crack, and went back to bed.

A hypochondriac can suffer in many different ways, but never in silence.

My wife always gives you a preamble to her constitution.

To get a child to take his medicine, label the bottle "Poison" and hide it.

Even when you're pushing 70, you still need more exercise.

Observe your dog--if he's fat, you're not getting enough exercise.

The best medicine for arthritis is to give thanks that it isn't gout.

My wife's health has me worried. It's always good.

People would be in better health if they didn't get sick so often.

A little honey is good for you--unless your wife finds out.

Socialized medicine: women talking about their operations.

To cheer myself up, I read the obituary notices.

One illness you can catch froma hypochondriac is a pain in the neck.

If an actor sneezes on television my wife thinks she's caught cold.

Many women who are the picture of health are just painted that way.

I told my doctor that I'm sick and tired of being sick and tired.

What do you send to a sick florist?

What do you say to God if he sneezes?

I sure hope I'm sick. I'd hate to feel like this when I'm well.

My wife's usual greeting is "Good moaning."

Some people look for a funeral whenever they smell flowers.

A hypochondriac is a rue-it-yourself expert.

"Doctor, doctor! I've just swallowed a spoon." "Sit down and don't stir."

My brother-in-law has an allergy. He's allergic to work.

My lawyer says that where there's a will, there's an ill.

They asked me to be a blood donor. I'm not even a blood owner.

The blood bank turned me down--they want plasma, not asthma.

I stayed up all night studying for a blood test.

I just got over the Egyptian flu--I got it from my mummy.

A frustrated hypochondriac is one who is allergic to medicine.

I'm sure I've got the chickn pox--I found a feather in my bed.

I always feel like a sick oyster at low tide.

Wives suffer as many ulcers as husbands do. The same ones.

Early to rise and early to bed makes a man healthy and socially dead.

One new miracle drug is so strong you have to be in perfect health to use it.

The only genuine red menace in America is sunburn.

Hay fever is much achoo about nothing.

Birth control is the evasion of the issue.

A convalescent is a patient who is still alive.

My wife collects ills and pills and always gets chills.

Some people always brood over their health, but never hatch.

I never use ice cubes because I can't boil them.

I won't kiss a girl unless her lipstick has penicillin in it.

Allow yourself to become run down and you'll wind up in the hospital.

I'll never die in my sleep--I don't sleep that well.

Dandruff: chips off the old block.

Show me a dentist's office, and I'll show you a drawing room.

Show me a dentist, and I'll show you a man who runs a filling station.

Dieting will take the starch out of you.

Dieting is the penalty for exceeding the feed limit.

Show me a man with a hangover, and I'll show you a man with a toot ache

You're healthy if you think that now is the best time of the year.

I take so many different-colored pills, I dream in Technicolor.

A hypochondriac is a woe-begonia.

A neurotic thinks you mean it when you ask him how he is.

If you ignore health in the chase for wealth you end up losing both.

The man given to early rising, does very little socializing.

He who eats an apple a day is frowned upon by the A.M.A.

A hospital is a place where they wake you up to give you a sleeping pill.

Hypochondria is a disease without a disease.

A hypochondriac is a person with an infinite capacity for faking pains.

"Mal de mer" is French for "You can't take it with you."

I've taken so many red and green pills I may get hired to direct traffic.

My doctor always puts on his best graveside manner.

A hypochondriac is a mis-fortune-teller.

Even cannibals have better sense than to eat themselves to death.

My medicine chest looks like a drug store, only there are no sandwiches.

A neurasthenic is a person always on pills and needles.

An operation is a surgical job taking minutes to do and years to describe.

A manic-depressive is the easy glum, easy glow type.

I'm so full of penicillin, every time I sneeze I cure ten people.

You could call reducing "wishful shrinking."

My wife loves to sunbathe--she's a fry in the ointment.

Show me a wrinkle, and I'll show you the nick of time.

I got out of a sick bed to get here--the bed is better.

Oversleeping will never make your dreams come true.

A dyspeptic is a person who can eat his cake and have it too.

Treat your nerves like a bank account. Never overdraw.

All is not bliss that blisters.

It takes backbone to become a successful chiropractor.

I've eaten so much wheat germ to stay healthy that I sway in the breeze.

Dandruff is small, whitish scales trying to get ahead.

Dyspepsia is the remorse of a guilty stomach.

Germs are usually caught on the fly.

Health is wealth is a rule that doesn't work both ways.

I have a heart murmur.It's off the beatin' path.

I have a perfect cure for a sore throat--cut it.

What really happens if you exercise daily is that you die healthier.

Health makes you feel it's a fine day when it isn't.

Insomnia is the triumph of mind over mattress.

People who have insomnia lie awake all night for an hour.

A rich man has acute laryngitis, but a poor man has a cold.

The best thing for halitosis is lockjaw.

Patent medicine is not what it's quacked up to be.

Show me an oculist, and I'll show you a man with an eye for business.

A plastic surgeon is one who maims to please.

Tapeworm: another mouth to feed.

Insanity is hereditary. You can get it from your children.

I never shake anyone's hand if it's more than 80 degrees.

Tell my wife how healthy she looks and you've made a mortal enemy.

I take a cold shower every morning--after my family has all taken hot ones.

Hollywood

In Hollywood, the multiple marriage is just a re-take.

A movie producer is one person who may truly thank his lucky stars.

A Hollywood producer is an ulcer with authority.

In Hollywood, an actress is anybody who's got a dimple.

Where an actor is a man who makes faces for money.

Movies are out of their infancy--but a lot of their stories aren't.

In Hollywood blood is thicker than talent.

The happy ending of some movies is the mere fact that they have ended.

For six years I worked for MGM. That's Mac's Grocery Market.

Marry in Hollywood and repeat indefinitely.

One actor likes his new wife enough to hold her over for a second week.

Hollywood executives used to pinch starlets, now they pinch pennies.

Stories about Hollywood marriages should end with a comma.

Girls in Hollywood don't live in sin--they just have unlisted husbands.

One actor has been divorced four times--he never could hold an audience.

Movie stars are marrying more, but enjoying it less.

In Hollywood they shoot too much film and not enough actors.

I've done some screen work--I fixed one on our kitchen door.

Movie photographers favor the clothes-up picture.

A Hollywood triangle is made up of an actor, his wife, and himself.

Hollywood is thickly populated, but to me it's still a be-wilderness.

A Hollywood marriage is much "I do" about nothing.

A modern miracle would be a diamond wedding anniversary in Hollywood.

Hollywood is a plastered Paris.

Hollywood is the most sensational merry-go-round ever built.

The land of yes-men and acqui-yes-girls.

A Hollywood marriage is a good way to spend a weekend.

I just returned from two weeks in Hollywood--looking for work.

It's spring in Hollywood when the smog gets greener.

Hollywood is Potter's field in neon lights.

The place bad plays go when they die.

The psychopathic ward of Art.

An asylum run by the inmates.

A director is a man who believes in victory through "yeah" power.

Hollywood is the world's most beautiful set in the lousiest scenario.

If a man's wife looks like a new woman in Hollywood--she probably is.

Hollywood is a gold rush in dinner jackets.

It's a warm Siberia.

Hollywood is a sunny spot for shady people.

At least one starlet has made it to the top because her clothes didn't.

A silver wedding anniversary in Hollywood means the twenty-fifth wedding.

Hollywood is sex suburbs in search of a city.

You have to see Hollywood to disbelieve it.

One well-known actor has a home where the kitchen alone has five rooms.

Hollywood is the Athens of Los Angeles County.

The movie industry finds out what you don't like, then gives it to you.

Hollywood is an emotional Detroit.

Hollywood is a state of mind surrounded by Los Angeles.

Hollywood is the musical comedy version of Cedar Rapids.

Hollywood is full of show-oafs.

In Hollywood, behind every successful husband is another woman.

A Hollywood actor is a refugee from life.

Where the wedding cake outlasts the wedding.

Where the bride keeps the bouquets and gets rid of the husband.

Where the girls ask their husbands for consent to marry.

Where people from Iowa mistake each other for movie stars.

Where a pal is someone who is around when he needs you.

Where people without reputation try to live upto it.

Where everyone is a genius until he loses his job.

Where the people accept you for what you're not.

Where they place you under contract instead of observation.

Where society moves in the best triangles.

Where no one gives their right age except in time of war.

Where they put beautiful frames in pictures.

Where they live happily, and get married ever afterward.

Where the girls are fit as a fiddle and ready to play.

Where they have secret weddings and catered divorces.

Home

These days a home is supplied with everything but a family.

The world may do for a hotel, but it will never do for a home.

I wonder what kind of home those home-made frozen pies come from.

In some homes the clock, like father, is always wrong.

Home is where you don't have to engage reservations in advance.

To a small boy, home is merely a filling station.

Home is a place to stay while the car is being serviced.

Home is the place where, when you are there, they have to take you in.

In today's home nothing can be accomplished if the electricity fails.

There's no place like home, and I, for one, am glad of it.

Be they ever so humble, there's nobody stays home.

Guests will happen in, in the best regulated families.

The old-fashioned girl, who married for a home, could be found in it.

The American home is sound as ever--thanks to television.

All men are not homeless, but some are home less than others.

Today's homes are built with every convenience except low payments.

Home is where we're treated the best and grumble the most.

There's no place like home, once in a while.

There's no place like home if you haven't got the money to go out.

You can't keep the home circle square with a triangle.

A guest never knows how much to laugh at a family joke.

Be there ever so many payments there's no place like home.

A model home isn't worth a thing without a model family inside.

God bless our scrappy home.

Nostalgia is longing for the place you wouldn't move back to.

My home is my castle--while my wife is out shopping.

Home is where you hang your head.

What is a home without a mutter?

The best home remedy is a good wife.

Home is a suit of clothes with a roof on it.

Home is where you take off your new shoes and put on your old manners.

My home has wall-to-wall carpeting and back-to-wall financing.

I appreciate the comforts of home most when my wife wants me to go out.

Henny with Jimmy and Gloria Stewart and Mr. and Mrs. Jesse White
(the "Lonely" Maytag Repairman)

First a man buys a home--then he buys a car to get away from it.

I built my wife an early American home--a teepee.

There's no place like home--thank heaven.

Home is where the mortgage is.

My wife and I never quarrel in public--that's what we have a home for.

A man's home is his wife's castle.

Home is where the heart is, and the car isn't.

The only way I can get away from my family is to stay at home.

In my home I run the show--my wife writes the script.

There's no place like home, which is why I go out nights.

Sooner or later everything wears out in a home, including your nerves.

Home is where you slip in the bathtub and break your neck.

There's no place like home, particularly when you're looking for trouble.

I go home when I'm tired of being polite to people.

Some men are never at home long enough to get homesick.

Home is the place to go to get reaty to do somewhere else.

This country needs more home-builders and less home-wreckers.

One way to make your home look better is to go out and price a new one.

Honesty

It pays to be honest. It pays even more than it costs.

One good thing about honesty is you don't need a confederate.

While it pays to be honest, it's often a long time collecting.

My handicap, in golf, is my honesty.

A lot of politicians give publicly and steal privately.

Common honesty should be more common.

My brother-in-law is a man of promise--broken promise.

Honesty isn't the best policy; but it is the safest.

Honesty is the best policy, but many are satisfied with less than the best.

Honesty pays--and dishonest gets paid.

It should be easy to make an honest living--there's so little competition.

Honesty is the best policy--for poor people.

Honesty is also the best foreign policy.

One thing a person can't keep on an empty stomach is principles.

Those who stay on the level rise higher in the end.

Honesty is the best policy, but not the best politics.

An honest confession is good for the soul, but bad for the reputation.

Honesty is the best policy--when there is money in it.

Opportunities lie on every hand. So do a lot of people.

Brassiere ads prove that honesty is not the bust policy.

White lies are usually yellow.

My brother-in-law has the gift of gab.

Honesty is mostly the fear of being caught.

He's so tricky, he could skin a flint.

Honesty is praised, and starves.

My brother-in-law is a gentleman to his fingerprints.

I'd be willing to earn my money honestly if it didn't take so long.

Nothing is as dishonest as a dentist's smile.

A lie in time saves nine.

Many people climb to considerable heights by remaining on the level.

An ambassador is an honest man sent abroad to lie for his country.

Diplomacy is the art of lying in state.

Some men will stand for anything they think you will fall for.

A hypocrite is a person who is honest when he has an audience.

I never go back on my word--without consulting my lawyer.

Your mirror doesn't lie to you. Why should I?

Some people can't even be honest in a diary.

Honesty is a state of mind, or else it isn't honesty.

My brother-in-law is a contact man--all con and no tact.

To many people honesty means undetected.

My boss carved his career by first-class chiseling.

No honest man will become a dog for a bone.

Some men talk on principles and act on interest.

My brother-in-law is long on promises and short on memory.

Remember when men were considered more honest than computers?

Horses

One day I played a horse so slow, the jockey kept a diary of the trip.

I once crossed a horse with a fish. I put a fin on its nose.

Race tracks attract people who have a talent for picking the wrong horse.

Horse sense isn't enough in this world, even for horses.

Horse sense dwells in a stable mind.

I bet on a horse named Lassie--but it never came home.

Horses are what more people bet on than get on.

When you bet on the horses you get nothing for something.

Never put the cart before the horse, unless you're backing up.

Many things run into money, except the horses I bet on.

Nothing is as uncertain as a sure thing in a horse race.

It's a wise horse that knows its own fodder.

The horse is a friend of man--until you start betting on him.

Woman's intuition never works at the race track either.

In pitching hoseshoes the first rule is to remove the horse.

No horse can go as fast as the money you bet on him.

If I put money on a horse's nose, the odds are he has sinus trouble.

Horsepower was much safer when only horses had it.

You can't make a fast buck on a slow horse.

The horse I bet on was so slow he was arrested for loitering.

I had a good day at the races. I didn't go.

Belmont has a special window for women bettors--a $1.98 window.

The race track is a place where windows clean people.

A tout is a guy who has nothing to lose and makes sure you do.

My girl is like a horse. She says "Nay, nay" all the time.

"I'm interested in the sport of kings." "Horses?" "No, queens."

My horse was so late getting home, he tiptoed into the stable.

My horse started from a kneeling position.

My horse was so slow--the jockey kept a diary.

Why is it that the favorite only wins when I don't bet on him?

I only play the horses for laughs. Last week I laughed away my car.

My horse was so slow they paid the jockey time-and-a-half for overtime.

It is possible to win money at the race track--if you're a fast horse.

That dumb wife of mine blew my racetrack money on the rent.

I bet on a polite horse. He kept holding out his hoof on the turns.

I bet on an aristocratic horse. He was the last of his race.

The horse was named "Fleabag"--he was scratched.

My horse came in twelfth--he said that 13 was his unlucky number.

I own a model horse. He poses for glue bottles.

My horse came in so late the jockey was wearing pajamas.

I always leave the racetrack with a nice clean feeling.

No horse is a man's best friend till he bets on him.

Dollars and sense seldom appear together at a race track.

A horse player buys $200 worth of hope for two minutes for $2.

I came to the track with faith and hope, I left needing charity.

No metter what racetrack you go to, you're always on the wrong track.

I know a fellow who always makes money at the track--he's a jockey.

There are always less horses on the track than asses in the stands.

The horse you put your money on usually runs away with it.

They had to photograph the track to find my horse.

The best way to stop a runaway horse is to bet on it.

If you want your troubles off your mind, go horseback riding.

If 50,000 people ran at a race track, not one horse would attend.

Money makes the mare go, but not if it's bet on her.

If you play the horses you're a gambler pure and simple. Especially simple.

A lot of people who wouldn't bet on a horse, turn around and get married.

Hotels

I have a lovely room with hot and cold running bedbugs.

I think the name of my hotel is"The Outstretched Palms."

My hotel is popular as a resort. A last resort.

My hotel is so swanky that room service has an unlisted number.

They're so tip-happy I ordered a deck of cards. They sent them up one at a time.

My hotel is so swanky they show movies in the elevators.

A hotel is where you stay when you have no relatives.

My hotel is so swanky they butter your toast on both sides.

My room is very musty. On a clear day I can see the window.

My hotel is so swanky they put out a red carpet on the beach.

For air conditioning two guys spray the room with empty Flit guns.

My hotel is so swanky you have to wear a tie to go to the swimming pool.

The best motel with a vacancy is the one you passed 50 miles back.

My hotel is so swanky even the guests have to use the service entrance.

One place you can make a name for yourself is in a hotel register.

My hotel is so swanky it costs 35 cents to change a quarter.

In my hotel everything is cold but the icewater.

My hotel is so dull, last night I sent down for another bible.

They change the sheets daily--from one room to another.

My hotel is very big. To call the desk you dial long distance.

I've got a room with a bath. Too bad they're in different buildings.

You don't need a reservation--unless you're an Indian.

It's called the Biltmore Hotel--it was built more like a stable.

The bath towels are so fluffy you can hardly close your suitcase.

Remember "motel" spelled backwards is "Let 'em."

One traveling salesman died and left his family 5,000 hotel towels.

My room has natural air-conditioning--a broken window.

A hotel is where you give up good dollars for bad quarters.

My room is so small . . .

. . . the mice are hunchbacked.

. . . I used a doormat for wall-to-wall carpeting.

. . . every time I bend over I re-arrange the furniture.

. . . when the sun came in, I had to get out.

. . . when I closed the door, the doorknob pinched my stomach.

. . . I couldn't even brush my teeth sideways.

. . . I have to go outside to change my mind.

. . . every time I put the key in the lock, I broke the window.

. . . when I go to bed my feet stick out the window.

. . . no matter where I stand I can always touch the walls.

. . . every time I blink I wash the window.

. . . when my girl friend visited, she couldn't even cross her legs.

. . . to brush my teeth I use a folding toothbrush.

. . . it gets overheated every time I turn on my electric toaster.

. . . I have to leave my suitcase in the hall.

. . . I can only fry one egg at a time.

. . . when a dog visited me, it had to wag its tail up and down.

. . . I have wall-to-wall furniture.

I'm looking for accommodations where I can put up with my wife.

I get all the hot water I want by asking for soup in the dining room.

My bed was so hard, I had to get up twice to get some rest.

Business is so bad, some hotels are stealing towels from the guests.

Human Nature

Poise is the power to raise the eyebrows instead of the roof.

Some people are good losers, and others can't act.

Luck is what enables someone else to succeed where you have failed.

Human nature makes a man find time to do the things he wants to do.

To avoid having enemies, outlive them.

At least an introvert spends his time minding his own business.

To cure insomnia, get a lot of sleep.

No two people are alike and both of them are glad of it.

It's easy to see through people who make spectacles of themselves.

Trade secrets--that's what women do.

The more I think of people, the less I think of them.

An inferiority complex would be fine if the right person had it.

My wife is so restless, she doesn't feel at home at home.

I always do the right thing too late, or the wrong thing too soon.

The division between the sexes is balanced by the multiplication.

People who throw kisses are lazy.

The best time to study human nature is when you are alone.

I would trust other people more if I knew myself less.

No one is as busy as the person who has nothing to do.

Why does a hostess insist on introducing us to people we don't know?

Why does everyone think he is an exception to the rules?

I like to hear the truth, no matter how flattering it is.

A meddler is a person who suffers from an interferiority complex.

Men and rivers go crooked by following the line of least resistance.

The best time to study human nature is when you are alone.

A neurotic is a person who, when you ask him how he feels, tells you.

A nuisance is a man you like better the more you see him less.

It's easy to pick out the best people--they'll help you do it.

The noblest quality of a human being is being human.

Very few people have the courage of my convictions.

It is human nature to do whatever human nature does.

Honest confession is good for the soul, but bad for the reputation.

A chip on the shoulder is usually a very heavy burden to carry.

"Be yourself" is the worst advice you can give some people.

It's a gay life if your "don't" weakens.

The way of the transgressor may be hard--but it isn't lonely.

To sell something, tell a woman it's a bargain; tell a man it's deductible.

Today people don't repent--even at leisure.

When you apologize you're being polite too late.

Wine, women and song ruined me. I didn't get any.

Rheumatism has kept many people on the right path in life.

Tears are the world's greatest water power.

Chivalry is the attitude of a man toward a strange woman.

If bankers can count, why do they always have 8 windows and 2 tellers?

Conceit is God's gift to little men.

Actions don't always speak louder than words, but they tell fewer lies.

A woman forgives only when she is in the wrong.

Getting up early is a triumph of mind over mattress.

If you mind your own business, you're an eccentric.

A fool and her money are soon courted.

Fidelity is a virtue peculiar to those who are about to be betrayed.

Flirting is paying attention without intention.

Don't be yourself--be what you should be.

A good citizen is one who behaves as if there were no laws.

Behavior patterns are trait jackets.

Jealousy is the friendship one woman has for another.

A lowbrow is a person who can't appreciate something he doesn't like.

Parents don't bring up children any more--they finance them.

To sing is human--to forgive divine.

Show me a man who carries a torch, and I'll show you a firebug.

Treat a girl like a hot-house flower and she'll come home potted.

The reason Robin Hood robbed the rich was: the poor had no money.

A girl with a nice stairway doesn't need much upstairs.

To make your dream come true, you've got to wake up.

The man who is stuck on himself seldom has any cause for jealousy.

The moment you think you've got humility, you've lost it.

It's easy for a somebody to be modest, but it's tough for a nobody.

If my wife doesn't stop nagging me, I'll let my insurance lapse.

My wife keeps a budget, so we'll know how much we owe.

Nobody ever knows a poet is alive until he is dead.

A wise man never laughs at his wife's old clothes.

The bigger a man's head gets, the easier to fill his shoes.

I wish I had been born rich instead of so darned lovable!

Never cross a bridge before it is built.

Never give coffee to a drunk, you'll end up with a wide-awake drunk.

Never pet a polar bear until he's a rug.

Never sleep with your eyes open.

Humor

If you want a girl to laugh at your jokes tell her she has a musical laugh.

Humor, like history, repeats itself.

Every humorist is an exhumerist.

A comic is a person, who, when he dies, is at his wit's end.

A joke is proof that the good do not die young.

My wife has a keen sense of humor. The more I humor her, the better.

It's a wise crack that knows its own father.

The lack of a sense of humor may make a person very funny.

A comedian is a man with a fun-track mind.

There are two sides to every story--one for men only.

Comedian's byword: Seek and ye shall file.

Some women show their sense of humor by their choice of husband.

Any comedian who indulges his audience, humors them.

I'm fast on the ad-lib. All I have to do is hear it once.

I wrote my own gags to keep the wolf from the door. I told them to the wolf.

A joke is a form of humor enjoyed by some and misunderstood by most.

A pun is the kind of humor that goes over with a groan.

A bad joke is a like a bad egg--all the worse for having been cracked.

He had a defect, which to a comic might be fatal. He wasn't funny.

I've been in show business thirty years, and I have the jokes to prove it.

A gag writer is a person who has hitched his gaggin' to a star.

He who laughs, lasts.

It's much easier to raise a laugh than a loan.

A real belly laugh is a mirthquake.

A comedian is a person who knows a good thing when he says it.

The field of humor is crowded when Congress is in session.

I know the secret of comedy--and I know how to keep a secret.

In literature it is the satirist who rules with an irony hand.

Some comedians couldn't cheer up a laughing hyena.

Man has a sense of humor to compensate for nature's law of gravity.

His jokes are not funny, but his delivery is terrible.

One man's wit is another man's poison.

Is he funny? He appears once and suffers from over-exposure.

He's a finished comedian--not only now, forever.

A comedian says things funny; a wit says funny things.

As our government deteriorates, our humor increases.

Women must have a sense of humor--look at the men they marry.

Brevity is the soul of wit, and wit is the brevity of levity.

Only his wife knows that a comedian is not always in good humor.

A good comic is worth his wit in gold.

A comic's ambition is to be healthy, wealthy and wisecracking.

My wife went on a diet, but all she lost was her sense of humor.

Many people live by their wits, but few by their wit.

Some comics employ wry wit, while others resort to corn.

A comic is a man who doesn't think he's funny but hopes he will be.

I'd tell a joke but you would only laugh at me.

A comic is a man who makes dough out of corn.

It's not funny if you get a quiet sitting ovation.

A comic is a man with a fun-track mind.

Old jokes never die, they just sound that way.

A comic is a man who originates old jokes.

Many a joke sounds too good to be new.

A comic is a man who has the gift of gag.

He who laughs last doesn't get the joke.

I hope to live to be as old as my jokes.

Whenever I tell jokes, I get carried away.

Don't stop me if you've heard this joke. I want to hear it again.

Humor is a hole that lets the sawdust out of a stuffed shirt.

My wife knows my jokes backwards--and tells them that way.

Husband

Today's husband is a do-it-yourself man with a get-it-done wife.

A husband has several mouths to feed and one big one to listen to.

A husband exchanges a bushel of fun for a peck of trouble.

The hand that darns the sock is the one that socks the husband.

Some men are born meek and others get married.

I wish I had as much fun as my wife thinks I do.

A good husband will wash up when asked and dry up when told.

An early bird gets up to serve his wife breakfast in bed.

She calls her husband "Henry." He's the eighth.

A husband is a man who was once in love.

She lost her husband ten years ago. He isn't dead--he's hiding.

A husband is a gay dog who has been spouse-broken.

Never try to pull the wool over your wife's eyes with the wrong yarn.

Given enough rope a husband will be tied up at the office.

My wife's reasoning is largely sound.

A checkmated husband is one who allows his wife to write the checks.

Any man who thinks he's smarter than his wife is married to a smart woman.

A husband can guess what his wife is going to say before she repeats it.

A "yes-man" is a husband who stoops to concur.

Tomorrow is a husband's greatest labor-saving device.

I wouldn't trade my wife for anything. Make me an offer.

I don't mind my wife walking on me, but she wears spiked heels.

My brother got a girl in trouble. He married her.

His marriage was a mistake--his wife's.

Keep a husband in hot water and he'll become hard boiled.

My only regret is that I have but one wife to send to the country.

Most husbands are generous to a fault--if the fault's their own.

Many a husband, in a family fight, is saved by the bell.

I married for love and then found out my wife has no money.

Some husbands buy expensive perfume as truce juice.

Give a husband enough rope--and he'll want to skip.

A husband is a polygamous animal in a monogamous trap.

I'm one husband who thinks twice before saying nothing.

The man who says his wife can't take a joke forgets himself.

A husband is the next thing to a wife.

My wife insists that I keep quiet while she is interrupting.

Some husbands don't snore in their sleep--they cackle.

Yawning is the only time some husbands get to open their mouths.

An agreeable husband is one who agrees with his wife.

He was her ideal before marriage--now he's an ordeal.

Married men are more inventive than single men. They have to be.

My wife and I have finally come to terms--hers.

A husband is a man who made a wrong turn in Lover's Lane.

A husband is a big shot at home until the company leaves.

I may not be the best-informed husband, but I'm the most-informed.

I'm a man of conviction--after I find out what my wife thinks.

She married a dreamer, and found he's just a sleeper.

A husband is the consummation of a woman's spousing project.

A girl needs a husband to share her joys, sorrows, and her friend's secrets.

If the husband isn't a self-starter, his wife becomes a crank.

In seeking a model husband, it's wise to be sure he's a working model.

He takes his troubles like a man--he blames them on his wife.

I run things in my house--the washing machine, the dishwasher...

My wife wanted a mink coat, so I bought her a trap and a gun.

I spend every afternoon with my wife--whenever they close the racetracks.

A husband is a man who gave up privileges he never knew he had.

I'm happiest when my wife is in bed, safe and soundless.

I love my wife so much, I won't even leave her to go to work.

I may be old-fashioned, but I expect my wife to help me with the dishes.

I always have the last word in my marriage--it's usually "Yes."

Some women will stick with a man through thick and gin.

He's really hen-pecked. His wife smokes but doesn't let him.

His timing is perfect--so is his two-timing.

She leads a double life--hers and her husband's.

I expect my wife to be perfect and to understand why I'm not.

I'm underfed, undernourished, and over-wifed.

My wife loves me so much, I can make her do anything she wants to do.

I wasn't born meek--I married and got that way.

I was a rake until my wife turned me into a lawn mower.

Many a man who is a big noise in the office is only a little squeak at home.

When she wants her husband's opinion, she gives it to him.

Many a husband, in a family fight, is saved by the bell.

The reason I stay home nights is because I have the house to myself.

Many husbands wear the pants in the house--under their aprons.

He comes right out and says what she tells him to think.

I can say anything I please in my home--nobody listens anyway.

I only regret that I didn't falter at the altar.

My wife has me on an allowance--fifty words a day.

I was crazy to get married, but I didn't realize it at the time.

I've been married for twenty awed years.

Everything he owns is hers--especially his nerve.

She jumps when he speaks--all over him.

Most husbands are generous to a fault--if the fault is their own.

I was a dude before getting married--now I'm subdued.

The worm turns--he turns over his pay check.

Some husbands have to ask permission to ask permission.

The ideal husband is heavily insured and dies on his wedding day.

The last time my wife said "yes" to me was when I proposed.

A husband never knows when he's well off because he never is.

I've given the best ears of my life to my wife.

Before we were married she knit for me--now she needles.

The best time to take out the garbage is when your wife tells you to.

It's a perfect love match. He loves her, and so does she.

When he asks her to darn his socks, she knits her brow.

It's a happy marriage if the husband gives and the wife forgives.

I have two chances of winning an argument with my wife--slim and none.

A husband starts out by handing out a line and finishes up walking it.

In the average home a luxury is anything the husband needs.

Silence is golden, but my wife is on the silver standard.

I went from a man-about-town to a mouse-around-the-house.

Married men are more inventive than bachelors. They have to be.

Tell your wife everything--especially before someone else does.

A husband is a man who has to grow old alone.

A husband is matrimony's silent partner.

I know my wife is outspoken, but by whom?

We have two cars and two TV sets, but only one opinion--hers.

A husband is a man of few words.

I run the show in my house--but my wife writes the script.

A model husband is any other woman's.

A considerate husband takes his wife window-wishing.

A husband becomes faithful after he has grown tired.

I owe my prosperity to push--my wife's.

A husband is a night owl who has been turned into a homing pigeon.

My wife can read me like a book--I only wish she didn't do it so loud.

My wife is never happier than when I'm poking funds at her.

I married my wife for her looks, but not the kind I'm getting.

Some husbands are comforters, others are just wet blankets.

A husband is the critic on the hearth.

Many girls who land husbands keep talking about the one that got away.

No respectable family should be without a husband.

A husband is a man who was once in love.

An ideal husband is one no other woman would have as a gift.

Most men would rather be the second husband of a widow than the first.

A husband is just a sweetheart who pushed his luck too far.

Her husband's not henpecked--just under good management.

I can tell when my wife has the car--by the tracks across the lawn.

A henpecked husband is one who is treated by his wife like a wife.

The best husbands aren't caught, they're made.

Marriage brings out the animal in some men, usually the chicken.

A married man is a bachelor whose luck finally ran out.

I married my wife 125 checkbooks ago.

I'm leaving my wife because of another woman--her mother.

A well-trained husband feels his pocket every time he passes a mailbox.

A husband's fate: hooked, booked, cooked.

Husbands are like fires: they go out when unattended.

A move star is known by the husbands she doesn't keep.

Married men make the best husbands.

I used to believe in dreams--but then I married one.

Being a husband is like any other job--it helps if you like the boss.

Every do-it-yourself husband has a do-it-now wife.

Most runaway husbands have been fed too many TV dinners.

I put a ring on her finger and she put one through my nose.

My wife jumps when I speak--all over me.

I know when and where I got married. What puzzles me is why.

Many a poor husband was once a rich bachelor.

Her husband is an accountant but he can't figure her out.

She used to work for her husband--until she got him.

More husbands would leave home if they knew how to pack their bags.

I'm so henpecked, I have to wash and iron my own apron.

Many times, the grouch a woman nurses is her husband.

The times a husband is right is when he admits he's wrong.

Clever men don't make good husbands because clever men don't get married.

A husband is what is left of the lover after the nerve has been removed.

All some women get out of their marriage is bed and boredom.

I hate to see a woman in cheap clothing, unless, of course, she's my wife.

Imagination

Ideas have to be hitched as well as hatched.

Castles in the air are fine until you try to move into them.

Imagination makes a politician think he's a statesman.

Imagination sits up with a wife when her husband is out late.

Imagination makes a man think he can run the business better than the boss.

Love and money make imagination work overtime.

Daydream: being lost in thought because you are a stranger there.

Imagination makes a man think one woman is different from another.

Women daydream but men dame-dream.

Do you think that Walter Mitty was on LSD?

Woman's chief asset is man's imagination.

An infant prodigy is a young child whose parents are highly imaginative.

A poet has a great imagination; he imagines people will read his poems.

You're famous when a crazy person imagines that he's you.

Daydreamers are the ones who dream while they are awake.

After a man reaches 60, his mischief is mainly in his head.

Truth is stranger than fiction, and also harder to make up.

What women's clothes leave to the imagination is what makes them dear.

The length of a man's kiss depends on the breadth of his imagination.

The play of imagination helps in the work of imagination.

A broken heart is really only a sprained imagination.

Every man is a hero to his imagination.

To make your dreams come true, you have to stay awake.

imagination can improve your driving--just imagine your family is in the car.

Dreaming is the time when you meet a better class of people.

A woman is more influenced by what she imagines than by what she is told.

Imagination drives a woman to find out something she'd rather not know.

Income

Income is a small matter to me--especially after taxes.

When you see red, start living within your income.

Saving is easy--just earn money faster than your family can spend it.

Income is something you can't live without or within.

Does your interest in life all come from your bank deposit?

Income always looks bigger coming than going.

All work and no play makes jack the dull way.

Married men tremble at the outcome of their income.

I made so much hush money, I had to whisper my bank deposits.

I'm selling furniture for a living--my own.

I may have the right aim in life, but I'm sure running out of ammunition.

I'm in the upper brackets. I stole $100,000 from my last employer.

Anybody with a quarter of a million dollars can always find a bargain.

Economy is a reduction in some other fellow's salary.

Income is the amount of money it costs more than to live.

A money-grabber is anyone who grabs more money than you can.

Debts are the certain outcome of an uncertain income.

The best place to spend a vacation is just inside your income.

Credit cards get you anything today--except an income.

I live within my income--even if I have to borrow to do it.

My agent gets 10% of everything I get, except my blinding headaches.

If ignorance paid dividends, I'd make a fortune in the stock market.

When a lot of credit goes with it, a little earning is a dangerous thing.

I don't live within my income because I can't afford it.

A man commands a salary and his wife commandeers it.

Nowadays a raise enables a man to live the way he is already living.

A man is known by the company he keeps--getting dividends from.

You can't tell a man's income from his clothes: look at his wife's.

The ideal income is a thousand dollars a day--and expenses.

Salary is the amount of money you are underpaid.

In the stock market a dividend is a certain per cent, per annum, perhaps.

Marrying for money is the hardest way to earn it.

My wife thinks it's my duty to earn money, and hers to spend it.

It isn't your income that counts, it's what your wife doesn't spend.

When your outgo exceeds your income, your upkeep is your downfall.

Courtship is another thing whose outcome depends on the income.

Behind every man who lives within his income is a wife who doesn't.

These days a person can't afford to make a living.

Inflation

The place where prices fall is at the end of the rainbow.

Maybe we can keep warm next winter by burning our bills.

Only statesmen of the loftiest vision can investigate high prices.

Declining to pay high prices can make them decline.

At any rate, the prophecies of lower prices make cheerful reading.

Nowadays money can buy happiness--what it can't buy is anything else.

Who can recall when he had to dig down so deep for potatoes?

Today you need a double-your-money-back guarantee just to break even.

My butcher doesn't sell meat any more--he rents it.

Inflation affects everything--including the wages of sin.

At today's prices you're lucky if you can make one end meet.

Another very annoying place to live is just beyond your income.

Inflation results in mini-money.

Inflation means that what goes up must keep going up.

Sugar would be just as sweet if it wasn't so dear.

The cost of living is still about the same--all a fellow has.

Declining sugar prices may be described as little drops of sweetness.

Falling prices, like falling stars, always fall someplace else.

About the only thing that will make gasoline drop is a leaky tank.

At today's prices very few people can afford to be poor.

At today's prices there are grounds for complaint in every cup of coffee.

This winter, the burning question is going to be what to burn.

Everything changes. Even high prices. They get higher.

Funny, the price of wool always fluctuates with the price of cotton.

Prices may be falling, but not fast enough to be seriously bruised.

Once price indicated value, now it's an indication of nerve.

The salary we used to dream of is the one we can't live on today.

If prices are coming down, they all have parachutes.

Everything is silly--even the dollar hasn't the same sense it used to have.

A kid can no longer get sick on a dollar's worth of candy.

Inflation has cut the dollar in half without damaging the paper.

Supply and demand sets prices. You pay what the store demands.

What used to cost $5 to buy now costs $25 to fix.

The airlines don't believe that less fare would be more fair.

Inflation is when you eat three square meals a day and pay for six.

Two can live as cheaply as one, and they generally have to.

Inflation is when you earn more and more of less and less.

Shoe prices should be expected to hold out to the last.

Inflation is when your pockets are full and your stomach isn't.

Apples are so expensive that you might as well have the doctor.

Inflation is a time when you can't keep a good price down.

The Great Beyond: living beyond your income.

Inflation is when you do more for the dollar than it does for you.

The pique of the buyer could be fatal to the peak of the prices.

Inflation is when the money you haven't got is worth less than before.

We call prices "prohibitive" because they never take a drop.

Inflation is when prices begin where they used to end.

People who want to can fruit find sugar prices positively uncanny.

Inflation is so bad now, I heard a golfer yell: "Five!"

Price cuts haven't yet reached the stage of quantity reduction.

Inflation is a shot in the arm that leaves a pain in the neck.

Let's hope the electric company never gets control of the sun.

Inflation has created a new economic problem: windfall poverty.

When building materials come down, more buildings will go up.

Inflation has changed things. Now one can live as cheaply as two.

The prediction of an early fall does not refer to prices.

Liberace joined by Jack Carter, Lena Horne, Henny and pals

Inflation raises everything but hopes.

Shooting at high prices seems only to scare them higher.

The hardest thing to get hold of these days is easy money.

Meeting expenses is easy--it's avoiding them that's difficult.

Oh, for the spirit of '76 and the prices of '66.

Things are so rough that one supermarket is putting in a recovery room.

When prices soar, so are we.

The peak of high prices looks more like a tableland.

To fight the rising cost of living, eat at your in-laws.

Prices seem to think there is plenty of room at the top.

Eat, drink and be merry, for tomorrow it will cost more.

Inflation means you never had it so good--or parted with it so fast.

Air is still free, but it costs much more to remain able to breathe.

Every year recently has been a leap year for prices.

Talk about the high cost of living is propaganda put out by people who eat.

There is so much inflation now, there's no money in money.

The only thing that comes down now is rain--and even that soaks you.

Money doesn't go as far as it used to, but at least it goes faster.

Business is on the up-grade. That accounts for the steep prices.

There's something much bigger than money--bills.

Highway robbery: the price of new cars.

Highway robbery: the price of gasoline.

Money can't buy a lot of things--for instance, what it did last month.

The cost of living is much too high, and so is the cost of dying.

Today a dollar saved is a quarter earned.

Drinking doesn't ruin a man any longer--today it's the price that does.

These days it's easier to earn money than to earn a living.

Gasoline prices have created a new class of drivers--the nouveau poor.

The cost of living is so high--a penny for your thoughts is now a quarter.

The law of supply and demand never seems to apply to money.

Whatever goes up must come down, except the cost of living.

Go figure! Blue Chip stamps are now worth more than Blue Chip stocks.

Two can live as cheaply as one--large family used to.

It takes twice as much money to live beyond your means as it used to.

The price of meat is so high--my butcher advertises "Easy Terms."

I shop at a friendly grocery. They not only deliver--they arrange financing.

Inflation may prove Columbus wrong--the world will be flat.

What I want is inflation of my income and deflation of everything else.

Inflation makes it easier to earn money than to earn a living.

Inflation wouldn't be so bad if prices wouldn't keep rising.

Inflation is what makes people pay more while they live on less.

The price of oil is high because the earth now charges storage.

Juvenile Delinquents

Today when a kid plays jacks, it's Jacks or better to open.

The only sure cure for delinquency is birth control.

My neighborhood is so tough, a cat with a tail is considered a tourist.

A good thrashing might get the wild oats out of some kids.

Heredity is what makes parents wonder about each other.

It's sad some parents don't burn their kid's britches behind them.

We spared the rod with our kid--and now he's riding it.

Kids would be better off if their doting parents were don'ting parents.

Juvenile delinquents are other people's children.

The kid next door joined a union--a teen-age mugger's union.

A delinquent is a kid who would rather steal hub-caps than third base.

Too many parents give their kids a free hand--but not in the right spot.

He's a delinquent health buff--only smokes filter-tipped pot.

My son takes more than understanding--he takes stamina.

One kid is too young to drive--so he steals taxi cabs--with the drivers.

Today's accent is on youth--but the stress is on the parents.

Today's kids would be smarter if they smarted in the right places.

I know a kid who is so tough, he makes his teacher stay after school.

Delinquents generally display their pest manners.

Imagine a kid so rotten, he's got a scholarship to reform school.

My kid makes me wish that birth control was retroactive.

A child who gets all he wants becomes a man who gets all he deserves.

Parents blame delinquency on anything except heredity.

Peculiar, but we never have spoiled brats in our own family.

My son was sweet during infancy but started to ferment during childhood.

A juvenile delinquent is a minor who creates a major problem.

Today's kids are very good at being no good.

Delinquency begins when kids start doing what their parents are doing.

In sixth grade I won the Academy Award for playing hooky.

In my neighborhood the kids used barbed wire for dental floss.

Talk about a tough kid! All his tattooing is done by a stone mason.

America will never be invaded--our delinquents are too well armed.

Spank your child every day--if you don't know why--he does.

When the kid next door goes to school, his teacher plays hookey.

Never give your kid his full allowance. Keep some to bail him out.

A delinquent tries to do right--but only when he thinks it is wrong.

One Texas delinquent was so rich he slashed his own tires.

We made our son cut his hair--he was giving our dog fleas.

My kid is so tough, he eats sardines without removing the cans.

My son was in school so long the principal had to frame him to graduate.

One way to curb a wild young man is to bridal him.

Kissing

People who throw kisses are hopelessly lazy.

There are two s's in kiss because it takes two to complete the spell.

Stealing a kiss may be petty larceny, but usually it's grand.

A kiss is the shortest distance between two.

Smart girls know how to refuse a kiss without being deprived of it.

It is better to kiss a Miss than to miss a kiss.

I learned to kiss by blowing up footballs.

A kiss that speaks volumes is seldom a first edition.

First kiss her--then argue about it.

Girls, never let a fool kiss you and never let a kiss fool you.

The shape of a kiss is a lip-tickle.

Kissing shortens life--single life, that is.

She screamed when I kissed her, but it was muffled.

I kissed her and she screamed from the bottom of her voice.

When I throw a kiss it's with a boomerang.

Kissing may be the language of love, but money still does the talking.

A kiss is the shortest distance between two.

Kissing a girl over the phone can be fun--if you're in the booth with her.

A kiss can never be taken back, but it can be returned.

A kiss is a contraction of the lips due to an enlargement of the heart.

A kiss is mutual interchange of salivary bacteria.

My nephew is so boring girls kiss him just to shut his mouth.

Mistletoe is never as green as the people you use it on.

A kiss is the time and spot where affection comes to the surface.

You told me that you loved me, why did you close your eyes?

Kissing her is like scratching a place that doesn't itch.

Kissing is the lip service to love.

When kissing a girl, don't give her a pain in the necking.

A kiss is an application for a better position.

Kiss me--I give Green Stamps.

I got a warmer kiss from the high school principal when I graduated.

I tried to kiss her, but she'd have none of my lip.

She's such a hot kisser, she melts the gold in a guy's teeth.

Kissing is the sincerest form of flattery.

A kiss is saying "I love you" in one syllable.

Kissing is still practiced in England--but is it worth the trip?

A kiss is what's left of the language of Paradise.

When some men get a kiss, they try to make a meal out of it.

I don't like lipstick. When I kiss a girl all I want to taste is girl.

I learned to kiss by drinking thick malteds through a straw.

A kiss is a report from headquarters.

He who kisses and runs away will live to kiss another.

In kissing, two heads are better than one.

To please them, don't tease them; first seize them, then squeeze them.

A kiss used to follow a nice evening; now a nice evening follows a kiss.

Kisses are more intoxicating if a man mixes his drinks.

I kiss my kids "Good night" no matter how late I have to wait up for them.

Every time some men plant a kiss they expect to reap a harvest.

Lots of things have been started by a kiss, especially young things.

I got a real kick out of kissing her--her husband caught me.

She has the kind of lips I like--one on top and one on the bottom.

My girl friend gives the kind of kisses that toast your tonsils.

It takes a lot of experience for a girl to kiss like a beginner.

Some men only kiss their wives when they can't find a napkin.

I take my wife everywhere I go--I hate to kiss her good-bye.

Now there's a cayenne-flavored lipstick--to make kisses burn like fire.

I knew her kiss was just puppy love--her nose was cold.

I've kissed so many women I can do it with my eyes closed.

I'll never forget my first wife's kisses--like opening a refrigerator.

A kiss over the telephone is like a straw hat--it isn't felt.

Every night my wife greets me with a dry martini and a wet kiss.

Whenever we kiss and make up, she gets the kiss, I get the make-up.

Knowledge

The person who knows everything has the most to learn.

What most people crave is an intelligence rest.

The most difficult intelligence test is to be a popular hero.

The less a man knows, the easier it is to convince him he knows it all.

Nothing annoys me more than a man who thinks he knows it all and does.

To some people a bright idea is beginner's luck.

In school I had underwater marks--below C level.

My brother-in-law is a fugitive from a brain gang.

Feel sorry for the man who has been educated beyond his intelligence.

The only successful substitute for a lack of brains is silence.

Existence is the toughest intelligence test.

Want of care does more damage than want of knowledge.

I may not know much, but I know it so fluently.

The more a man knows himself, the less he says about it.

A man thinks he knows--but a woman knows better.

Imagine a girl so dumb, mind readers only charge her half-price.

My uncle is recovering from an odd accident. An idea struck him.

All too often one of those mighty minds is just mighty empty.

Some people stop to think and then forget to start again.

Some drink at the fountain of knowledge--others just gargle.

A little knowledge is a dangerous thing, especially when playing cards.

Today, if you're not confused, you're not well-informed.

To learn how to invest your money ask a man who has none.

First-hand knowledge does not become second-hand when used.

Most people believe most what they know least.

To brag of learning is a badge of ignorance.

If you know all the answers, you probably misunderstood the question.

A wise man never blows his knows.

What some men lack in intelligence they make up for in stupidity.

Everything I knew before I reached 30 I had to unlearn again.

If a little learning is a dangerous thing, then most people are safe.

Every argument proves that someone has been ignorant.

A moron is a guy who wrinkles his brow while watching television.

My boss is just as smart as he can be--unfortunately.

I have a neighbor whose mind wanders--unfortunately he just goes along.

There's no value in having brains if they're in dead storage.

My mother-in-law isn't scatterbrained--she hasn't any brains to scatter.

My brother-in-law was in a fight once, and was knocked conscious.

Knowledge is power--if you know it about the right people.

Knowing a lot is of no value if what you know isn't so.

The surest way to spoil a good story is by sticking to the facts.

To keep up with the neighbors, just listen to their children's conversation.

A word to the wise is sufficient, but not to the wise guy.

A word to the wise is--unnecessary.

Get the facts, or the facts will get you.

Some guys are wise, and some are wise guys.

My boss is an M.D.--Mentally Deficient.

Somehow when two know-it-alls get together, they always disagree.

An ignorant person is one who doesn't know what you just found out.

A "wise guy" knows more about everything than you know about anything.

You become wise by noticing what happens to you when you aren't.

Nothing is more disputed than an indisputable fact.

Knowledge is power, but not for the man who knows it all.

The man who knows how to do everything never does.

Many a knowledgeable word is spoken in ignorance.

A smart aleck knows things without having to learn them.

The wise man knows a little, but the wise guy knows it all.

A smart man can always catch on, the wise man knows when to let go.

The man who thinks he knows everything irritates those of us who do.

An intelligent man knows everything, a shrewd man knows everybody.

Many a man has a lot of knowledge, but doesn't let it go to his head.

Most men can detect a rattle in the car faster than one in their head.

Law, Lawyers

Justice is all too often hampered with mercy.

Mass production cheapens everything--even laws.

We don't need more judges in America, but more judgement.

Scales are too often on the eyes of Justice instead of in her hands.

You can't flout all the laws--there are the in-laws.

Circumstances alter cases, especially legal cases.

If there were no bad people, there would be no good lawyers.

Man's inhumanity to man makes countless numbers of lawyers.

Anyone can sit on a jury, but it takes a lawyer to sit on a witness.

One eye-witness never seems to see eye to eye with another eye-witness.

Lawyers sometimes tell the truth--they'll do anything to win a case.

When money talks, all too often it says: "Not guilty."

Justice is never blind at a beauty contest.

If you think there ought to be a law, there probably is.

Ignorance of the law is no excuse for the man who retains poor counsel.

A lawsuit is generally a matter of dollars and suspense.

My lawyer was hurt--the ambulance backed up suddenly.

One law we don't have to enforce is the law of gravity.

My lawyer once got a jury so confused, they sent the judge to jail.

A jury is twelve people chosen to decide which side has the better lawyer.

My lawyer will stay up all night to break a girl's will.

In court, wrangling between lawyers is nine points of the law.

The prouder a man is of his citizenship, the more he evades jury duty.

One lawyer joined a nudist colony and never had a suit again.

My brother is a real lawyer--he even named his daughter Sue.

I don't want a lawyer who knows the law, I want one who knows the judge.

Justice often triumphs in spite of all the publicity issued to support it.

Suppression is nine points of the law.

Divorces are arranged so lawyers can live happily ever after.

A lawyer is a person who helps you get what's coming to him.

A divorce lawyer is the referee in a fight who winds up with the purse.

A man never admits he is a physical wreck, except when suing for damages.

Lawyers prevent someone else from getting your money.

The last guess of the Supreme Court becomes the law of the land.

Hell hath no fury like the lawyer of a woman scorned.

The man who said talk is cheap never hired a lawyer.

You can't live without lawyers and you can't die without them.

When judge and jury are against the defendant, 13 is an unlucky number.

Do it now--there may be a law against it tomorrow.

Quite often a witness makes a jury wonder what lies ahead.

Some men court, then marry, then go to court again.

Judges without conviction are the most generous in handing it out.

I don't like to serve on a jury, unless it's in a beauty contest.

All things come to him who waits--even justice.

Every time Congress makes a mistake, a new law is born.

Truth is stranger than fiction, especially in lawsuits.

Some men inherit money, some earn it, and some are lawyers.

Lawyers help those who help themselves.

In times of trial, nothing is as comforting to a man as an acquittal.

A jury is one thing that never works properly after it has been fixed.

It takes a thief to catch a thief, and a jury to let him go.

A lawsuit is generally a matter of dollars and suspense.

When there's a will there's a lawsuit.

A witness has to swear to tell the truth before he starts to lie.

Many are called, but few are chosen--for a jury.

When better laws are made, Americans will break them.

It takes a lot of suits to keep a lawyer well dressed.

A law firm is successful when it has more clients than partners.

Ignorance of the law excuses no man--from practicing it.

I thought I was intelligent until I was tried by a jury of my peers.

In court, some witnesses tell half-truths, while others tell whole lies.

A judge is a man who ends a sentence with a sentence.

My mother-in-law dislikes jury duty because it's all listening.

The portion of the law usually found unconstitutional is the teeth.

Look before you leap--into litigation.

A lawyer is a man who profits by your experience.

Honesty is the best policy, because good lawyers are expensive.

Witnesses will testify to anything, even the truth.

The truly successful lawyer owns his own ambulance.

Lazy

Laziness is like money; the more you have of it the more you want.

My feet have been known to fall asleep while running for a bus.

The less I have to do, the less time I find to do it in.

Very few men have character enough to lead a life of idleness.

I'm not lazy--I'm just naturally tired.

The only time a lazy man succeeds is when he tries to do nothing.

Hard work never killed anyone--neither did not working.

What I know best is how to rest with zest.

I prefer to earn my daily bread by the sweat of someone else's brow.

My brother-in-law's life work is to avoid it.

Doing nothing is tiresome because you can't stop and rest.

I like to sit and think--mainly sit.

Some people are so lazy they get in a revolving door and wait.

My wife is too lazy to walk in her sleep--she hitch hikes.

Some people get up early so as to have more time to loaf.

Man is lazy by nature, so God gave us children to get us up early.

Some people are always looking for less to do and more time to do it in.

My problem is that I'm too heavy for light work and too light for heavy work.

Any man who does nothing is usually doing somebody.

Laziness travels so slowly, poverty easily overtakes it.

Even though I never do anything, I still get criticized.

In the lives of lazy people there is nothing doing every minute.

Some people are lazy; others suffer from voluntary inertia.

If work is a virtue, my brother-in-law is living in sin.

Many people are too lazy to work, but my brother-in-law is too lazy to fish.

My wife only uses drip dry dishes.

My mother-in-law is so lazy, she washes her dishes in bed.

The only thing my brother-in-law ever does fast is get tired.

It takes my wife five minutes to boil a three-minute egg.

I found a great way to start the day--I go back to bed.

My brother only opens his mouth to put something in it.

They named the loafer shoe after him.

He couldn't catch a cold in Alaska.

Even his car is shiftless.

What some people need is a kick in the seat of their can'ts.

My brother-in-law is so lazy he only eats loaf sugar.

Imagine! A college boy who is too lazy to write home for money.

My brother is a miracle worker--it's a miracle when he works.

He's two-dimensional--he has loung-itude and lassitude.

I always look forward to the yawn of a new day.

It's a great life if you don't waken.

My wife is the power behind my drone.

If I were any steadier as a worker I'd be motionless.

I only throw kisses.

He even married a widow with four children.

Maybe hard work never killed anybody--but I'm not taking any chances.

I'm not afraid of hard work--I've fought it successfully for years.

My boss's son has a malady that malingers on.

I do most of my work sitting down--that's where I shine.

My brother-in-law is as active as a leftover fly in January.

The greatest labor saving device is tomorrow.

I like the parable about the multitude that loafs and fishes.

I get my exercise pulling ice trays from the refrigerator.

One thing you can say for me--I put in a good day's work--each week.

He has as much life in him as a mummy.

He's as active as an oyster on the beach in August.

He's so lazy that he even finds loafing to be hard work.

Regularly every day I do my daily dozing.

My brother is so lazy he won't even exercise discretion.

He sleeps as soundly as a night nurse on duty.

I'm treading water until my ship comes in.

My brother is so lazy he's become a landmark.

The only action I ever see from him is a delaying one.

I like to have my work cut out for me, entirely.

I'm superstitious--I won't work in any week that has a Friday in it.

My brother is so lazy that his self-winding watch ran down.

I've got a bad case of insomnia--I keep waking up every few days.

Nature provides lazy people with a big cushion to sit around on.

My brother is the family idol. He's been idle for the past five years.

He has an excellent background, and he's always leaning on it.

It's a great life so long as you don't waken.

I walk in my sleep so I get my rest and my exercise at the same time.

I even get winded playing chess.

In December I work my fingers to the bonus.

I joined six unions to be sure of always being out on strike.

I do push-ups three times a day--from my chair, for meals.

Remember, even loafing can be hard work.

My greatest pleasure is having lots to do, and not doing it.

I've been out of work so long I forget what I do for a living.

I even hire a gardener to take care of my window-box plants.

It is better to have loafed and lost than never to have loafed at all.

When day is done, be sure that something else has also been.

Laziness is the habit of resting before you get tired.

Whenever I have nothing to do I give it my personal attention.

Some people are like blisters--they don't show up until the work is done.

I don't mind being laid off, especially when compensation sets in.

The lazier a man is, the more he is going to do tomorrow.

Even if his ship would come in, he wouldn't bother to unload it.

Even his nose is lazy. It won't even run when he has a cold.

He's so lazy his feet hurt before he gets out of bed.

He can fall asleep even while running for a bus.

He puts in a good day's work--but it takes him a week to do it.

Romantically he may have notions, but he never makes motions.

He's so lazy he won't even exercise discretion.

Lazy! He wouldn't even help his mother-in-law move out of his house.

When laziness attacks a woman, it always avoids her tongue.

A lazy man is judged by what he doesn't.

I always find it difficult to start but easy to stop.

My wife puts popcorn in her pancakes so they'll turn over by themselves.

Librarians

I had to pay $25 to get my library card back. I didn't return the librarian for two weeks.

Life

Life is the process of getting used to the unexpected.

Most men live on the cafeteria plan--self-service only.

So live that you'll live longer.

Life is made up of sleeping, eating, working, and interruptions.

Living is cheaper in the city--for that matter, so is life.

Naturally women live longer than men--look how long they remain girls.

Take care of your life--without it, you're dead.

We throw flowers at the dead, and mud at the living.

All too often a man who has too much to live on, has too little to live for.

The world is full of men making good livings but poor lives.

Half the world doesn't know why the other half lives.

Half the world doesn't know how; the other half lives.

Some men can write the story of their lives on a piece of confetti.

Life must be worth living. The cost has doubled and we still hang on.

The least understood art is the art of living.

Life is the popular endurance contest.

Life and hash are what you make them.

Life is one long process of getting tired.

Life is too serious to take too seriously.

Life is a predicament which precedes death.

People are living longer now; they have to--who can afford to die?

Dad was fond of high living, so he slept on the roof.

The best thing a man can make is a living for his family.

Never have so many people lived so well, so far behind, before.

Live your life like a fried egg--with your sunny side up.

It is better to live rich than to die rich.

When life hands you a lemon, make lemonade.

Life is made up of trials, appeals, reversals, but few convictions.

Life was once what you made it--now it's a case of if you make it.

If you live at a rattling pace you end up with loose joints.

It is better to make mistakes than not to live at all.

Life is what passes you by while you're making other plans.

Life is really wonderful; do your best not to miss it.

Life is like a shower--one wrong turn and you're in hot water.

Is there life after marriage?

To live to a ripe old age, never waste any energy resisting temptation.

To live a long life get somebody else to worry for you.

All men are born free and equal--some are a little too free.

Would you call life in Hollywood mere sexistence?

The tree of liberty will not survive too much grafting.

Recipe for a long life: don't exceed the feed limit.

Man's fate is to keep growing older long after he is old enough.

Life wouldn't be worth living if we didn't keep our enemies.

Too many of my neighbors enjoy the right of free screech.

Life is just one stop sign after another.

The liberty loving are hard pressed by the liberty taking.

Life is a sentence that man serves for the crime of being born.

Men fight for liberty, then make laws to take it away.

So live that you'll live longer.

Ten per cent of life is what you make it and 90 per cent is how you take it.

Life is a banquet, but most of us are starving to death.

All golfers are entitled to life, liberty, and the pursuit of golf balls.

Life is like an artichoke--you go through so much to get so little.

Most people go through life expecting to be disappointed.

Life is what happens to us while we're making other plans.

Life is the original do-it-yourself project.

Life is an "L" of a thing with a big "IF" in the middle.

One difficult problem in the business of life is minding your own.

Living it up is always a prelude to trying to live it down.

Man does not live by bread alone. He's got to have gasoline, too.

An autobiography is the story of how a man thinks he lived.

Life is a dead-end street.

Leading a double life will get you nowhere twice as fast.

No one cheers his own birth, and no one mourns his own death.

You can always live on less when you have more to live for.

It's true that women live longer than men--especially widows.

An autobiography is the story of a person whose life is an open book.

Life is not fate but fatal.

Life isn't all beer and skittles; in fact, I haven't touched a skittle in years.

Every man dies, but not every man has lived.

Even when a man has nothing to live on, he still lives on.

Half the world knows how the other half ought to live.

Sometimes the best way to prolong life is to throw up your hands.

Life is a trivial comedy made up of important tragedies.

By the yard, life is hard; by the inch, life's a cinch.

Half the world doesn't know with whom the other half lives.

Tis better to have lived and loved than never to have lived at all.

Man is illogical--he wishes for a long life but never for old age.

Women need to live longer than men because they have more to say.

You get out of life exactly what you put into it--less taxes.

Life is made up of three things: pretense, suspense, and expense.

I don't consider living within my income, living.

My father lived to be ninety, but liquor and women finally got him.

A good liver and a bad liver often go together.

Breathing is the secret of longevity--but only if you keep it up long enough.

Man does not live by bread alone, even pre-sliced bread.

Some people go through life standing at the complaint counter.

I was having the time of my life until my wife found out.

She gave me the best years of her life. Now come the worst years.

My life is so dull, I have to count sheep to keep awake.

You can't make a hit if you have no aim in life.

Losers

My brother has a steady job. He's a picket.

My brother, Lester, is a loser. He just opened a Tall Man's Shop in Tokyo.

If I inherited a pumpkin farm, they'd outlaw Halloween.

If I bought General Motors stock, wagon trains would come back.

My bank account is my shrinking fund.

I had a forward spring--and an early fall.

I seem to go through life pushing doors marked "Pull."

Ten years ago I was an unknown failure--now I'm a known failure.

My Dad had more pipe dreams than an organist.

I'm as broke as a pickpocket at a nudist camp.

Pity the poor kleptomaniac who found himself in a piano store.

I'm going to the dogs faster than a flea.

Dad gave failure a bad name.

I started life as a human dynamo, but I got short-circuited along the way.

Two companies are fighting for my services. The loser gets me.

I'm in the hole more often than a gravedigger.

My brother is a genius--he can do almost anything except make a living.

I always take my salary to the bank. It's too little to go by itself.

There is a lot less to some people than meets the eye.

I've got ulcers without being a success.

Love

If you can't love your enemies, compromise: forget them.

If you can't make a girl melt in your arms, maybe you're not so hot.

If you fall in love make sure it's someone you like.

I love her for what she is--rich.

Love is like an x-ray. It has to be developed in the dark.

It was a beautiful night; the moon was out and so were her parents.

It's better to have loved and lost--yeah, lots better.

Love is being stupid together.

Love is the tie that blinds.

Love is happiness given back and forth.

To fall in love you must have an open mind--a hole in the head.

Love is having the wool pulled over your sheep eyes.

My wife and I fight just so we can kiss and make up.

The best way to hold a man is in your arms.

Love is perpetual emotion.

A love story is a comedy of Eros.

Love conquers all things except poverty and toothaches.

Love is when two people, with their eyes shut, can see heaven.

Undying love is the kind you wouldn't die for.

Love is like war--easy to begin--but how do you stop it?

All the world loves a lover--except the husband.

I know a couple who are as inseparable as a screen test and a proposition.

Lover's leap: the distance between twin beds.

First it's boy meets girl, and then it's man waits for wife.

She turned her back on love, so she got it in the neck.

Your knowledge of love depends on the way you grasp the subject.

The course of two loves never does run smooth.

Lovers follow nature--when lilacs bloom in Spring, they lilac anything.

All the world loves a lover until he complicates the parking problem.

Love makes the world go 'round-looking for a job.

My girl friend calls me "Tall, Dark and Hands."

Nothing increases affection's value like being alienated.

You don't have to be a hunter to want a girl who's game.

Love at first sight usually ends with divorce at first slight.

The trouble with blind love is that it doesn't stay that way.

Many a favorite son shows you how blind maternal love is.

There is at least enough in love to keep everybody hopeful about it.

A bachelor girl is a girl who is looking for a bachelor.

Love often leads to marriage--and almost as often to divorce.

If love is blind, how can there be love at first sight?

I tried everything: candy, flowers, furs jewelry--and they all worked.

Absence makes the heart grow fonder--of the other fellow.

Love is a conflict between reflexes and reflections.

Love may be blind--but the neighbors aren't.

Love is the only game that two can play and both win.

Love is man's insane desire to support a woman.

Love at first sight saves a lot of time and money.

We're only half serious about getting married: she is, I'm not.

A girl can always tell when she's in love and usually does.

Fall into a woman's arms and soon you fall into her hands.

Love makes time pass, and time makes love pass.

I go on pick-up dates. I pick up my girl, then she picks up the check.

To save money at the movies we buy one ticket and take turns sitting.

Love is like a well--all right to taste of, but bad to fall into.

The quickest way to go broke is to start loving beyond your means.

Love is a disease that begins with a fever and ends with a pain.

A girl's best bait, whether for man or mouse, is a little cheesecake.

I got a safety belt in my car--my date belted me for her own safety.

Any girl can live on love--if he's wealthy.

All the world loves a lover--he never complains about the price.

Love birds are married couples that are always flying at each other.

Love is a feeling of affection toward your enemies' enemies.

One way to waste breath is to try to be reasonable about love.

When a girl begins to count on a man, his number is up.

Money may not buy love, but it sure can add zest to the shopping.

A bigamist spends half his life in love and half his life in jail.

Platonic love is like being invited into a bar to sample the water.

Love is like a game of chess. One false move and you're mated.

If a man's tie remains in place, he can't be too affectionate.

When a man loses his heart, his head has to do double the work.

Love is a disease usually cured by marriage.

Love makes the world go around looking for a divorce lawyer.

Hot food on the table does a lot to keep love warm.

The game of love is one that usually ends in a tie.

Love may laugh at locksmiths, but it doesn't run food markets.

Love is the only behavior that does not lend itself to statistics.

Love makes time pass and marriage makes love pass.

Life would be happier if love were as easy to keep as it is to make.

Platonic love is love from the neck up.

The man who loses his heart usually loses his head as well.

Love is a state of mind which has nothing to do with the mind.

Love is the last and most serious of the childhood diseases.

Few men marry their first love, and fewer marry their last.

If you do not love, what can you betray?

Love-sick couples usually wind up consulting Doctors of Divinity.

Love is propaganda for propagation.

You can't buy love, but you can pay heavily for it.

Lover's lane is the route of all evil.

Platonic love is possible, but only between a husband a wife.

The best combination is a hard head and a soft heart.

First a man sweeps a girl off her feet, then he has her on his hands.

People fall in love, but they have to climb out.

In love, a woman knows her heart; in marriage, her mind.

True love never runs up a big light bill.

Love is like a vaccination; when it takes you don't have to be told.

Love is a beautiful story, and marriage is the vocal version of it.

*Henny makes it a threesome with legendary jazz greats Sarah Vaughn (left)
and Cleo Laine*

Love at first sight never happens before breakfast.

Love makes the world go 'round--usually when it should be asleep.

Lover's lane is a secluded place with indoor-outdoor car-petting.

A nature lover is a man who goes into the woods without a girl.

Just call me "Chestnut" because I'm nuts about chests.

Sleep is the best thing in the world--next to a woman.

I'm a Yes-man with no interest in a No-girl.

If you know your oats you can talk a girl into a serial.

All I ask of life is a little peach and quiet.

In Platonic love, a lovely friend never becomes a friendly lover.

A man in love shows great ingenuity in making a fool of himself.

It's a good thing that love is blind, otherwise it would see too much.

Every woman marries for love, even if it's only love of money.

Love is the only kind of fire which is never covered by insurance.

I may be old, but I'm still in there pinching.

Love isn't blind--but there are times when you can't bear to look.

Puppy love is the prelude to a dog's life.

I worship the ground her father struck oil on.

When I kiss a girl I do it the hard way--no lips.

Much of the fun of being in love is the worry of it.

Some men fall in love, but they get out of it by marrying the girl.

When a man is in love for the first time he thinks he invented it.

Love flatters your ego while it flattens your wallet.

Love makes time pass, and time makes love pass.

Platonic love is like a gun that seems not to be loaded--but it always is.

I knew it was puppy love because her nose was always cold and damp.

See those two birds in the tree? Know what they're thinking of? Worms.

If I ever win the girl of my dreams what will I do with my wife?

It was love at first sight. She first saw him in his Mercedes.

The game of love can't be played with all the cards on the table.

Every lover is a liar.

The mark of a great lover is mostly lipstick.

Love letters should always be dictated to a secretary.

When I'm in love I think almost as much of the girl as I do of myself.

My sister is in love with a garbage man. He has an air about him.

My sister is down in the dumps--she's in love with a garbage man.

It's love that makes the world go around--with a worried expression.

Love has its own alphabet--it consists of avowals and consents.

Love at first sight is possible, but it always pays to take a second look.

Money can't buy love, but it can put you in a better bargaining position.

Falling in love is awfully simple, but falling out is simply awful.

All the world loves a lover, but not while the love-making is going on.

Money can't buy love, but it makes shopping for it a lot easier.

The cure for love at first sight is second sight.

If this isn't love, it'll have to do until I get some sleep.

A woman's heart strings have been known to follow a man's purse strings.

In love you're either supremely happy or supremely miserable.

A fork in the road may lead to a spoon in the park.

Everyone has someone, but all I have is you.

If my love affair was on television--I'd change channels.

I had to propose to my wife in the garage. I couldn't back out.

If at first you don't succeed--call another girl.

In making love I'm a caveman--one kiss and I cave in.

The course of two loves never runs smooth.

Love is just a lot of dame foolishness.

Love is the delusion that one girl differs from another.

Most of those love triangles are wreck-tangles.

Every time I find a girl I love, my father marries her.

Love is a feeling that makes a woman make a man make a fool of himself.

All's fair in love and war and they are alike in other ways.

Love is blind. That's why I use the touch system.

Pity the two red corpuscles. They loved in vein.

I'm too much of a coward to ever fall in love with a woman again.

The hard part is to love your neighbor as your self.

The love that passeth all understanding is on television.

The easiest way out of one love affair is into another.

Love is a form of government under the two-party system.

The way to tell if a girl is ripe for love is to squeeze her.

When some men aren't chasing jack, they're after Jill.

As long as women have curves, men will have angles.

To me, love is just a passion fancy.

I love my neighbors--especially their wives.

It used to be love at first sight; now it's love at every opportunity.

Love is blind. That's why a man has to depend so much on his feelings.

Ours was a garden romance: she was an old tomato and I was a dead beat.

Love is the wine of life, and marriage is the morning after.

Love is a thing of beauty. Too bad people get married and spoil it.

If a girl has the time, I have the place.

Love is the only game never postponed on account of darkness.

Some men start with roses and end up with forget-me-notes.

Central Park is a famous battle ground in New York City.

For every man over 65 there are seven women--but by then it's too late.

I don't know much about love. I was an incubator baby.

Love is a wonderful thing and highly desirable in marriage.

Love is blind to everything but fat.

Love in a cottage is all right if you can sell the movie rights.

I believe in treating all women as sequels.

In Spring a young man's fancy turns to anything that passes.

I'm very broad-minded--in fact, I think of nothing else.

This I believe: nothing risque, nothing gained.

Give some men an inch, and they take the whole 38-27-38.

I've always been a man of single purpose, and double talk.

I usually treat a woman to rum and coax.

I'm counting on a reduction in the wages of sin.

In college, I signed up for all the romance languages.

Love is the art of assisting nature.

Love is a disease of the nymph glands.

It's love when she looks at him as if he's a coat she can't afford.

Love is just sentimental measles.

She fell in love with me. She wrote every week--for one week.

Love is an itch around the heart that you can't scratch.

Love is a compact with sorrow.

Love is propaganda for propagation.

Love is a mutual misunderstanding.

A love nest is an exhibition of etchings.

Love is the softening of the hearteries.

True love is friendship set on fire.

I just can't play it straight with a girl who is all curves.

To be an expert on love you've got to grasp the subject.

As far as I'm concerned, love is just a passing fanny.

I prefer well-formed women to well-informed ones.

Love is soft music, soft lights, and soft soap.

I'd be in clover if it wasn't for my wild oats.

I never pass up a chance to mix business with pleasure.

All I know about women is what I pick up.

I always whistle while I lurk.

I can only count up to sex.

I'm waiting for the right girl to come alone.

It's romantic to be a man's first love, but it's safer to be his last.

I have two hobbies: collecting old masters and young mistresses.

As to seduction, I'm always ready, villain, and able.

The trouble with my hands is that they go from pat to worse.

Luck

The less luck some of us have, the more we believe in it.

In playing cards a good deal depends on a good deal.

Luck is a very good word if you put a P before it.

Luck is when preparedness catches up with opportunity.

Luck draws us for jury duty, but never for the sweepstakes.

Three cigarettes on a match isn't unlucky--it's unlikely.

Luck explains the success of people you don't like.

Miss Fortune visits me more often than Lady Luck.

A rabbit's foot may be lucky; but the original owner wasn't.

You can't spend all your time growling and be a lucky dog.

The only sure thing about luck is that it will change.

I bought a waterproof, shockproof, unbreakable watch--and lost it.

Anyone who has the time to look for a four-leaf clover needs to find one.

Luck is the idol of the idle.

When a man is engaged, the lucky woman is the girl's mother.

Other people's good luck makes us dissatisfied with our own.

Lady Luck smiles on a few of us, but laughs at the rest of us.

A lucky man doesn't need advice.

Depend on luck and you'll soon have nothing else to depend on.

A horseshoe is good luck, but only when it's on the winning horse.

Many men are not superstitious because they think it brings bad luck.

If I didn't have bad luck I wouldn't have any luck at all.

Beginners' luck is happiness during the first two weeks after marriage.

A rabbit's foot is a poor substitute for horse sense.

Talk about bad luck! I opened a fortune cookie and found a summons.

Lying

You can't believe some people, even when they swear they are lying.

Truth may not be stranger than fiction, but it's scarcer.

My boss is a man of proven liar-bilities.

I can tell when my wife is lying--if her lips are moving, she is.

I once dislocated both shoulders describing a fish I caught.

Some people can't even tell the truth in a diary.

My neighbor is like a harp struck by lightning--a blasted lyre.

I know a confirmed liar--nothing he says is ever confirmed.

Truth is like a woman's girdle--it's made to be stretched.

The trouble with cooked-up excuses is that they are half-baked.

No one can lie like a man with a second-hand car to sell.

I'm the kind of fisherman who catches fish by the tale.

I swear at myself after eveything I say--I hate liars.

I know a microscope expert--he magnifies everything.

The truth is mighty and will prevail, but it is very hard to find it.

Some people take the bull by the horns--I shoot it.

Actually, I'm just too modest to speak the naked truth.

I'm a second-story man. No one ever believes my first story.

At a party, I'm the guy who always starts the bull rolling.

Most people need a partition between their imagination and their facts.

The light that lies in a woman's eyes--lies.

Clever liars give details, but the cleverest don't.

I guess a monumental liar is a guy who writes epitaphs.

A lie never passes my lips--I talk through my nose.

My wife can tell more lies than falsies.

My brother-in-law is full of soft soap--mostly lye.

At college, he majored in alibiology.

My father-in-law lies like an affidavit.

A lie never passes my lips--I talk through my nose.

Unfortunately cooked-up excuses are usually half-baked.

I don't really exaggerate--I just remember big.

I've never been known to burn the candor at both ends.

I enjoy a cold shower every morning--I lie about other things, too.

Be careful when you stretch the truth too far--it may snap back.

There are more liars in this country than you would believe.

The man who says he never tells lies is telling one.

If you want to be thought a liar, always tell the truth.

Exaggeration always makes the truth more acceptable, and the lie less so.

A pathological liar will always tell you where the truth lies.

Not every husband lies to his wife--some men prevaricate.

Never tell a lie when the truth is more profitable.

Truth is what's left over when you run out of lies.

Most fish would be bigger if fishermen's arms were longer.

Never exaggerate your faults--your friends will do that for you.

If there were no listeners, there would be no liars.

Pretending that you believe a liar is also lying.

Tell your child to lie for you, and he will learn to lie to you.

The big advantage of being truthful is that your lies are believed.

The most important part of lying is to know when to tell the truth.

Actions lie louder than words.

The perjurer's mother probably told white lies.

Children learn to lie by watching adults who pretend they don't.

Some people love the truth, and some hate to get caught in a lie.

The safest of all lies is sometimes the truth.

Opportunities lie at every hand, and so do a lot of people.

If at first you're not believed, lie, lie again.

Allow your child to tell white lies, and he'll grow up color-blind.

In a psychiatrist's office you lie on a couch to tell the truth.

The way he handles the truth, he should work for the weather bureau.

You can believe half of what he tells you--the question is: which half?

Money talks, but it doesn't always tell the truth.

One good lie requires another.

It isn't lying to compliment a woman.

Half the lies that they tell about me are not true.

White lies are usually yellow.

I always tell the truth, even if I have to lie to do it.

Ask some people a direct question and you get a direct lie.

Half the world doesn't know how much the other half lies about it.

We're all liars--even if you never lie to others, you lie to yourself.

Malcontent

If I smile when things go wrong, it means I have someone to blame it on.

One thing an alarm clock never arouses in me is my better nature.

I had three phones installed, so I can hang up on more people.

Talk about disagreeable, hs own shadow won't keep him company.

My wife is so contrary, she does everything versa vice.

I'm the kind of guy who gets sick on his day off.

Some people can see viruses in the milk of human kindness.

Today the human race is a race for a parking place.

My mother-in-law never wipes her opinion off her face.

I may not be disgruntled, but I'm certainly far from being gruntled.

I had such a long face, the barber charged me double for a shave.

Please don't tell me anything--I have a soundproof head.

When I was in the hospital, I got get-well cards from all the nurses.

My boss follows the straight and narrow-minded path.

The idea for whiskey sours came from a look at my wife's face.

My wife hasn't been herself lately--and I hope she'll stay that way.

My wife is very quick on the flaw.

The thing my wife finds hardest to do is give in.

My boss is so disagreeable, his own shadow won't keep him company.

My boss's tactics are a combination of needles and threats.

My boss is so narrow-minded, he has to stack his ideas vertically.

I hate the kind of hostess whom you have to thank for her hostility.

Some people have comebacks that are as snappy as their checks.

Lately my wife has been as glum as a tongue-tied parrot.

My brother-in-law is always down on everything he's not up on.

My mother-in-law has the disposition of an untipped waiter.

A man who never made a mistake in his life, usually has a wife that did.

My brother-in-law thinks the world is against him--and it is.

My wife is all right in her own way--but she always wants it.

Arguing with my wife is like trying to read a newspaper in a high wind.

My mother-in-law looks through rose-colored glasses with a jaundiced eye.

If you win all your arguments you'll end up with no friends.

Always keep your words soft and sweet--one day you may have to eat them.

Everyone has a good word for the boss-they all whisper it.

All the women living in our neighborhood belong to the meddle class.

Some people pay you a compliment like they expected a receipt.

Even what's eating me has a case of indigestion.

Some people have a unique talent for invading an issue.

I never hit a man when he's down--I kick him.

My wife is blower-upper without any countdown.

Last night my mother-in-law dreamed she was dead--the heat woke her up.

When it comes to helping someone, I stop at nothing.

Eating your own words can give you an acute case of indigestion.

My mother-in-law is a very sneer-sighted person.

The narrower a man's mind, the broader his statements.

Some people get up on the wrong side of the floor every morning.

Arguing with your wife is like trying to blow out an electric light bulb.

Life is a mirror to my wife, and she's always looking for cracks in it.

Some people have as much use for anyone living as an undertaker.

If I ever become deaf I'm not going to tell my barber.

Some people look for faults as if they were buried treasure.

I've got a neighbor who is a chip off the old glacier.

Many people who think themselves broad-minded, are really thick-headed.

Every man feels the need of a good-natured woman to grumble to.

The chronic complainer is a man whose like is seldom seen.

My boss has a testimonial plaque from Simon Legree.

I told my kids Santa Claus is too old to get around any more.

My wife can make more cutting remarks than a surgeon.

Everything looks yellow to my mother-in-law's jaundiced eye.

I heat the knive so my family won't use too much butter.

A grouch is a man who spreads good cheer wherever he doesn't go.

Some men would look unhappy even if they weren't married.

The man who is always kicking seldom has a leg to stand on.

My boss is always unpleasant, even when you catch him off-guard.

A chronic complainer gets all his exercise out of kicking.

The meaner a man is, the harder it is to make him feel mean.

The only thing my mother-in-law shares willingly is a disease.

Want some fun? Send a get-well card to a hypochondriac.

I couldn't warm up to my boss if I was cremated with him.

What I need is a good-natured woman to grumble to.

If you can't bite, don't growl.

You should see a psychiatrist about your infuriating complex.

One poor guy was shipwrecked on a desert island with his own wife.

I don't mind criticism just so long as it is unqualified praise.

My only fault is that I have none.

There is more kicking done with the tongue than with the foot.

My wife is like an angel, always harping on something.

The worst fault of some people is telling other people theirs.

Actually, I'm never satisfied unless I'm dissatisfied.

Some husbands would look unhappy even if they weren't married.

I've lost heart--now I have to depend wholly on my liver.

I think my mother-in-law was weaned on a pickle.

I won't be contented with my lot until it's a lot more.

I always take bad luck like a man--I blame it on my wife.

I hate those people who tell you off by going on and on.

Marriage

We're as compatible as a cat and a goldfish.

Our home is frequently closed for altercations.

We're as unlike as a yacht and a coal barge.

The current trend is towards shorter honeymoons, but more of them.

We get along like two peeves in a pod.

In the word "wedding" the "we" comes before the "I."

It's a trial marriage--nothing could be more of a trial.

The bridegroom spends a ot of money on a new suit that nobody notices.

The honeymoon is the morning after the knot before.

I'll never forget the first time we met--but I'm trying hard.

I put a ring on her finger and she put one through my nose.

My wife always forgives me when she's wrong.

A bridegroom is a man who has just lost his self-control.

Our parakeet gets to talk more than I do.

I worship the ground she gives me to run around on.

I gave my wife an inch and now she's the ruler.

I have my will, but she has her way.

My wife is all peaches and scream.

The honeymoon is the short period of doting between dating and debting.

A word to my wife is never sufficient.

The hand that socks the husband rules the pocketbook.

I'm mad about my wife--I love every hair on her lip.

My wife opens cans, just like her mother.

Today's wife tries to love, honor and display.

It's dangerous to marry a woman who looks good in black.

Wives of great men all remind us of it.

A married man is one who uses two hands while driving.

Even on our honeymoon we had our ups and downs.

I have the courage of my wife's convictions.

A bridgroom is a wolf whose whistle got stuck.

A honeymoon is something that happens only once every few years.

I married her for her looks--but not the kind she gives me.

They didn't marry for love or money--but for a short time.

All men are born free and equal--marriage comes later.

My wife is my booin' companion.

A honeymoon is the thrill that comes but once in a wifetime.

I can make my wife do anything she wants to do.

I wish that Adam had died with all his ribs in his body.

I married my wife for her money, and I earn every dollar of it.

I never realized how unimportant I was until I went to my own wedding.

The cooing stops with the honeymoon, but the billing goes on forever.

I avoid getting up with a grouch--by getting up before she does.

When she threatened to divorce me I shed a few cheers.

When I ask my wife a question, I have to take a lot for grunted.

We're inseparable--it takes several people to pull us apart.

My wife has a sobering effect on me--she hides the bottle.

The bridegroom begins by handing out a line, and ends up walking it.

I believed in dreams until I married my wife.

My wife has no minor voices.

I've given my wife the best ears of my live.

Every time I argue with my wife, words fail me.

When we have words I never get to use mine.

I have several mouths to feed, and one big one to listen to.

Honeymoon cooking: only the brave deserve the fare.

Every bride likes to take her husband with her on her honeymoon.

Nothing is written about less than a June bridegroom.

I have two mouths to heed--hers and her mother's.

I'm happiest when my wife is in bed, safe and soundless.

To get a word in with my wife, I have to sit sideways.

I married my wife 211 checkbooks ago.

Man worships woman, and then sacrifices himself at the altar.

What becomes of the honeymoon when it goes into eclipse?

My wife is a human dynamo--she charges everything.

Without my wife, I'd never be what I am today--broke.

Marriage is just another union that defies management.

The only time my wife didn't try to reform me was on our honeymoon.

I'm more interested in spice than spouse.

My wife is very gifted--and I've got the bills to prove it.

My wife's clothes make her, but they break me.

A woman's upkeep can be her husband's downfall.

After our honeymoon I felt like a new man. My wife said she did too.

My mother just got married again. Medicare is paying for the honeymoon.

My wife can dish it out, but she can't cook it.

I was introduced to my wife by a former friend.

When the honeymoon is over the necking changes to pecking.

The honeymoon is over when the man stops wearing his toupee at home.

A new groom sweeps clean, and also washes the dishes.

We never have pot roast--only roast pot.

We run our marriage like a business--I'm the silent partner.

The groom is never important at a wedding unless he doesn't show up.

Solomon was the one who loved not wisely, but too many.

My wife deserves a lot of credit--but she demands cash.

I was too poor to get married, but I found it out too late.

Marriage is the billing after the cooing.

No other co-educational institution equals matrimony.

It's a happy marriage if he gives and she forgives.

When the minister asked: "Do you take this woman?" I replied: "I'll try."

Marriage is the gateway of romance into the real of reality.

Most marital arguments could be stopped by the timely use of arms.

Marriage is an unequalled intelligence test.

Marriage is a man's afterthought and a woman's all-thought.

In marriage you make progress if you just break even.

A marriage license is a treaty pledging two powers to coo-existence.

Marriage doesn't promote thrift--it exacts it.

The secret of a happy marriage remains a secret.

No man who would make a perfect husband is married.

Another thing this country needs is fewer self-made widows.

The world's prime example of double jeopardy is marriage.

Don't neglect your wife--a kiss in time saves nine.

A widower is the only man who has an angel for a wife.

The landed gentry is made up of men who are either married or engaged.

Checkmate is the girl you marry for her money.

Marriage is a souvenir of love.

Marriage is for people who are afraid to think for themselves.

Today a marriage contract is just a short-term option.

The trouble with marriage is it can break up a good romance.

Marriage is a form of quarantined love.

Marriage is the hangover from the intoxication of passion.

Marriage is proof that two can live as bitter as one.

Marriage is the original on-the-job training institution.

A married couple is an example of two minds without a single thought.

Babies are the little rivets in the bonds of matrimony.

A bad husband is the only thing that beats a good wife.

A nagging wife is one who keeps a swivel tongue in her head.

A perfect man is a wife's first husband.

Since "Here comes the bride" I've been constantly facing the music.

Marriage is the union that makes estranged bedfellows.

We have a dictionary marriage--one word leads to another.

Marriage guarantees that your troubles will be over--little things.

A smart wife is one who can get her way without half crying.

Marriage is a state of antagonistic cooperation.

Children read fairy tales, married women listen to them.

It's a successful marriage if the wife is the boss but doesn't know it.

It only takes a few years of marriage to change necking to pecking.

Today's thought: I wonder why I got married.

Before marriage, bushels of kisses; after, a few measly pecks.

I impulsively proposed on the purr of the moment.

Matrimony is a wonderful thing--no married couple should be without it.

The only time my wife gives me a helping hand is in tying my apron.

Ideal marriage: the wife is a treasure, and the husband a treasury.

Many people marry in Las Vegas because it's such a good place to gamble.

Marriage begins when women stop dating and start intimidating.

Deciding to marry was the last decision I was allowed to make.

There's nothing like a wedding to bring two married people together.

Marriage is a premature punishment for those who get divorced.

My wife and I are well-matched--we fight each other to a standstill.

Marriage is a knot tied by a preacher and untied by a lawyer.

Matrimony is the root of all evil.

My wife's mind is just a scheme engine.

My wife just added a room divider--she sent for her mother.

Never argue with your wife--if you win you're in real trouble.

I got married because I wanted a large family, and I got one--my wife's.

The secret of a happy marriage: Don't go to bed angry--stay up and fight.

I'm true to my wife for three reasons: love, respect and fear.

Marriage is like a long banquet, with the dessert served first.

Is there life after marriage?

Ours was love at first sight, and it ended at the first slight.

For breakfast I get a three-minute egg and a five-minute argument.

Does my wife talk? I had laryngitis for three weeks, and didn't know it.

To entertain my wife all I have to do is listen to her.

For me, life is one canned thing after another.

It's not who you know that's important--it's how your wife found out.

My wife always lets me have the first word in an argument.

I'm sending my wife away for a rest--God knows I need it.

Marriage is a mutual partnership, if both parties know when to be mute.

Most wives are awakened from love's young dream with a snore.

Marriage is the intermission between the wedding and the divorce.

Marriage is all right--it's living together afterward that's so difficult.

When we were married we were mispronounced man and wife.

My wife dresses to kill, she cooks the same way.

A girl who marries a man with money to burn makes a good match.

You know what they say: Marry in haste, repeat at pleasure.

Know what I did before I was married? Anything I wanted to.

Married life is great! It's my wife I can't stand.

Marriage is like a quiz show, but you lose if you give the right reply.

Marriage is an association of two people for the benefit of one.

Marriage is two toothbrushes with a single tube of paste.

Marriage is give and take. If you don't give it to her, she takes it.

My wife is a doll. She's a little effeminate, but very sweet.

My marriage has been a mutual misunderstanding.

Marriage is love parsonified.

My wife hit the ceiling yesterday--she's always been a lousy shot.

Marriage is a sort of friendship recognized by the police.

Men who aren't born meek, get married, and get that way.

They say that marriage encourages thrift. Demands is more the word.

Marriage turns a bachelor apartment into a dog house.

Marriage is a meal where the soup is better than the dessert.

Marriage is the tie that blinds.

Marriage is a legalized way of suppressing free speech.

I saved her from drowning and she married me--that's gratitude?

Marriage is a process where love ripens into vengeance.

Marriage is a rest period between romances.

I never kept any secrets from my wife--even when I tried.

Always marry an ugly girl--in ten years she'll be as pretty as ever.

What a marriage! I bring home the bacon and she burns it.

It's advantageous to marry late--there's less of it.

When I got married again I took a new leash on life.

It's a formal wedding when the shotgun is painted white.

Just tell your wife who's boss. Say, "You're the boss."

Her husband is a writer--she edits his pockets.

Marriage is a life sentence that's suspended for bad behavior.

Women are fools to marry--but what else can a man marry?

Marriage is the end of love at first sight.

The man of the hour is the one whose wife told him to wait a minute.

Marriage is the original duet-yourself project.

A stitch in time is usually a surprise to a married man.

Marriage is like soup. When you get through spooning, it cools off.

Embark on the sea of matrimony and you wind up with a raft of kids.

People don't marry as early today--but they marry oftener.

A second marriage is the triumph of hope over experience.

On the sea of matrimony I got a leaky boat.

If you have her mother for dinner--make sure she's well done.

I'm married--as a bachelor I weakened.

I can't get along with my wife--she understands me.

He married so often he has an altar-ego.

I eat out of my wife's hands--she hates to do the dishes.

Every time I meet a pretty girl, either she's married or I am.

It takes two to make a marriage--a single girl and an anxious mother.

An optimist thinks the world owes him a living and gets married on it.

Married men don't live longer than single men--it just seems longer.

My marriage didn't bring blessings, it brought consequences.

When a fellow needs a friend he often makes a mistake and gets a wife.

A woman's mouth is like a rosebud--after marriage the bud opens.

My marriage is in a state of antagonist cooperation.

It takes two to make an argument--unless you have a wife.

I wrote my girl friend every day--so she married the mailman.

Marriage makes loving legal.

You look as if you got up on the wrong side of your wife.

Marriage is a two-handed game of solitaire.

In marriage, the first sex years are the toughest.

Marriage is the most expensive hobby.

I wish my wife was my mother--so I could run away from home.

Marriage is a fire-extinguisher.

Most men marry for life, and then want a girl to be able to show some.

Marriage is an expensive way to get your laundry done free.

My wife and I are married and happy--she's happy--I'm married.

Marriage simplifies life and complicates living.

The most popular labor-saving device today is a husband with money.

A girl's dream today is to go out with every Tom, Dick, and marry.

I'm opposed to early marriages. I've always been married in the afternoon.

Marriage is an attempt to change a night-owl into a homing pigeon.

Imagination sits up with a wife when her husband is out late.

My wife doesn't pick my suits--just my pockets.

A husband is never interrupted when talking in his sleep.

Yawning enables a husband to open his mouth.

There's nothing like marriage to break up a good romance.

I meet any marital crises with a firm hand--full of flowers.

Two people can live as cheaply as one what?

The difference between marriage and a circus is two rings.

When a man isn't a mouse, his wife keeps her trap shut.

Anniversary: the day on which you forget to buy a present.

The matrimonial bark is wrecked by the matrimonial barking.

The trouble with blind love is that it doesn't stay that way.

You can never trust a woman; she may be true to you.

Sometimes a wife drives a man to distinction.

Some wives awaken with a pain in the neck--others prefer twin beds.

How can they outlaw gambling as long as marriage is legal?

Love is intoxication, but marriage is the hangover.

Marriage is like a 3:00 a.m. phone call. It jolts you awake.

Behind every famous man is a woman to tell him he's not so good.

Wisdom is the decision to close your mouth before your wife wants to.

A wise woman always lets her husband have her way.

Time, money and marriage separate the best of friends.

A pessimist is a man who buys a one-way ticket to Niagara Falls.

In marriage, two live more cheaply than one wants to.

Success is what comes faster to the man your wife almost married.

Marriage is the greatest adventure of all.

The world's a stage, with husbands playing the supporting roles.

Marriage is a perfect moment frozen for a dull eternity.

Once we have a joint bank account--my wife beat me to the draw.

It's a happy marriage when both mates get better than they deserve.

Give a girl enough rope and she'll ring the wedding bell.

Marriage is a mutual partnership with the husband as the mute.

My marriage is just a reciprocal tirade agreement.

Marriage is not a gamble--in a gamble you have a chance.

Some women marry only for love and securities.

The three "R's" of marriage are: Romance, Rice, and Rocks.

They make a good match--they're both always lit.

Our unhappiness is due to illness--we're sick of each other.

Once we swore to love--now we love to swear.

We're a pair of lovebirds--always flying at each other.

We're not just drifting apart--we're under full sail.

We're very compatible. We both dislike each other.

After the dating comes the intimidating.

There is a lot to be said about marriage, but who has the nerve?

Research tells us that 50% of all married people are women.

Marriages are made in heaven--so is thunder and lightning.

We went steady for 10 years, then we broke our engagement and got married.

My best friend married my sister--now he hates me like a brother.

One way for a man to acquire a large vocabulary is to get married.

I asked one girl to marry me so she put me on her wedding list.

Ours is a give-and-take marriage--I give and she takes.

Marrying a woman for her beauty is like buying a house for its paint.

Married men can't understand why every bachelor is not a millionaire.

Marriage is like a tourniquet--it stops your circulation.

I'm one of the silent majority--I'm married.

To be honest, I owe everything to married life--ulcers, headaches...

Marriage is the hangover that lasts a lifetime.

It's better to marry for money than for no reason at all.

He who marries a chicken gets henpecked.

*On the set of "You Can't Run Away From It," a remake of "It Happened One Night,"
with Jack Lemmon*

Our unhappiness is due to illness--we're sick of each other.

Our marriage started as puppy love, but it's since gone to the dogs.

Compatible couple: he's a pill and she's a headache.

He's paunchy and she's punchy.

The thing they have in common is that both of them are.

They're proving that two can live as bitter as one.

He's a past master and she's a past mistress.

Women aspire to marriage, men submit to it.

A common law marriage is one where a couple lives in unholy wedlock.

Common-law marriage is when a woman mates a man halfway.

The shortest marriage bedtime story: "Move over!"

The marriage system created a new sport--adultery.

I was married by a judge--I should have held out for a jury.

My father wanted me to marry one of my own kind, but I married a girl.

Don't marry for money--you can borrow it cheaper.

It takes two to quarrel, and the same number to get married.

A marriage license gives a woman the right to drive a man.

If you want to keep your husband home, ask him to take you out.

My wife is so fussy she even irons shoelaces.

They are a fastidious couple. She's fast and he's hideous.

I seem to have entered into marriage for better or for wars.

My wife and I see eye to eye--we're the same height.

I may live in a man's world, but it's in my wife's name.

An expert is a married man away from home.

I take my wife to a witch doctor--because she is.

I'm hoping for a blessed event--my wife's next pay raise.

With my wife money is not the object--only the subject.

My wife thinks she'll spoil me if she lets me have my own way.

He's a has-been, and she's a been-had.

Marriage is a way to get a woman to work for you for nothing.

Marriage is singular--you add one and one and make one.

Fools rush in where bachelors fear to wed.

Wives are people who feel that they don't dance enough.

It's always better to have your wife with you than after you.

A married man never knows when he's well off because he never is.

Husbands give allowances, and wives make them.

The sea of matrimony is filled with men over-bored.

Every time I look at my wife I'm sorry I learned how to whistle.

My marriage didn't work out--everywhere I went I kept running into my wife.

To my wife the law is known as demand and supply.

My wife does bird imitations--she watches me like a hawk.

I can always put my boss in a good humor--by doing the dishes for her.

Only a newlywed tells his wife when he gets a salary raise.

At my wedding I lost complete control of myself.

When my wife is away, I wash the dishes--both of them--every day.

I was broke when I got married and I've held my own ever since.

My wife only wins half of our arguments. Her mother wins the other half.

It's a beef-stew marriage. She's always beefing, and he's always stewed.

On Valentine's Day she eats my heart out.

She drives from the back seat, and he cooks from the dining room table.

We have a fifty-fifty marriage. She signs the checks; I sign the receipts.

We have nothing in common--we don't even hate the same people.

My wife is 45 going on 37; I'm 49 going on pep pills.

We get breakfast together. She makes the toast and I scrape it.

Ours is a nip-and-tuck marriage. I take a nip, and she tucks me in.

We have a fifty-fifty marriage. She buys $50 dresses, and I buy 50-cent shirts.

Politics doesn't make strange bedfellows--marriage does.

I've got my wife trained--she makes her own breakfast.

My wife knows all my jokes backwards--and tells them that way.

My wife changed a lot after marriage--my hours, my habits and my friends.

The honeymoon is over when she gets flabby, gabby, and crabby.

A groom is a man who's fit to be tied--down.

One of the things that puzzle married men is married women.

Many people are unhappily married, but fortuntately they don't know it.

Husbands are like fires--they go out when unattended.

My wife will go anywhere for dinner, except to the kitchen.

Married life isn't so bad--once you get to be a trusty.

Whoever said marriags is a 50/50 proposition didn't know the half of it.

I save myself a lot of trouble by marrying my second wife first.

To the young, marriage is a heaven; to the old, a haven.

Men

A gentleman is a man you don't know very well.

Time tells on a man--especially a good time.

A man who talks like a book can be easily shut up by a woman.

Man is a species of the second-toughest sex.

A successful man is one who can earn more than his family can spend.

Silence is golden--that's why so many married men are prosperous.

Men and women chasing each other is what makes the human race.

Man is the only creature that refuses to be what he is.

Every man has his price, and every woman has her figure.

He's her white-haired boy--she turned it white.

History records only one indispensable man: Adam.

Man is the only animal that can be skinned and still live.

A small man usually talks big.

Married men are more inventive than single men. They have to be.

Some men are like a watch--hard to regulate.

A man about town is usually a fool about women.

Men who go out on the loose frequently end up tight.

Counting sheep is no fun. Most men would rather count calves.

I kiss the ground she walks on; it's a lot better than kissing her.

A man will always pay a fancy figure for checking his hat.

Women have their permanent waves, men just want permanent hair.

The Mann Act is a law that discourages travel.

Man is a perpetual-notion machine--and it's always the same notion.

The three sexes are: masculine, feminine, and nuder.

The three sexes are: men, women, and social workers. (Change to fit.)

Man is the only animal that can make a beast of himself.

It takes two women to raise one man--his mother and his wife.

Man wants a great deal here below, and woman even more.

A man criticizes his enemies behind their backs; a woman, her friends.

All women like to be loved, all men love to be liked.

When it comes to women, no man can be both logical and biological.

Man may be the head, but woman is his headache.

A man can drop a lot of money trying to pick up a little honey.

Nothing so unmans a man as a woman.

A man in love is bound to be bound.

A man likes to feel he is loved, a woman likes to be told.

A man in love is no judge of beauty.

Life is full of troubles, and most of them are man-maid.

A man is incomplete until he marries--then he's really finished.

For every man there is a woman--with luck his wife never finds out.

A man is known by the company he is trying to avoid.

One man who didn't kiss his wife in years shot a man who did.

A man is known by the company he thinks nobody knows he's keeping.

A man who falls in love with himself has no mother-in-law.

A man is known by the company his wife keeps.

A man who gives in when he's right is married.

Men worry more about losing their hair than losing their heads.

Business must be bad--men are all wearing their Christmas neckties.

Men who are run down generally wind up in a hospital.

Men are the cause of women's dislike for one another.

Man is the only animal that cooks.

I've been up all night nursing a grouch--my wife.

Man is a horse's best friend.

Man is a somewhat elegant form of ape.

Men prefer blondes because they are afraid of the dark.

A man who is buried in thought usually has a grave appearance.

Man is an animal that throws peanuts to his ancestors.

By the time a man is rich enough to sleep late, he's too old to enjoy it.

Nothing upsets a man's balance as much as a wife who writes checks.

Nothing is impossible to the man who doesn't have to do it.

Any man who misses his mother-in-law doesn't throw straight.

Most young men know how to kiss a girl, but not when.

Any man who never makes a mistake isn't very busy.

Man was created at the end of the week, when God was tired.

Some men carry a torch for a girl simply because they aren't very bright.

I've got three suits: non-support, separation, and breach of promise.

All men are created free and eager.

Man is woman's last domestic animal.

Is he important? Why, the Mafia hears from him.

A handsome man is the answer to a maiden's stare.

Man is the only creature with a nasty mind.

Man is the lord of the home--if he's under three years old.

Any man who puts his nose to the grindstone is a bloody fool.

One man's telephone is another man's wrong number.

A man can't think straight when he only has curves on his mind.

The first thing a man makes in his workshop is a mess.

The best way to make a monkey out of a man is to ape him.

The first thing most self-made men owe themselves is an apology.

I never swear before ladies. I let them swear first.

Show me a man who beats his wife, and I'll show you a good bridge player.

Many a man thinks he's being cultivated when he's only being trimmed.

Show me a man with very little money, and I'll show you a bum.

Never hit a man when he's down. He might get up again.

A wise man is one who is smarter than he thinks he is.

A gentleman won't strike a woman with his hat on.

The more I see of mankind, the more I like my dog.

Women like the silent type man because they think he's listening.

Men prefer women who don't "no" too much.

A man will leave the straight and narrow for a few exciting curves.

Some men depend entirely upon themselves. Others marry.

Middle Age

I still chase women, but I can't remember why.

At middle age our tripping becomes less light and more fantastic.

Middle age spread is the destiny that ends our shapes.

Middle age is when winking is closing one eye to reality.

It's middle age when you go all out and end up all in.

The middle aged woman is all bleaches and creams.

You begin to develop scales resistance in your forties.

Middle age is when you're reduced to reducing.

You're middle aged when you feel your corns more than your oats.

Middle age is the time to start mending your weighs.

I can still do as much as I did before--but I don't.

In middle age you walk around a puddle instead of through it.

These days I only chase girls if it's downhill.

Nowadays, when the phone rings, I hope it's not for me.

Middle age is when you begin to clash with the furniture.

It now takes me as long to get over a good time as it does to have it.

A middle aged man talks about what a fool he used to be.

Middle age comes later than you think and sooner than you expect.

In middle age, weight-lifting consists of standing up.

If you look forward to a dull evening--you're reached middle age.

Middle age is when you're thin on the top and not on the bottom.

It's called "middle age" because that's where it shows.

Middle age is when getting ahead means staying even.

I can't decide which I have more of: age or middle.

Middle age is when you laugh at photos you once prized.

I'm as young as ever, but it takes a lot more effort.

Middle age is when you're going to start saving next month.

When I step on a scale the balance is no longer in my favor.

Middle age is when you feel fit as a fiddle, but bulge like a bass.

I winked at a girl today and she thought I had something in my eye.

Middle age is the roaring forties.

The only exercise of middle-aged people is caution.

This is the time when your thoughts turn from passion to pension.

Middle age is the time between graduation and retirement.

The time when your favorite nightspot is in front of the TV set.

Middle age is when you are reduced to reducing.

In middle age work is no longer play and play is getting to be work.

The time when you use one bend-over to pick up two things.

At middle age a man starts to feel friendly toward insurance agents.

My wife's been pressing thirty so long, it's pleated.

She still looks like a million dollars--but now it's after taxes.

My wife's age ranges from thirty to secrecy.

My wife's not what she was 15 years ago--she's ten years older.

Middle age is when you decide you look better in glasses.

At my time of life, each day makes me feel two days older.

Middle age comes later than you think, and sooner than you expect.

At middle age you start to use the count-down method of calculating age.

My wife still looks like a million--every year of it.

These days I get exhausted simply by wrestling with my conscience.

At middle age you start talking about what a fool you used to be.

Middle age is when a man returns a wink with a blink.

My wife's hardest decision is when to start middle age.

In middle age you're too old to be fired, but too young to be retired.

Lately I burn the midnight oil about 9:00 p.m.

The time when a woman's dangerous curves become extended detours.

I've given up exercising--pushing fifty is enough exercise for me.

My wife's 42, going on indefinitely.

Middle age is when a lot of dreamboats give up the shape.

I'm beginning to think that my gray hair isn't premature.

I feel I get less for my money each time I go to the barber.

Middle age is a time of life that a man first notices in his wife.

The worst thing about middle age is that you outgrow it.

Middle age spread is what might be called the fullness of time.

Middle age is the age dominated by the middle.

Middle age is when it takes longer to rest than to get tired.

Of course I'm against sin--I'm against anything I'm too old to enjoy.

My wife won't lie about her age--she just refuses to talk about it.

My wife found the secret of youth--she lies about her age.

Minds

Ever notice how narrow-minded people are thick-headed?

Minds, like streams, may be so broad that they're shallow.

A man who doesn't know his own mind hasn't missed much.

A mind, like a parachute, functions only when it is open.

Sales resistance is the triumph of mind over patter.

An open mind may be too porous to hold a conviction.

A man who can't make up his mind may not have a mind to make up.

My wife always asks my opinion after she has made up her mind.

People with open minds should wear warm hats.

A man with a mechanical mind should remember to wind it up.

My nephew has a photographic mind--unfortunately it never developed.

My mother-in-law went to a mind reader--she was only charged half-price.

Some people think they have an open mind when it is really their mouth.

I like a woman to have a narrow waist and a broad mind.

The best way to change a woman's mind is to agree with her.

Most bathing beauties have no more on their minds than anywhere else.

People's minds are changed through their pockets.

Too many people have dream-lined brains.

If both sides make you laugh, you are broad-minded.

The single-track mind is seldom well-ballasted.

The "best minds" are not those who mind best.

Some so-called "open minds" should be closed for repairs.

My wife can make up her face easier than her mind.

One way to get ahead and stay ahead is to use your head.

A man who has more money than brains doesn't have it for long.

The influence of our mind over statistics is another remarkable thing.

No man is half as smart as he wants some woman to believe he is.

Too bad that so much that broadens the mind also hardens the arteries.

A frame of mind is about all some people have of it.

The trouble with most open minds is that they are open at both ends.

When my wife's mind wanders, it never has far to go.

When a man and wife are of one mind it's not hard to guess which mind.

Brains are what make a man think he's smarter than he is.

Active minds and hens aren't discouraged by infertile eggs.

To pay for success you must tax your brains.

Very few people are as broadminded as we think we are.

My boss is a mental tourist. His mind wanders.

My boss has a mind like a water-bug--it just skates over the surface.

My boss would have to step out of his mind to get an idea.

Ingenuity is getting others to do the work you dislike.

The mind is a cloud no bigger than a man's brain.

My brother can never make up what little mind he has left.

My boss has a one-track mind, and the traffic on it is very light.

A brilliant extremist is a person whose mind is short-circuited.

To make up her mind my wife powders her forehead.

Some men who have open minds let the wrong kind of stuff in.

A genius is a man with a closed mind--closed to distractions.

Anything preying on my mother-in-law's mind would starve to death.

She doesn't know her own mind--if she did, she'd hate it.

My wife's mind is always fresh. It should be. She never uses it.

Strange, but a filthy mind is usually sterile.

A single-track mind is seldom well-balanced.

The world's troubles are often caused by one-track minds meeting head-on.

The man with a mind like a steel trap better watch his step.

The best kind of mind is that which minds its own business.

There are two sides to every question--my side, and the screwball side.

My wife never speaks her whole mind. She only gives me a piece of it.

Like computers, human minds are subject to goofs in programming.

The two types of smart women are the highbrows and the low necks.

Some folks have minds as sharp as tacks--and just as small.

A brain is no stronger than its weakest think.

Often a man who doesn't know his own mind hasn't missed much.

Don't give others a piece of your mind unless you can afford it.

Too many of us just aren't equipped to attend a meeting of the minds.

The narrower the mind, the louder the accusation.

Too many of us are broadminded about the wrong things.

If you haven't much education, you've got to use your brains.

The head never begins to swell until the mind stops growing.

You never know how intelligent some people are until they tell you.

Man's reason for existence is the existence of his reason.

There's no tax on brains--the revenue would be too small.

Many men would reach greater heights if they had more depth.

There are two kinds of fools: mindful and mindless.

Misfortune

Fortune knocks once, but misfortune has more patience.

Every time I'm in a hurry my car won't start.

Trouble is the one thing you can borrow without references.

Every time I'm in a hurry my shoelaces break.

Trouble, like bananas, often comes in bunches.

Every time I answer the phone the call isn't for me.

One way to keep happy is to learn to enjoy trouble.

Every time I buy an orange I get a lemon.

He's nursing a grouch. His wife is sick.

Every time I came home from school, my parents had moved.

Being a round man is hard when square holes are the style.

Every time I come up with a fresh idea my secretary slaps me.

You can save yourself a lot of trouble by not borrowing any.

Every time I dial a number I get a busy signal.

Nothing but troubles seem to hatch out of a love nest.

Every time I find a parking meter I have no change.

When you look for trouble, you don't need a search warrant.

Every time I find a taxi it's off duty.

If you can't make light of your troubles keep them in the dark.

Every time I go to the race track I lose my shirt.

Troubles are like babies--they only grow by nursing.

Every time I have a light lunch my wife serves a dark dinner.

The trouble with trouble is that it always starts out like fun.

Every time I kiss my secretary my wife walks in.

Never borrow trouble; the interest on the loan is too high.

Every time I look at my wife, I'm sorry I learned how to whistle.

Worry is the interest paid on trouble before it falls due.

Every time I look at my wife I lose my appetite.

Trouble is something that many are looking for, but no one wants.

Every time I open my mouth my wife interrupts.

Misfortunes never come singly; sometimes it comes married.

Every time I play Bingo I get cards without numbers.

Trouble is opportunity in work clothes.

Life's worst misfortunes are the ones that never happened.

I fell on my back and broke my nose.

Sweet are the uses of adversity--your enemy's adversity.

I had the seven-year itch for eight years.

Misfortune is the kind of fortune that never misses.

I went bankrupt three times and didn't make a cent once.

In the divorce I got custody of my wife's parents.

My bank account is my shrinking fund.

I used to be a tree surgeon, but I kept falling out of my patients.

If it weren't for the misfortune of others, life would be unbearable.

Bad luck never lasts; it continues for a while, and then gets worse.

Marriage, twins and other misfortunes never come singly.

I took my wife to an antique show and someone tried to buy her.

When misfortune comes, take it like a man--blame it on your wife.

My wife found a blonde hair on my coat and saw red.

I'm not a good loser; in fact, that's all I ever do.

No matter when I want my wife, she's out shopping.

The trouble with men is their trouble with women.

The quickest way to get into trouble is to be right at the wrong time.

Just thinking about the price of aspirin gives me a headache.

A man's in real trouble if both his wife and his TV set aren't working.

Whenever I take a trip I forget something. Last time I forgot my wife.

One thing you can get without a lot of trouble is a lot of trouble.

Whenever I put my foot down my wife steps on it.

People who look for trouble usually don't know what to do when they find it.

I put a seashell to my ear and got a busy signal.

If I didn't have bad luck I wouldn't have any luck at all.

I have hard luck. Every time I meet a married woman she's got a husband.

Money

A sign saying "Jesus Saves." Underneath it somebody wrote, "Moses Invests."

Am I rich? Why my bank account is named after me.

Money doesn't grow on trees; you've got to beat the bushes for it.

Money is something that brushes by you on its way to Washington.

A fool and his money are soon parted--just like the rest of us.

Save your money and buy yourself a calculator--that's what counts.

All you can get for a dollar today is change.

No man is a hero to his wallet.

No man is a hero to a bill collector.

Money works the other way, too. It stops talk.

Money doesn't go very far these days, or come very near.

Money is the route of all evil.

Money talks most when a man marries it.

Money talks, but it doesn't always talk sense.

You can't take it with you, but where on earth can you go without it?

A borrower is a person who exchanges hot air for cold cash.

Money is constantly changing hands--and people.

Money is what things run into, and people out of.

A happy wife is one who has everything that credit can buy.

The only thing you can do on a shoestring today is trip.

The love of someone else's money is the root of all evil.

Money is all right, but you have to waste a lot of time making it.

Today I'm celebrating an anniversary--I've been broke for seven years.

I just read a book with nothing in it: my bankbook.

I always take my salary to the bank--it's too small to go by itself.

Rome isn't the world's most beloved capital--money is.

There are bigger things in life than money--for instance, bills.

Pay as you go, unless you are going for good.

A bargain is anything that only costs twice as much as it did 5 years ago.

The man who can't pay as he goes is going too fast.

A man who can afford to pay the interest today doesn't need the loan.

The only kinds of books I really like are checkbooks.

There's no place like home, if you haven't got the money to go out.

The only thing you can get without money is sick.

Money isn't important as long as you have it.

My credit rating is so bad, my cash isn't even accepted.

The trouble with money is that you can't use it more than once.

Money isn't everything, but it's a sure cure for poverty.

Our floating currency is a sign of a sinking economy.

Cold cash has a way of making the approach a little warmer.

Two can live as cheaply as one, but only half as long.

When my wife writes a check she draws on her imagination.

Ever notice that by the time you get a raise it's not eough?

If it's a small world, why does it cost so much to run it?

Yesterday I tried to get change for a quarter and it cost me fifty cents.

The reason coins are round is because they were made to circulate.

A dollar goes very fast these days, but not very far.

A penny saved gathers no moss.

Two can live as cheaply as one--large family use to.

At today's prices very few people can afford to be poor.

Money isn't everything--but look at how many things it is.

Man can not live on bread alone--he has to have credit cards.

Money is not the root of all evil--no money is.

By the time a man has money to burn, the fire has gone out.

It's easy to save pennies today--what else can you do with them?

The hardest thing to get hold of these days is easy money.

My paycheck is like the tide--it comes in and goes out.

Money is not for poor people.

Saving money isn't a challenge--it's an out-and-out victory.

If you think today's dollar doesn't go far, try to get one back.

Money doesn't go very far today, or come very near.

Money isn't everything; in fact, after taxes, it isn't anything.

Money isn't everything; sometimes it isn't even 99%.

It's easy to make money. It's hard to make a living.

The other fellow's wallet always looks greener.

I give my wife everything credit can buy.

They say you can't take it with you. I can't even afford to go.

Money isn't everything--for one thing, it isn't plentiful.

They say a poor man can be happy--but a happy man isn't poor.

Money can't buy everything--poverty, for example.

A man never realizes the blessing of being poor until he gets over it.

Poverty is no disgrace, but that's all one can say in its favor.

Money isn't everything; usually, it isn't even enough.

Money isn't everything, but it's way ahead of any of its competitors.

If poverty is a blessing in disguise, the disguise is perfect.

One man's money burns a hole in another man's pocket.

My girl friend's favorite book is Dun and Bradstreet.

The mint makes money first, it's up to us to make it last.

Remember the poor--it doesn't cost a thing.

If you have money you don't have to worry about not having it.

Money talks, but it doesn't always talk sense.

Money can't buy happiness--that's why we have credit cards.

Money constantly changes hands--and people.

There is nothing as long as a short-term debt.

When a man says money can do anything--he hasn't any.

After paying my taxes, all I have let is a deficit.

I'm in favor of capital punishment; capital deserves it.

What this country needs is a good five-cent quarter.

Money talks, but poverty just pinches.

A dollar saved is a dollar earned, but seldom vice versa.

Money talks, and poverty also has a way of telling.

Today you can't live on love--without refinancing.

Her husband is rich and old--what a combination!

Money only brings misery--but with it you can afford misery.

A financier is always ready to back his decisions with your last cent.

A budget is an attempt to live below your yearnings.

I had a sinking fund--it just went down for the third time.

These days a man can't afford to make a living.

Money is legal tender--when you don't have it, it's tough.

Money is like a sixth sense--you can't use the other five without it.

Money makes a dirty old man a man-about-town.

Money can't buy happiness--but then, happiness can't buy groceries.

My ambition is to be able to afford to spend what I'm spending.

I've been broke so long that I can't get used to money.

When I buy a new suit I have them put a patch in it.

I'm as sound as a dollar--been to a grocery with a dollar lately?

I've got what no millionaire has got--I've got no money.

The tighter the money, the soberer the business world.

My wife loves to spend money, but she hasn't any other extravagances.

Check stubs are a record of how you managed to overdraw your account.

More rabbits than people have made their million.

All work and no play makes jack the dull way.

Money is like men. The tighter it gets, the louder it talks.

Money used to talk. Now it only whispers.

Money talks, but the people who know how to keep it don't.

To clean up a man must use soft soap.

Sound money is that which talks the loudest.

Some girls marry for money to make their dreams come true.

Some people make money--others earn it.

My uncle is so rich--he begs with two hats.

Anyone who has $100,000 can always find a bargain.

A millionaire is a billionaire after he pays his taxes.

Breadwinner: you have to win it--it's too expensive to buy.

Strange that we call money "dough." Dough sticks to your fingers.

Money can be lost in more ways than won.

Money isn't everything, it just quiets the nerves a little.

I don't want to take it with me, I just want enough to get me there.

A philanthropist gives away what he should be giving back.

A fool and his money--are invited places.

Money, like fertilizer, is no good unless you spread it around.

Some people think money grows on trees--as they did.

I like fancy things--like monogrammed aspirins.

If money talks, why isn't it doing some explaining?

I'm saving my money for a rainy day--that's why my checks are rubber.

A debutante is a tomato with plenty of lettuce.

Hush money is the proof that silence is golden.

A dollar saved is a pocket burned.

I know money isn't everything--but try to convince my wife of that.

The salary we used to dream of is the one we can't live on today.

It's the woman who pays and pays--but look at whose money she uses.

Economists have a new truism that I've known for years: money is tight.

He's money mad. He hasn't got a cent--that's why he's mad.

I make as much money as a hat check girl in a nudist camp.

Money doesn't mean everything, but everything seems to mean money.

Hush money does not guarantee a quiet life.

Money has wings, but it is not a homing pigeon.

At a really high class wedding they throw puffed rice.

Even the price of bread has gone up--pumpernickel is now pumper-dime.

Money goes further than it did--and stays away longer.

A miser is what might be called a "dough-nut."

Money is the principal export of the United States.

A dollar to doughnut bet today is even money.

He had everything she wanted in a man--money.

Am I wealthy? Why my bank account is named after me.

He who steals my purse, steals I.O.U.s.

Inflation is so bad now that there's no money in money.

Money may not be everything, but it's a wonderful substitute.

Money is the most expensive thing these days.

The best tranquilizer is money.

Money is still the most efficient labor-saving device.

My financial problems are simple. I'm short on money.

My boss throws money away like it was an anchor.

Rich or poor, it's always best to have money.

Girls don't marry for cash--they'll take checks.

An income is what you can't live without or within.

If you don't know what's up--you haven't been shopping lately.

Two can live as cheaply as one--and today they have to.

A check dodger is a man with a slight impediment in his reach.

When money talks, my wife doesn't miss a word.

Cash is the poor man's credit card.

Hard cash is the softest thing to fall back on.

These days a billion dollars is just a drop in the budget.

Money isn't everything. Sometimes it isn't even enough.

The only thing you can get for a quarter today is a dime.

Money is one commodity that doesn't grow on sprees.

Instead of a tax refund they sent me a bridge they couldn't find a river for.

A wealthy playboy is a "Cashanova."

Money is what you swap for what you think will make you happy.

If you don't know where your money goes--you're probably single.

The best way to jingle coins in your pocket is to shake a leg.

Thieves demand your money or your life--women require both.

I know a girl whose motto is: "Dough or die."

Overeating can turn you black and blue--just eat more than you can pay for.

Save your money--you never know when it may become valuable again.

Money can talk, but it doesn't hear very well when you call it.

When it does talk, all my money says is "Goodbye."

Say this for pickpockets--they try to keep money in circulation.

By the time a man learns money doesn't grow on trees, he's up one.

You could buy something for a dime 10 years ago--dimes sure have changed.

Mother-in-law

A mother-in-law is what you inherit when you marry.

A mother-in-law is a woman who is never outspoken.

My mother-in-law rarely goes without saying.

A mother-in-law is a referee with an interest in one of the fighters.

My mother-in-law is coming to visit--another mouth to heed.

Every day at breakfast I have two lumps--my wife and my mother-in-law.

My mother-in-law isn't so bad. She's fair to meddling.

I just came back from a pleasure trip--I took my mother-in-law to the airport.

Adam had no mother-in-law--that's how we know he lived in Paradise.

A mother-in-law should be careful not to go too far, unless she stays there.

They named a flower for my mother-in-law: the snapdragon.

I sent my mother-in-law a present on Mother's Day--her daughter.

She has a great figure for swimming. She's built like a submarine.

My mother-in-law never needs a permanent wave. Her skin is naturally curly.

She has a nice, steady disposition. Nasty all the time.

Her voice sounds like the 10-second warning at the Army-Navy game.

She has an iron deficiency. I hope the doctor puts a knife in her.

Her voice sounds like the all-clear signal at a floating crap game.

Mother-in-law sandwich: cold shoulder and hot tongue.

My mother-in-law forgets that she was a daughter-in-law.

A mother-in-law is one of the disadvantages of marriage.

Be kind to your mother-in-law. Babysitters are expensive.

My mother-in-law has the same effect on me as a wet holiday.

A man's mother-in-law is a relative, and always on his wife's side.

Divorce is the most popular way of getting rid of a mother-in-law.

I sent my mother-in-law to the country--they refused her.

My mother-in-law even talks louder than money.

A young man can't be too careful in his choice of a mother-in-law.

I've REALLY got troubles. My mother-in-law has a twin sister.

Absence makes the heart grow fonder, unless it's your mother-in-law.

Surplus means something you have no need for--like a mother-in-law.

A mother-in-law is the matrimonial kin that gets under your skin.

Simile: as welcome as a mother-in-law on a honeymoon.

I always tell my wife: "I like your mother-in-law better than mine."

Simile: as cold as a mother-in-law's kiss.

Behind every successful man is a surprised woman--his mother-in-law.

Johnny gets roasted by (l. to r.) Alan King, Milton Berle, Henny, Don Rickles, George C. Scott, Dick Cavett

Love is blind, but your mother-in-law isn't.

You're not really successful until your mother-in-law admits it.

The worst part of a second marriage is breaking in a new mother-in-law.

I just had the 24-hour virus--a visit from my mother-in-law.

Actually, I'd like to smother her in diamonds--or with anything else.

We had a blessed event at our house today--my mother-in-law finally left.

No man is a hero to his mother-in-law.

Motion Pictures

I'll never forget my first words in the theatre. "Peanuts, Popcorn!"

It was a super picture. It looked like a super made it.

Today a movie hero is the person who sits through it.

When they said they shot the picture--they weren't kidding.

Her last film isn't as good as her bad pictures.

Crime doesn't pay--in the movies.

An action movie is one where there is lots of squirming in the seats.

Many a movie has to be seen to be depreciated.

I photograph plaid.

We wanted a sneak preview--but we couldn't round up enough sneaks.

Seeing is believing--except in the movies.

Some people love to go to the movies--others go to the movies to love.

The happy ending in many films is the fact the picture has ended.

Incognito in Hollywood means: "I wish someone would recognize me."

She's been in a lot of pictures. Two of them were movies.

Hollywood has two seasons: the rainy season and the divorce season.

A Hollywood producer is a man who knows what he wants, but can't spell it.

In motion pictures blood is thicker than talent.

Movies are out of their infancy, but a lot of their stories aren't.

One starlet is ashamed of how she got her mink coat--she bought it.

Most film actors can't stand success--especially if it's someone else's.

A film director always knows where his next reel is coming from.

Hollywood is where they have secret weddings and catered divorces.

Dracula films are fang-tastic.

All the dummies in the movies don't get thrown over cliffs.

Hollywood is made up of "Yes" men and acqui-yes woman.

A Hollywood wedding is, as a rule, a retake.

I saw a Danish sex film--they spoke English, but the sex was dubbed in.

A motion picture is art simplified, purified, and hog-tied.

A movie star is a guy with a swimming pool and a worried look.

A movie theater is where people talk behind your back.

Hollywood shoots too much film and not enough actors.

Old films are sold as junk. Some of them started that way.

I saw an adult film so sexy, cops were standing in line to raid it.

An artistic movie is an accident that happened in a camera.

Movies are stories written by the half-educated for the half-witted.

In Hollywood you ask a girl's husband for her hand in marriage.

When two movie stars get married, their lawyers live happily ever after.

Millionaire movie directors can thank their lucky stars.

In Hollywood, you are a genius until you lose your job.

Most of today's movies aren't worth stacking the dishes for.

A movie actor is a man whose head is too big for his toupee.

I saw a refreshing movie last night--I felt like a new man when I woke up.

Motion pictures have ruined a lot more evenings than morals.

Some stars are heavenly bodies, but most stars have them.

You seldom realize how good the book is until after you see the movie.

All's well that ends well, except in the movies.

When a starlet is going places, it's probably with the producer.

A movie star is a woman who has a weakness for wedding cake.

A movie star's background is never as important as her foreground.

A movie actress lives happily and gets married forever after.

One movie was so bad it curdled the butter on my popcorn.

My brother has a leading part in the theater--he's a head usher.

I went to a drive-in movie and somebody stole my car.

One adult film was so disgusting I walked out the third time I saw it.

The movie was so bad, people were standing in line to get out.

All you need to be a star in films today are the bare necessities.

Once actresses used to play parts--now they reveal them.

The films we slept through in theaters now keep us awake on TV.

Movies today are not only bigger than life, they're dirtier than life.

They shot the film in a hurry--previewed it, and then shot the director.

If you want to be alone, drop in to see my latest picture.

The only star most adult films will ever get will be on the sheriff's vest.

One good thing about Hollywood--you can starve without an overcoat.

Music

Musicians who play by ear should remember we listen the same way.

They were a three-piece band. They only knew three pieces.

The piano player wasn't part of the regular band, but he owned the car.

If he's a conductor I want a transfer.

I'm buying a piano. I don't play, but I love to whistle.

Our orchestra is from the grill room of the Automat.

To write a hit song take an old composition and decompose it.

A folk singer is one who warbles through his nose by ear.

Fortunately popular songs are not popular for very long.

The Star Spangled Banner is a song without words.

A coloratura is a singer who carries a tune too far.

The only instrument I play is second fiddle at home.

This is Chopin's Third Movement--for not paying his rent.

Then came Beethoven's Fourth. A boy, as I recall it.

A little softer, please. Softer, I said. I can still hear you.

You don't have to be tone deaf to write a popular song, but it helps.

People who have a lot to say shouldn't go to a concert to say it.

A drum is the one toy you never give a child more than once.

There are more bad musicians than there is bad music.

No one should be allowed to play a saxophone until he knows how.

Now music by (name) and his all-girl chasing orchestra.

Now a solo by Joan and her magic comb and tissue paper.

Play on the black notes--the white part is the paper.

Are you playing my music as is? Try it is as this time.

Very good, but I didn't know you couldn't play the piano.

He thinks a bar's rest means the bartender's night off.

Pianist: one who practices for hours on end.

I know he's a musician--but what does he do for a living?

If you can't face the music, you'll never get to lead the band.

A piano is harmless as long as people leave it alone.

One of the most difficult instruments to play well is second fiddle.

Two heads are better than one, but only if you're a drum.

Teen-agers love good music, no matter how bad it is.

I've played the piano for years--on and off. I've got a slippery stool.

What kind of a dirty piano is this? Half the keys are black.

What are you doing? Playing with your knuckles?

Our band has many accomplishments, but music isn't one of them.

This is the only orchestra in the world where the drums carry the melody.

The old songs are best, because no one sings them any more.

Song hits are notable for what they miss.

What I enjoy most about a harp is that its strings break.

Never blow your own horn--unless you're in an orchestra.

An upright piano can be a downright nuisance.

The greatest martial music ever written is the wedding march.

Good musicians execute their music--bad ones murder it.

Some performers take pains with their music, others give them.

The life of a popular song is brief, but not too brief.

Music isn't a luxury. It's a habit--like smoking or spitting.

A quartet is four people who think the other three can't sing.

Some people can carry a tune, but they seem to stagger under the load.

Some women are music lovers--others can love without it.

I've got music in my veins--I just wish I had blood.

I can play the Minute Waltz in forty-five seconds.

Today I'm going to play as I never played before--in tune.

A violinist is a man who is always up to his chin in music.

Many a child pretends to sleep to make its father stop singing.

Xylophonists must be superstitious--they go around knocking on wood.

What this country needs is more short-haired music.

Our band consists of six pieces: one piano player and five sheets of music.

Some piano players should be moving them instead.

I compose music in bed. It's called "sheet music."

He plays the violin exactly like Heifetz. Under his chin.

Why is it that you look so sharp and play so flat?

He tied his hands so he could play the piano by ear.

Music isn't always as bad as it sounds.

She is so knock-kneed, she has to play the cello sidesaddle.

Our fiddle player has the only Stradivarius made in Japan.

I worked hard all week on an arrangement--then my wife stayed home.

There should be music in every house--except the one next door.

I must have lots of music in me, as none of it ever came out.

A musical ignoramus is one who doesn't know his brass from his oboe.

The men in the band not only can't read music, they can't read lyrics.

An opera house is a jukebox with a chandelier.

And now, for your pleasure, we have a small musical aggravation.

Singing in the bathtub is called a "soap opera."

Our vocalist has pear-shaped tones, and a figure to match.

She couldn't be on key if she sat on a Yale lock.

She made her debris in grand opera.

Musical notations are a collection of extensive hints.

When I listen to chamber music I keep hoping it will turn into a tune.

If it isn't worth saying, it'll be made into a popular song.

A cool musician is one who flats his fifth.

It's an ill wind that blows a saxophone.

I play piano by ear, but I'm quite deft.

A trombone looks better in my derby than I do.

A musician can help a poor singer with his playing--by drowning him out.

All a musician does for a living is play around.

Banjo players get $50 an hour. That's pretty easy picking.

Music hath charms to soothe a savage beast--but I'd try a rifle first.

Anyone who can fold a road map can play an accordion.

An organ grinder is a man who walks around with a chimp on his shoulder.

An impresario is a promoter with an opera cape.

One soprano has to take any note above A with her eyebrows.

The viola is an instrument played by a disappointed second violinist.

The guitar is a hillbilly harp.

Transistor radios wear out popular songs faster than they do batteries.

Some song writers can't carry a tune, but they lift a lot of them.

Two things kill a popular song: playing it and singing it.

No Laughs

I told that joke last night and three empty seats got up and walked out.

This microphone is A.C. and my voice is D.C.

You'll notice that I'm doing a very fast show.

That's the last joke I buy from the men's room attendant.

You may as well laugh now, this act doesn't get any funnier.

This is no laughing matter--and you seem to share that opinion.

How can so many people sleep with all these lights on?

Look at watch. Is this place open?

Are you sure my time isn't up?

That's funny when you think of it--but, let's not think of it.

Well, it's not really funny--but it shows that I'm friendly.

Don't blame my writers; they've been dead for thirty years.

There's only one thing I can do now--ask for a vote of confidence.

Did you ever get the feeling that you were in the wrong business?

Forgive me--I'm breaking in a new set of teeth.

How about that? I had my nose fixed and now my mouth won't work.

It's getting tense in here, isn't it?

This is the kind of act where there's nothing doing every minute.

That doesn't get much of a laugh, but it does kill time.

You folks actually planned on a quiet evening like this, didn't you?

Could you make that smile a little louder?

I've got a speech impediment. I just can't seem to say anything funny.

That was your last chance to laugh. I know the rest of the material.

There's nothing like new material; I wish I had some.

That was a throw-away gag; I should have before this show.

Don't blame me, I'm in here pitching--you're not catching.

Services for that gag will be held at 10:00 a.m. tomorrow.

Hurry up and laugh; the spotlight is fading my new suit.

Eleven more lines like that and I'll have an even dozen.

That's enough of the good stuff, now I'll do something different.

I'm trying to make you laugh, and you're trying to make me cry.

Excuse me while I check one of my tongues.

I seem to have gotten that joke versa vice.

That didn't stop the show, but it sure slowed it down.

I wish you'd laugh faster. I could stay out here longer.

I've still got my typewriter in my mouth.

Now that I've got you hysterical.

I'll keep telling you these jokes and you pick out the ones you like.

I had my tongue in my typewriter when I told that joke.

I just put that in. We needed a laugh. We still need one.

Oh, I could keep you going like this for hours.

Thank you, you've been a grand bunch of seats.

We hear stories--I wish we heard one now.

I know I had an audience when I came in here.

I may not have talent--but I do have guts.

Don't laugh now, lady. Either laugh when the rest do or go home.

Did you hear that splash? Well, it wasn't the weather.

Don't force anything.

I'll wait for that. Maybe someone likes it well-done.

I must have my plate in backwards.

Pardon me for talking so fast, but I don't like this material either.

Oh, I could keep you quiet like this for hours.

What ever made me get into show business?

Anyone know the number of Dial-A-Prayer?

After repeating gag. That was an egg with a double yolk.

This show could become the last of a series of one.

It's wonderful to be able to lay an egg while standing.

Difficulty in reading. I love this white type on white paper.

If you think that's bad, wait'll you see the rest of the show.

It was because of jokes like that that Burr shot Hamilton.

You only have to listen to this material--I have to say it out loud.

So you're going to pout all evening, right?

Who booked this audience?

Take a good look at me, you'll never see me here again.

I'd like to try a change of pace. By that I mean get some laughs.

Don't stare at me with those bloodshot eyes.

This is a live show. I wish we had an audience to match.

You have no idea how lonely stardom can be.

This could be worse--I could be here in person.

I want to thank you all for coming to my funeral.

Hm-m. I seem to be having trouble with my vowels.

This program is like an old girdle. It falls apart in the stretch.

We had a bet on that one, and I win.

I should have stopped on the other laugh.

There will be a short pause for audience resuscitation.

I will now lower my tie to half mast in honor of that joke.

I know about two people who are enjoying this.

We'll wait three minutes for that last egg to be boiled.

That's what I get for wearing my wife's false teeth.

I don't use a laugh-track--the silence you hear is absolulutely genuine.

Don't laugh please--I have a headache.

This reminds me of Sunday in Philadelphia.

I'm having a wonderful time up here. Won't you join me?

What this show lacks in entertainment, it makes up for in monotony.

You keep acting like this and I won't tell you the funny stuff.

What is this, a staring contest?

I hope my Blue Cross covers something like this.

I'd better butter my throat--this corn is dry.

After this I'm taking a ride in a leaky submarine.

I'd like a little cooperation on your part.

And I thought that was going to go so good, too.

Take your time--it's raining out.

I'll leave that one out of the next show.

I overrated that one.

And now to continue on this serious note.

Here's another joke you might not care for.

Don't laugh--and who didn't?

You people are looking at me as if I invented the income tax.

I could wait for the laugh--but this club closes in four hours.

I wouldn't give this spot to a dry cleaner.

That's the last gag I'll ever buy from a minister.

All you need with that joke is a tombstone.

Is this an audience or an oil painting?

That was told to me by a very unfunny friend.

Well, anyway, that's neither here nor funny.

Nudists

Nudist national anthem: "You're An Old Smoothie."

A nudist is a person who grins and bares it.

I was the nudist camp athlete--I ran 100 yards in nothing.

Nudists suffer from clothes-trophobia.

I grew a long beard so I could go to the village for supplies.

I became a nudist to see life in the raw.

I could never be a nudist. I always spill hot coffee in my lap.

For a nudist, every morning marks the dawn of a nude day.

Nudists go hatless and coatless, with trousers to match.

Some nudists are accused of wrong undoing.

A nudist is someone wrapped up only in himself.

When two nudists fight they're barely talking.

I took my girl to a nudist camp and nothing looked good on her.

I was ostracized because my breath came in short pants.

Even my wife's sewing machine is without a stitch.

I always try to be as careful as a nudist crossing a barbed wire fence.

To join our nudist colony, just leave your name and dress.

Where does a nudist put his keys after he locks his car?

A nudist never has to hold out his hand to see if it's raining.

Some nudists won't even ask for dressing on their salads.

Nudism is a back to form movement.

I was expelled from a nudist camp--they found a coat on my tongue.

A nudist is a person who is barely proper.

In a nudist camp you learn that all men are not created equal.

Nudism is life in the raw.

I'd like to be a guide in a nudist camp--I like to show people all over.

Most nudists have acquired nothing since birth but nerve.

Nakedness is good for the eyes. Have you ever seen a blind nudist?

A nudist is a person who wears a one-button suit.

A nudist colony is where people are all together in the altogether.

I was the most handicapped man in the camp. I'm near-sighted.

A nudist is a person who runs around in his silhouette.

I became a nudist because I'm interested in the naked facts of life.

My girl friend is a fine specimen of the nuder gender.

Nudists must be right--they have millions of followers--mosquitos.

Nudists are people who peel first and get sunburned aftrwards.

At the nudist camp I had a room with a sudden exposure.

A bleached blonde has a real problem in a nudist camp.

The nudist's theme song is "Stares and Strips Forever."

I was attracted to one camp because of its name: "Bearskin Lodge."

Nudism is only a skin game.

Nudists on horses always ride bare back.

Cushions are the only underthings nudists go for.

The only thing a girl nudist wears are beads--of perspiration.

To become a nudist I had to give up my favorite game--strip poker.

I brought my wife with me so we could air our differences.

I was expelled from one nudist camp for putting on airs.

Nudists are never in the nude for work.

Even in the nudist camp my wife told me what not to wear.

The police arrested one nudist but they couldn't pin a thing on him.

Ever since one lawyer joined our nudist colony he hasn't had a suit.

The first time I drove into camp I even had to strip my gears.

My nudist girl friend and I split up--we were seeing too much of each other.

A nudist is a girl who doesn't wear a bra--with slacks to match.

A nudist camp is a kind of do-it-yourself burlesque show.

One nudist colony calls itself a "de-nude ranch."

The apparel off proclaims the woman.

The trouble with a nudist camp is that it leaves nothing to the imagination.

In a nudist colony, a person's face doesn't matter.

Another man you don't catch with his pants down is a nudist.

Two can live as cheaply as one, but only if both are nudists on a diet.

Clothes make the man, except in a nudist colony.

I became a nudist so that my wife can't tell me what to wear.

Don't criticize nudists--remember they were born that way.

Old Age

Old age is an incurable disease.

You're getting old when all girls look alike to you.

My wife has antique jewelry. She got it when it was new.

You're getting old when you're more interested in pension than passion.

My wife is very mature--in fact, she's past that.

You're getting old if you consider simplicity an unpowdered nose.

Statistics say women live longer than men. Paint is a good preservative.

Don't speak ill of the aged--you may grow old yourself.

It's terrible to grow old alone. My wife hasn't had a birthday in six years.

I'm not the man I used to be--now my age is really showing.

My wife says she's just turned 30--it was a U-turn.

At my age it's not so hard to avoid temptation as it is to find it.

My youth has changed from the present tense to pre-tense.

You're getting on when your kids become depressingly middle aged.

There's spring in the air, but not in me.

Sunday night is the weak end of my weekend.

I still pick up a woman's hanky, but I no longer pick up the woman.

I consider the 10 o'clock television program the Late, Late Show.

My wife won't live to fifty. Not at the rate she's been overstaying at forty.

Nowadays my feet hurt even before I get out of bed.

It's getting so that just making a long-distance call tires me out.

The hardest things for me to raise in my garden are my knees.

There were enough candles on my birthday cake to give everyone a tan.

I must be getting old--all my dreams about girls are re-runs.

It's not how old you are, but how you are old.

In youth we run into difficulties, in old age difficulties run into us.

At sixty-five you begin to regret the sins you did not commit.

I'm not as young as I used to be--and I never was.

I follow my daily dozen by several days of daily doesn't.

You're getting old when you walk around a puddle instead of through it.

I find it hard to make ends meet--ends like my fingers and toes.

After a night on the town, I feel my oats--and my corns.

I feel like the day after the night before--and I haven't been anywhere.

Like a cigarette lighter--my spirit is willing, but the flash is weak.

No one tries the patience of his relatives as much as a rich old man.

The trouble with old age is that there's not much of a future in it.

Geriatrics tries to solve the age-old problem of old age.

Youth is the happiest time of all, but only age knows it.

Growing old has one advantage: you'll never have to do it over again.

Now that I finally know my way around, I don't feel like going.

I feel like a million--every year of it.

Lately I get tired just wrestling with temptation.

I'm chock-full of pep--for an hour or two a day.

Before some women age a lot, they age a lot of men.

The way to live to be 100 is to reach 99, and then live very carefully.

The trouble with old age is it comes when we're too old to enjoy it.

In old age you begin to smile at things you used to laugh at.

A man is as young as he feels, a woman is as old as she looks.

To this day, I still chase women--but only if it's downhill.

My forehead is getting higher and my energy is getting lower.

My wife says I'm a WOW--that's a Worn-Out-Wolf.

I'm more interested in a "Yes" from my banker than from a blonde.

I've begun to have thoughts about women instead of feelings.

Lately I'm done before the day is.

Unfortunately we keep on growing older long after we are old enough.

Geriatrics helps you to live longer without growing older.

At 60, you realize that grandfather wasn't so old when he died at 80.

Calling a man a "sexagenarian" sounds like flattery.

A man is never too old to learn, but he is sometimes too young.

Growing old isn't so bad, especially if you consider the alternative.

A woman seldom gets old enough to admit she is that old.

To make a success of old age, you've got to start when you're young.

No matter how old you are, you're younger than you'll ever be.

An old man is a man who is ten years older than you are.

In youth we pursue physical culture--in age, fiscal fitness.

You are never too old to learn, but that's what makes you old.

To the old, no people are old.

Nowadays when I turn out the lights, it's for economy--not for romance.

I not only have rheumatism--I have reminiscences.

My head keeps making dates that my body can't keep.

My wife powders and I puff.

Everytime I think "Why not?" I end up figuring "Why bother?"

A man is as old as his arteries, a woman is as young as her art.

Now when a girl flirts with me in the movies--she's after my popcorn.

I don't have to learn history--I remember it.

My mother-in-law's Social Security number is 2.

On my last birthday the candles cost more than the cake.

I tried to count the candles on my birthday cake, but the heat drove me back.

I'd retire rich if I could sell my experience for what it cost me.

I'm so old that I get winded playing chess.

Spring may be in the air, but it's not in me.

I'm buying a pair of moccasins so I won't have to lace my shoes.

In youth, everything matters too much--in old age, nothing matters much.

At last she admitted she was forty--but she won't say when.

You're getting old if you creak when you walk and squeak when you talk.

Have you noticed how the younger generation keeps getting younger?

If you want to live a long time, become a centenarian.

These days I have an off day after my day off.

Lately I'm done before the day is.

Now when I proposition a girl, I hope she says "No."

At 65 you putter around the garden and mutter around the house.

My wife has the nerve to say she's 39, but that's not the half of it.

He was named after General Sherman--not long after him either.

My wife hides her age better than a torn-up birth certificate.

She is so old she doesn't celebrate her birthday--she just knocks wood.

He says he's 53--and there are very few people alive to contradict him.

A man is as old as the women he feels.

Her age is her own business, and she's been in business a long time.

Old Maids

With some girls rice means a wedding--With an old maid, it means pudding.

An old maid is a girl who lives alone and looks it.

An old maid is a woman who has been good for nothing.

The only dates some women get are on their tombstones.

A maiden aunt is a girl who never had sense enough to say "Uncle."

An old maid is a girl who never learned how to tie a beau.

An old maid is an unemployed back seat driver.

An old maid is a girl of 24 where she should be 36.

An old maid is an unlusted number.

Old maid's prayer: Now I lay me down to sleep--darn it!

An old maid is a woman in the prim of life.

The old maid sighed when she died, "Who said you can't take it with you?"

An old maid is a girl with a faulty ignition.

Some girls are overlooked after they have been looked over.

I know an old maid whose hope chest is growing moss on the north side.

An old maid is a woman who has been missed too long.

A myth is a woman who hasn't got a husband.

An old maid knows all the answers, but is never asked the question.

Show me an old maid, and I'll show you a vintage virgin.

An old maid remains single out of choice--but not always her choice.

An old maid in baby dolls is like a malted milk in a champagne bottle.

Show me an old maid, and I'll show you an uncalled for package.

Old maids are girls who talk of boy-gone days.

An old maid is a girl whose father never owned a shotgun.

It isn't dying an old maid that worries a woman, it's living that way.

Remember ladies, it's never too late--instead of giving up--give in.

Women will not stay single, and they won't stay married either.

Old maids make mistakes, but not in front of a clergyman or judge.

An old maid does not always miss as much as others think she does.

Spinsterhood is sometimes a misfortune, but more often an achievement.

An old maid is a woman who regrets that she was so sensible.

Old maids are born, not made.

An old maid is a woman of un-altar-able views.

All an old maid's romances have been carried off without a hitch.

Show me an old maid, and I'll show you a woman with a wait problem.

Old-timers

An old timer can remember when...a bureau was a piece of furniture.

the most popular family on the block was the one with the TV set.

virtue was not a vice.

you didn't need a guide to find the prescription counter in a drug store.

a garage housed a car and not a boat.

children learned to count up from 1 to 10, not down from 10 to1.

an allergy was something you scratched.

there were no deductions in your pay until you got home.

horsepower was something to do with a horse.

a summer vacation was one day at the countyfair.

power steering consisted of a buggy whip

a shoemaker stuck to his last, and a wife stuck to her first.

a kid who got a licking at school got another at home.

callers rang the door-bell instead of blowing their horn.

the fall-out problem was something kept under your hat.

folks sat down to dinner they counted their blessings instead of calories.

guided missiles were rolling pins and frying pans.

women had no figures to speak of.

the only skin-diver was a mosquito.

a baby-sitter was called a mother.

movies and breakfast cereals were silent.

marriage problems were solved--not dissolved.

no lipsticks were kissproof and most girls were.

people were more intelligent than machines.

typing a love letter was an insult.

people who wore blue jeans worked.

the day was done before you were.

the medicine man came to town on a wagon instead of on television.

dirty words in books were dots and dashes.

a child had more brothers and sisters than fathers.

a car didn't wear out before it was paid for.

a housewife put food into cans instead of taking it out.

a woman didn't have to be old to be middle-aged.

you couldn't eat a dollar's worth at a cafeteria.

being a parent required more patience than money.

dancing was done with the feet.

kids were juvenile delinquents but didn't know it.

any man who washed dishes worked in a restaurant.

the woman you left behind stayed there.

he could remember.

you could go barefoot without going to bed.

a man could kiss a girl and taste nothing but the girl

kids received their counselling in a woodshed.

marriages produced triangles on the clothesline, not in the courtroom.

baths were taken once a week and religion every day.

a woman wore the same face she got up with in the morning all day.

radio activity consisted mostly of static.

a woman would stay home when she had nothing to wear.

a service charge included service.

a woman who had never been kissed would admit it.

when Senior Citizens were known as Old-Timers.

people criticized the government's extravagance for giving away free seeds.

children who misbehaved to get attention got it.

rockets were part of the fun on July Fourth.

you could make the merchandise outlast the payments.

a day's work took only a day.

the only red menace was long winter underwear.

you paddled your own canoe because there were no outboards.

five dollars worth of groceries filled two bags.

you could promise your kid the moon.

the hero only kissed the heroine in the end.

you weren't judged a good driver just because you hadn't killed anyone.

the telephone was a convenience.

you could distinguish betwewen a bathing beach and a nudist camp.

a job was the first thing you went steady with.

there were other hand-me-downs for the kids besides money.

things in ten-cent stores were ten cents.

women dressed on the beaches as they now do in markets.

wives rocked the cradle instead of the boat.

a girl didn't demand white sidewalls on spinning wheels.

it paid to make a lot of money.

the sky was the limit.

unmentionables were also un-seeables.

girls walked backward in a high wind.

you didn't have to buy what you couldn't afford.

a woman looked the same after washing her face.

a baseball game was called on account of darkness.

Opinions

A radical is anyone whose opinions differ radically from mine.

My wife asks my opinion after making up her own mind.

Whatever your opinion is of me--I don't deserve it.

My wife catches an opinion like she catches a head cold.

Popular opinion is usually based on prejudice and ignorance.

Some people fall for everything and stand for nothing.

It's easy to spot a well-informed man--his views coincide with yours.

Liberty of opinion is often just laziness of mind.

My wife has concrete opinions--thoroughly mixed and permanently set.

"Positive" means mistaken at the top of one's voice.

An obstinate man doesn't hold opinions, they hold him.

Public opinion is what people think other people are thinking.

Brains were made to think with--but money forms most of the opinions.

For the truth about yourself listen to your enemies.

The weakness of public opinion is that so many express it privately.

If your stomach is out of order, your opinion is likely to be too.

My wife has her own opinions, but she wears whatever is in style.

A beautiful girl can get almost anything--except your point of view.

A fool and his opinions are soon parted.

Every question has two sides, unless your wife holds one of them.

A stranger's word is opinion, yours is truth, your wife's is law.

Some people base their opinions on fact, others base them on prejudice.

A slap in the face is the shortest distance between two opinions.

If you never change your opinions you'll never correct your mistakes.

How do I know what my opinion is until I hear what I say?

To find out a girl's opinion of you, marry her.

When my wife wants my opinion--she gives it to me.

My wife is wonderful--that's not just my opinion--it's hers too.

When expressing your opinion always give credit to the source.

Many people are unprejudiced--by the facts.

If you want my opinion--you've got excellent taste.

Opportunists

Some people always go through a revolving door on someone else's push.

Opportunities lie on every hand, and so do opportunists.

He's like French bread--not much dough, but lots of crust.

An opportunist's oily tongue goes with his slick mind.

He's the kind of man who picks up your chick instead of the check.

Merv Griffin, Georgie Jessel and Henny share a chuckle

An opportunist never forgets a favor--if he did it.

I never do anyone harm--unless I can do myself good.

When an opportunist lays his cards on the table--count them!

The only time to deal with him is when he isn't himself.

I started as an unwanted child, but now I'm wanted in seven states.

An opportunist is a man who tries to substitute brass for brains.

He has the human touch--it conceals an itching palm.

I never go back on a friend as long as I can use him to advantage.

This guy is polished--in a slippery sort of way.

Did you ever see a guy pick up a girl on another fellow's whistle?

An opportunist can hand out baloney disguised as food for thought.

He wouldn't hesitate to drive up to the gate of heaven and honk.

An opportunist can change sides faster than a windshield wiper.

He would flirt with a woman standing in a bus while he's sitting.

The best time to deal with an opportunist is when he isn't himself.

Opportunity knocks only once, but not opportunists.

An opportunist remembers what he gives and forgets what he gets.

An opportunist always tries to land on someone else's feet.

You can always depend on an opportunist--to depend on you.

An opportunist is a person who isn't himself on Sundays.

An opportunist will always help you get what's coming to him.

I'm looking for a rich girl who's too proud to have her husband work.

He's getting a stoop from living up to his ideals.

An opportunist carves his career by first-class chiseling.

Give an opportunist a free hand and he'll stick it right in your pocket.

An opportunist is always around--when he needs you.

An opportunist is always ready to back his hot tips with your cash.

An opportunist talks on principles and acts on interest.

An opportunist can talk in stereo--out of both sides of his mouth.

An opportunist has as much conscience as a fox in a chicken farm.

An opportunist stands for anything he thinks you'll fall for.

An opportunist has a lot of grit. He can take it--no matter who owns it.

Taking an opportunist's conscience out is a minor operation.

An opportunist always does his best--including his best friends.

The only use some people have for a friend is to use him.

An opportunist is always close to you until you try to touch him.

Opportunity

Why are opportunities always bigger going than coming?

Some people wait for opportunity to break the door down and come in.

A grapefruit is a lime that took advantage of its opportunities.

It's hard to say if opportunity is at the door or just another salesman.

Opportunity is a favorable occasion for grasping a disappointment.

Opportunity knocks, but last night a knock spoiled my opportunity.

Opportunity differs from neighbors--it only knocks once.

Opportunity is hard to find because it is usually disguised as hard work.

The sign on the door of opportunity reads "Push."

If life hands you a lemon, make lemonade.

Golden opportunities are not found in the realm of slumber.

When I have words with my wife I don't get the opportunity to use them.

Opportunity knocks; to a woman it comes with a ring.

When opportunity knocked I complained about the noise.

If you find yourself in hot water--take a bath.

If the door to opportunity does not open to polite knocks--kick it in.

To get ahead don't wait for opportunity to knock before opening the door.

Opportunity taps lightly, but temptation seems to pound away.

A lot of people miss opportunity because it is dressed in work clothes.

Opportunity must exist in a land where a horse can make a million bucks.

Opportunity is something that goes without saying.

Man's importunity is woman's opportunity.

One man's outing is another man's inning.

Circumstances alter cases, especially reduced circumstances.

This is a land of opportunity, explaining why husbands get into trouble.

Opportunities are never lost; if you don't grasp them, another will.

Things don't turn up in this world until someone turns them up.

Opportunity would have to advertise to get some people's attention.

Opportunities are like eggs; they come one at a time.

Opportunity doesn't knock for people who don't give a rap.

Opportunity always seems to be where I was, never where I am.

In life you make more opportunities than you find.

There are two doors to opportunity: push and pull.

Optimism

An optimist...believes a fly is looking for a way to get out.

recalls that life is short when he receives a life sentence.

lights a match before asking for a cigarette.

goes downstairs with a fishing pole when his basement is flooded.

looks forward to enjoying the scenery on a detour.

is a woman who mistakes a bulge for a curve.

is a man who wolf-whistles through false teeth.

is a hope addict.

is a happy-condriac.

keeps the motor running while waiting for his wife.

has more fun guessing wrong than a pessimist can have guessing right.

always talks about what a fool he used to be.

wipes his eye-glasses before starting to eat grapefruit.

is a person who marries a pessimist.

is a bridegroom who thinks that he has no bad habits.

expects the IRS to believe that he is the head of the house.

doesn't care what happens--as long as it doesn't happen to him.

believes his wife when she threatens to go home to mother.

is the kind of man who marries his sister's best friend.

is a bigamist.

thinks his wife has given up when she has given in.

is a bridegroom

is a single man contemplating marriage.

asks his wife to help him with the dishes.

sends a package by parcel post and marks it "rush."

is convinced he will never again do anything stupid.

is happy because he isn't one of his many creditors.

is a man who doesn't know what's coming to him.

is a man who has never had much experience.

believes everything he reads on the jacket of a new book.

is an anti-skeptic.

thinks that love is a game of chance.

is a man who looks forward to marriage.

is a man who is happy to feel rosy.

goes on a fishing trip carrying a camera and a frying pan.

is the fellow who first called it "free love."

drops a quarter in the collection plate and expects a five dollar sermon.

gets treed by a lion but enjoys the scenery.

is a girl who goes into Tiffany's with a shopping cart.

can always see the bright side of other people" troubles.

opens a bottle of liquor at a New Year's Eve party and saves the cork.

is anybody who expects change.

digs dandelions out of his lawn.

makes a motel reservation before a blind date.

is a man who hasn't gotten around to reading the morning papers.

plans what to do with the money he'll have left over after taxes.

thinks the dry cleaners are shrinking the waistband of his trousers.

still looks forward to the day when two can live as cheaply as one.

feels kindly toward everyone because he hasn't been cheated yet.

always seems to have the right feelings for the wrong reasons.

goes grocery shopping with $10 in his pocket.

will spend his last dollar to buy a new wallet.

maintains that everything is right when it is wrong.

will leave his door unlocked and hope his wife will walk out on him.

gets married at 85 and then buys a house near a school.

sits in the tenth row and winks at a chorus girl.

sends his income tax return in an unstamped envelope.

thinks marriage will end his trouble.

lets his creditors do the worrying.

believes that matrimony will be cheaper than the courtship.

goes to a summer resort that a friend recommended.

is a man who has never had much experience.

gets married on Independence Day.

waits for his ship to come in when he hasn't sent one out.

figures that by the time his shoes wear out, he'll be back on his feet.

makes the best of it when he gets the worst of it.

goes to the courthouse to find out when his marriage license expires.

thinks that a word to the wife is sufficient.

looks for the pork in a can of pork and beans.

counts his change while running for a bus.

Optimism is the noble temptation to see too much in everything.

Optimism is the belief that all peas are sweetpeas.

If a man doesn't believe the world is getting better, he isn't.

The place where optimism flourishes most is the lunatic asylum.

Remember the teakettle--when it's up to its neck in hot water, it sings.

Optimism helps in achieving success, or in getting along without it.

I used to think I was in a rut, but now I've decided I'm just in orbit.

At bridge, an optimist calls a spade: two spades.

Overweight

A man always loses weight when his wife is dieting.

Worry makes people thin, except when they worry about being fat.

My wife is too thin to enjoy eating, and I'm too fat to enjoy walking.

My wife is always trying to take off weight, put it on, or rearrange it.

Just once I'd like to be weighed and found wanting.

When I take a shower, my feet don't get wet.

My wife has to wear two girdles, one upper and one lower.

Imagine being able to answer the front door without leaving the kitchen.

It takes two dimes to weigh my wife.

I'm one man who carries a lot of weight--in my stomach.

No matter where my wife sits at home, I'm always near her.

The one thing bigger than my stomach is my appetite.

She had the mumps for two weeks before we noticed it.

The only thing about me that's getting thinner is my hair.

My wife has to put on a girdle to get into a bathrobe.

I have to take two trips to put my arms around her.

I can eat anything and never gain a pound--over 250.

I love intimate little dinners for two. Unfortunately, I eat them alone.

I've been going to some length to change my width.

The trouble with the bulk of women is where it shows.

My idea of exercise is to move food from my plate to my palate.

With me, a moment on the lips is a lifetime on the hips.

Two more pounds and I'm going to have to wear license plates.

To go through a revolving door, I have to take two trips.

I'm thinking of buying a violin so I'll have a place to rest my chin.

When I go to have my picture taken they charge me group rates.

If you're stout, you look very silly in a dress that's frilly.

My idea of interior decoration is an enormous meal.

My fondest wish is to be weighed and found wanting.

I live by dinner time instead of inner time.

I could help myself more by helping myself to less.

I must be eating army food. Everything I eat goes to the front.

My wife's bathing suits let her swim, but not slink.

My doctor put me on a seven-day diet, but I ate the whole thing at one meal.

My wife stretches the truth when she wears those tight ski pants.

I'll eat anything that won't bite first.

My wife's like a foreign car--all her weight's in the rear.

I didn't think of myself as fat until the police used me as a roadblock.

My wife has a shape the world should be in.

My girl friend is so fat, she outnumbers herself.

I once boarded a boat and it became a submarine.

Every time I stand up my heels flatten out.

I had to sign up for group insurance all by myself.

In my high school graduation picture I was the front row.

I'm unable to contain myself.

Anything you say about me has to take in a lot of territory.

I've got stomach trouble. There's too much of it.

I want on a fourteen-day diet, but all I lost was two weeks.

The only well-rounded thing about my wife is her figure.

My wife has a figure like a pillow.

She's a real Oomph girl--when she sits on a couch, it goes oomph.

I'm really watching my weight--watching it go up.

My wife's trouble is she's not sylph-conscious.

When my wife gets into an elevator it had better be going down.

The trouble is that my stomach has no memory.

My wife is very prominent in society circles, and around the hips.

She makes up a crowd all by herself.

One time four girls threw their arms about me. It took that many.

Don't think of me as a sight--think of me as a panorama.

It's not easy to support all this weight out of water.

All I have to do is sit on a bar stool to have a hangover.

Girls, the more snacks--the tighter the slacks.

If my wife was worth her weight in gold we'd be very rich.

Either my wife goes on a diet, or we will have to let out the living room.

I used to be spic and span, now I'm more span than spic.

When my wife and I walked down the aisle, we had to walk single file.

You realize that if I fall down I rock myself to sleep trying to get up.

Minutes at the table don't put on weight--it's the seconds.

When it comes to food, I'm all will and a yard wide.

When my wife wears slacks she reveals stern facts.

The reason I'm unhappy is because I only have one mouth.

With this stomach, you know I'd never stoop to anything low.

I have an optimistic stomach and a pessimistic digestion.

Lately my wife's been wearing a stretch bathrobe.

My wife is the only person I know who has an unlisted dress size.

They put me on the critical list at Weight Watchers.

When I get on a scale I get two fortunes.

The only thing they had in my size in the store was the dressing room.

My wife doesn't mind being fat--she's a model for slip covers.

When my wife takes off her girdle her feet disappear.

When she cries her tears run up.

I've tried many diets, but let's face it--I'm a poor loser.

My wife is enlarging not only her sphere, but her circumference.

The doctor says I could help myself more by helping myself to less.

The cheese cake I like so much is fast turning into pound cake.

Face it--I grew up when meat was cheap.

I've given up dancing. I can't find a concave woman for a partner.

When I have my shoes shined, I have to take the bootblack's word for it.

I was a food taster, but I quit. I didn't get enough time off for lunch.

My wife can sit around a table all by herself.

Everybody loves a fat man until he sits down next to them in a bus.

When a fat woman steps on a scale, she always has a sinking feeling.

Nowadays a girl is never "fat." She's just overemphasized.

The way I eat it's no wonder I get thick to my stomach.

My wife has a big heart, and a stomach to match.

A stout person lives shorter, but eats longer.

The more you overeat, the harder it is to get close to the table.

Unfortunately what melts in your mouth, bulges lower down.

The fastest way to reduce is to eat nothing and then walk it off.

Only one kind of exercise helps you reduce--the exercise of will power.

Destiny shapes our ends, but a reducing diet also helps.

I found a sure way to reduce--never eat when your wife is talking.

I have to keep fit as a fiddle or look like a bass viol.

Reducing slogan: "A word to the wide is sufficient."

She was fat in places where most girls don't have places.

For her slips, the laundry charges her for sheets.

I've seen chain smokers but this guy is a chain eater.

This guy eats more for breakfast than I weigh.

Try a garlic diet--you don't lose weight--just friends.

One million American women are overweight. These are round figures.

I'm living way beyond my seams.

Driving over street car tracks his double chins applaud.

Someone ought to invent lo-cal hair tonic for fatheads.

Rockefeller diet: for six months you eat nothing but money.

My wife not only kept her girlish figure--she doubled it.

Candy can put an end to a thin girl.

The perfect diet: eat all you want--chew--but don't swallow.

You develop "sandwich spread" from eating between meals.

Eat like a horse and you'll soon begin to look like onw.

She used to be stout--but that's all behind her now.

Parents

A parent believes the words "progeny" and "prodigy" are interchangeable.

Parents are one of the hardships of a child's life.

Mother is a baby's bosom friend.

At one time it took more patience than money to be a good parent.

A mother is a woman whose life is disorganized around her children.

A doting parent is never a don'ting parent.

The only thing found at a mother's knees these days is her skirt.

Modern parents should be seen but never hard.

A smart mother knows a pounce of prevention is worth a pound of cure.

Rich parents usually make poor parents.

Home economics means going home to mother.

Parents should be on spanking terms with their children.

An extravagant girl makes a poor mother--and a bankrupt father.

Children first love their parents, then judge them, then forgive them.

A mother of ten is a woman who has gone stork-mad.

Parents bear infants, bore teen-agers and board newlyweds.

One mother calls the maternity hospital a delivery stable.

A parent is one who thinks he's old enough to know better.

A modern mother is one who worries if her daughter gets in too early.

Parents are such simple things that even a child can operate them.

Every mother knows that her most spoiled child is her husband.

We get our parents when they are too old for us to change their habits.

Today's mother considers the maternity hospital a place of confinement.

The economic law reverses for parents to Demand and Supply.

And one mother calls the maternity ward the heirport.

Some parents only hit their children in self-defense.

The hand that rules the cradle rocks the world.

Parents are what children wear out faster than shoes.

These days a girl is usually as old as her mother looks.

A father is a man who is working his son's way through college.

Maternity is a fine thing--especially in a woman.

Parents are people with problems--not all of them unpleasant.

Mother never saw me before I was born. I wonder how she recognized me?

Parenthood requires infinite experience to perform and none to achieve.

I have a terribly heavy beard. I take after mother.

We're the posterity our parents worried about. Can you blame them?

On the day I was born mother wired everyone--apologies.

Fathers replace the cash in their wallets with photos of their kids.

Mother is the necessity of convention.

Becoming a parent is one way to give yourself heirs.

Parenthood is the most difficult career entrusted to amateurs.

Most fathers have several mouths to feed--and listen to.

Most parents' lives are disorganized around their children.

Many problem children go by the name of "parents."

Most parents begin by giving in, and end by giving up.

There are no illegitimate children--there are only illegitimate parents.

No one is more helpless than a new-born father.

A father is a banker provided by nature.

A parent who really loves his children won't have them.

Mother's yearning capacity was greater than father's earning capacity.

The skin you love to touch. Dad's old pigskin wallet.

We put mother on a pedestal--to keep her away from father.

Today, it's a wise father who knows as much as his own child.

The father is head of the family, and he's the one that gets the headaches.

It's the running expenses that keep father out of breath.

Pedestrians

Life is what you make it, for the pedestrian it's if he makes it.

A pedestrian is a man with a wife and grown daughters.

A jaywalker is a man on his way to become a statistic.

I'm a pedestrian when my wife beats me to the garage.

A pedestrian is a person walking or lying in the street.

Pessimists

A pessimist...is a man who tells the truth prematurely.

avoids looking at the bright side for fear of getting eyestrain.

is never happy unless he's miserable, and even then he's not pleased.

is a man who really knows what's going on nowadays.

builds slums in the air.

is always good for bad news.

thinks everyone is as nasty as he is and he hates them for it.

is one who, regardless of the present, is disappointed in the future.

is a man with a difficulty for every solution.

is a person who looks at things as they are.

expects nothing on a silver platter except tarnish.

is sure the world is against him--and he is probably right.

feels bad when he feels good for fear he'll feel worse when he feels better.

is a man who thinks all women are bad--an optimist hopes they are.

is a man who has been intimately acquainted with an optimist.

is a person to borrow money from--he never expects to be repaid.

is a man who says things are going to get worse.

is a person who believes life isn't worth leaving.

makes difficulties of his opportunities.

is a man who financed an optimist.

is afraid women's necklines will go higher this year.

is a cured optimist.

keeps an optimist from becoming satisfied with himself.

is a person who, when he has the choice of two evils, takes both.

likes to listen to the patter of little defeats.

is a woman who thinks she can't get her car into the only parking space.

goes through life wearing morose-colored glasses.

always looks both ways before crossing a one-way street.

when smelling flowers, looks around for the funeral.

always expects the worst and makes the most of it when it happens.

is a man who once tried to practice what he preached.

sees only the dark side of the clouds and mopes.

turns out the light to see how dark it is.

lives on the fret of the land.

fills up every time he sees a gas station.

is never content with his lot, even if it is a corner one.

suffers from skeptic poisoning.

never worries about tomorrow--he knows everything is going to turn out bad.

is one whom you give an inch--and he measures it.

is always pulling tomorrow's cloud over today's sunshine.

manages to find a little bad in the best of things.

is afraid to build castles in the sky for fear they'll have mortgages on them.

is so fond of hard luck he runs halfway to meet it.

is afraid to use saccharine for fear of getting artificial diabetes.

only sees the hole in the doughnut.

always sees microbes in the milk of human kindness.

is always building dungeons in the sky.

says: "Good morning, probably."

is a man who wears a belt, as well as suspenders.

is a misfortune teller.

is afraid the optimist is right.

thinks no trouble is as bad as no trouble.

is always trying to put his alarm around you.

is a well-informed optimist.

complains about the noise when opportunity knocks.

is seasick during the entire voyage of life.

is a man who sized himself up and is sore about it.

is seldom as tired of the world as the world is of him.

doesn't expect to be better off next year.

is a man who, even when he gets the best of it, makes the worst of it.

dreads the evil day when things will get better.

Playgirls

My girlfriend runs the gamut of emotions from "Yes" to "Yes."

The perfect secretary types fast and runs slow.

My girl keeps whispering those sweet nothing-doings in my ear.

I'm looking for a thoroughly sexperienced secretary.

Then there was the local girl who everybody made good.

A playgirl has a Sunday-school face with Saturday-night ideas.

A girl's salary goes up as her neckline goes down.

A playgirl is a miss who doesn't miss much.

A playgirl's clothes go to extremes--never to extremities.

At fifteen, her voice started changing--from no to yes.

We went to a night club that had a minimum--and she was wearing it.

A playgirl makes good impressions on the guys--with her lipstick.

One girl could hardly wait until she got married--in fact, she didn't.

Most playgirls lead a date-to-date existence.

A girl is never positionless if she's always inhibitionless.

To a playgirl, pregnancy is a miss-conception.

Some women take to a man only if they can take from him.

When a man gets fresh, a playgirl counts to ten--thousand.

My girl is dangerous around machinery--too many moving parts.

A playgirl can give you a beau-by-beau account of her affairs.

Girls are attracted to the simple things in life, like men.

A playgirl with a sylphlike figure rarely keeps it to her sylph.

She was insulted when I offered her a drink--but she swallowed the insult.

A girl doesn't have to be able to add if she can distract.

A fast playgirl can make five laps during a short party.

Before money, what did women find attractive about men?

A playgirl drinks sloe gin and is made fast.

At school she was voted the girl most likely to concede.

I know one playgirl who has been around more than a merry-go-'round.

Of all creatures hunted for sport, woman is most popular.

A playgirl's sunny disposition may hide a shady past.

A flirt is a girl whose sex appeal springs from her eye cue.

A playgirl believes in affair play.

A girl can collect an expensive wardrobe by starting with a little slip.

A playgirl believes that girls who do right get left.

I'm looking for a girl who has been tried and found wanton.

She's very shy--the kind you have to whistle at twice.

One line can make any girl popular--the line of least resistance.

She may not be able to swim, but she knows every dive in town.

A wise playgirl keeps her hair light and her past dark.

A playgirl knows where bad little girls go--everywhere.

Anyone can get her number--it's on phone booth walls all over town.

She never uses four-letter words, like: can't, won't, stop, or don't.

The only thing a playgirl ever gives is in.

Marriage isn't important to her--she'd mate a man half-way.

A playgirl is a thing of beauty and an expense forever.

Most playgirls like to be taken with a grain of assault.

She has a figure that men give the once-over twice.

We met in a most unusual way--we were introduced.

She failed the typing test but passed the physical.

A playgirl isn't picked out--she's picked up.

Everyone knows her to be a lady in her own wrong.

A playgirl advances pulses by not repulsing advances.

The girl who is easy to get is usually hard to take.

A playgirl never no's what's wrong.

To catch either a man or a fish a girl has to wiggle her bait.

The reason for her popularity can be summed up in one word: "Yes."

She's one for the book--every man's little black book.

Little girls today believe that they should be seen.

She leads a simple, natural life. Her won'ts are few.

I call her "rumor"--she goes from mouth to mouth.

"She is such a nice girl, wasn't she?"

Good girls are born, but playgirls are made.

A playgirl has shapely legs and proclaims the fact from her hose-tops.

Men don't meet a playgirl--she overtakes them.

One playgirl speaks six languages and can't say "No" in any of them.

Once she let her shoulder-strap slip. It was her first undoing.

A playgirl in a car is worth more than five in the phone book.

A playgirl can go out on a lark and end up in a bird's nest.

Many a man is in bad shape because of a playgirl in good shape.

Her boy friend's car stalled, but she didn't.

A girl in your lap is worth two in your mind.

Boys take out a playgirl hoping to take her in.

A playgirl who plays with fire seldom strikes a match.

A playgirl is more to be petted than censured.

A good girl is good but a bad girl is better.

Playgirls have bad grammar--they can't decline.

A miss in the car is worth two in the engine.

She was a well-bred girl--all the men buttered her up.

Playgirls with figures make the best dates.

A playgirl thinks she is sitting pretty when her knees show.

The playgirl who skates on thin ice can end up in hot water.

A playgirl looks for a husband with a fat wallet and a slim stomach.

One playgirl could hardly wait until she got married--in fact, she didn't.

A playgirl is never complex--anyone can grasp her.

A playgirl lets her boy friend's conscience be her guile.

To be popular a playgirl should have tight sweaters and loose morals.

A playgirl is a girl that's game--everybody's.

A playgirl is broad-minded when it comes to a narrow sofa.

She's so kind to animals--she'd do anything for a mink--or even for a fox.

Some girls count on their fingers' playgirls count on their legs.

A playgirl has what it takes, to take what you have.

To most playgirls, men are not a problem, but a solution.

She's a capable girl--capable of anything.

The best years in a playgirl's life are figured in man hours.

She's the proverbial good time that was had by all.

She knows how to raise a hem to get a him.

Poverty

The easiest way to remain poor is to pretend to be rich.

These days there's money in poverty.

Poverty is an allergy that makes a man unusually sensitive to paper money.

My family was so poor we only had one car to our name.

Poverty prevents you from going anywhere--except into debt.

It's no disgrace to be poor, but it is inconvenient.

We try to hide our poverty when we're broke, but brag about it afterwards.

You never realize the blessing of being born poor until you get over it.

To be poor is no disgrace--provided no one knows it.

Poverty is no disgrace, but that's all you can say for it.

Not only did I see poverty in Europe--I brought some back with me.

Poor people think more about money than rich people.

If poverty is a blessing in disguise, the disguise is perfect.

One reason so many poets are poor is that there are so many poor poets.

Poverty is a state of mind caused by a neighbor's new car.

It's easy to tell if a man is poor--he washes his own car.

Poverty isn't a crime; but it counts against you if you commit one.

The only thing I like about rich people is their money.

Remember the poor--it costs nothing.

The rich suffer from lack of appetite, the poor from too much appetite.

It's no disgrace to be poor; it doesn't attract that much attention.

The poor have to work so hard making a living, they haven't time to get rich.

The poor feel want, the rich want feeling.

The poorest hour is just before the pawn.

I must look down and out--last night a hold-up man gave me money.

Cheer up! The less you have the more there is to get.

Blessed are the poor. The more you own, the more things you have to dust.

Once, when we got a loaf of bread, we had to ask how to cut it.

On my birthday, my parents used to give me a picture of a birthday cake.

Burglars used to break into our house and leave things.

My mother bought one meatball and made hamburger for the family.

The one good thing about being poor is that it's inexpensive.

Poor? I could afford to play golf only once a month.

One thing that money can't buy is poverty.

Poor? I could only have one measle at a time.

I was so poor I only bought one shoe at a time.

Poor? I have to wash my Cadillac myself.

We used old newspapers for wall-to-wall carpeting.

Poor? I have to watch TV by candlelight.

My parents were so poor, as a kid I thought knives and forks were jewelry.

Every time I lose a dime it's my last one.

Money talks--mine only stutters.

It is easy for me to meet expenses. I just turn around and there they are.

Poverty is no crime, but it is more certain in its punishment.

Money talks, but poverty just pinches.

The poor have more children, but the rich have more relatives.

It's hard to be poor, but much easier than to be rich.

Poverty is a crime of which the rich are never guilty.

Poverty isn't a crime--it is much worse.

Money talks, and poverty also has a way of telling.

There are two classes of people: the have-nots and the have-yachts.

I'm not ashamed of my poverty; I acquired it honestly.

I've got enough money to last me a lifetime, unless I buy something.

God help the rich--the poor can sleep on park benches.

If everyone were rich, the world would be poorer.

Prosperity

He is so rich...he has bookcases for his bank books.

he just bought another yacht--the old one got wet.

his kids play Little League polo.

he just had his gums capped.

he has a different dentist for each tooth.

he bought a boy for his dog.

he has two secretaries--one for each knee.

he has Swiss money in American banks.

he has an unlisted Zip code number.

he has an unlisted wife.

he has monogrammed money.

he uses money as wallpaper.

he has to pay storage charges for his money.

his butler has his own butler.

he has wall-to-wall carpeting in his garage.

at parties he only serves money.

he has two swimming pools, one for rinsing.

he even had his car wallpapered.

he has two cars, one for driving and one for parking.

even his garbage is gift-wrapped.

his station wagon is bigger than the station.

he has four cars, one for each direction.

he has one suit just for the moths.

his sable coat has a mink lining.

he has wall-to-wall carpeting in his swimming pool.

he has an air-conditioned swimming pool.

even his kitchen has five rooms.

he could retire and live off the interest on his interest.

he has solid-gold silverware.

his office is on an unlisted floor.

he flies his own jet plane in his living room.

the finance company owes him money.

he goes to a drive-in movie in a taxi.

he has wall-to-wall furniture.

he hired a chauffeur for his motorcycle.

he has an unlisted Social Security number.

the rings under his eyes have diamonds in them.

he has wall-to-wall parties.

he never counts his money, he weighs it.

he owns an unlisted telephone company.

his telephone has a 24-karat ring.

the water in his swimming pool has a permanent wave.

Frank Gifford (left), Henny and a couple of "big mouths," Martha Raye and Joe E. Brown clown around

his bank is named after him.

he won't even ride in the same car with his chauffeur.

even his bathroom has a picture window.

when he cashes a check the bank bounces.

his bath has three faucets: hot, cold, and luke.

he has two hot water bottles, one for each foot.

his birthday party lasts from birthday to birthday.

he carries an attache case with credit cards.

his son in the army has an unlisted serial number.

he has his own sleep-in television repairman.

Prosperity comes in cycles, the best of which is the try-cycle.

The horn of plenty starts a lot of men on a toot.

Only Americans have mastered the art of being prosperous though broke.

I can't stand prosperity--if it's some other fellow's.

Prosperity means paying installments on ten things instead of one.

To me, waves of prosperity are generally breakers.

Prosperity is when people go into debt for things they don't need.

Businessmen create prosperity--politicians take the credit for it.

No plan to restore prosperity will work if the people can't.

To me prosperity is a matter for posterity.

Prosperity enables us to pay more for things we shouldn't buy anyway.

The first sign of prosperity are the excavations for new buildings.

In prosperity our friends know us; in adversity we know our friends.

Women who go shopping bring back everything exept prosperity.

Prosperity is being in a rut, while depression is being in a hole.

In the matter of making fools, prosperity has it all over adversity.

Some people are so prosperous, they have no neighbors.

Keeping on your toes and being well heeled usually go together.

It is harder for a rich man to enter heaven--or jail.

If you are prosperous all your faults are called eccentricities.

People with many friends are rich--they have to be.

It's okay to show off--but a Rolls Royce with stained-glass windows?

If there is one thing better than marrying a millionaire--it's divorcing him.

Rich is rich--but a split-level Cadillac?

Imagine a man with a three-room Jaguar.

Prosperity can be a curse--especially if your neighbors have it.

It is better to live rich--than to die rich.

Prosperity is largely confined to drug pushers and gangsters.

Prosperity is a buy-product.

Prosperity will return in the sweet buy and buy.

Suggestion to business: money is a boomerang--turn it loose.

Psychiatry

My psychiatrist told me I was crazy. I said I wanted a second opinion. He said, "O.K., you're ugly too!"

Guy to psychiatrist, "Nobody talks to me." Psychiatrist says, "Next!"

My analyst is so expensive--for $50 he sends you a get-well card.

When a billing clerk goes psycho he hears strange invoices.

I'm not troubled by sexual fantasies--in fact, I rather enjoy them.

A neurotic is a person who has discovered the secret of perpetual emotion.

One analyst specializes in teen-agers--he uses the back seat of a car.

I've got privy-phobia--I can't resist writing on walls.

I'm a-Freud he isn't all there.

Anyone who's not neurotic these days is probably disadvantaged.

I work 25 hours a day--I get up an hour earlier.

Psychiatrist's ad: "Satisfaction guaranteed or your mania back."

Have I told you about my aberration?

A psychopath is a path where a psycho walks up and down.

My analyst is so famous all the world beat a psychopath to his door.

Anyone who goes to a psychiatrist should have his head examined.

I listen to my analyst and then draw my own confusions.

My brother is getting a jacket for his birthday--the strait kind.

When Dad was born, no bells were rung--a pot was cracked.

My boss is as happy as if he were in his right mind.

Last December I got a card from my analyst reading: "Happy Neurosis!"

I drink psychopathic coffee--it's weak in the bean.

I'm girl-crazy. Girls won't go out with me--that's why I'm crazy.

If I was insured--I'd kill myself.

You're never alone with schizophrenia.

A psychiatrist is a mind-sweeper.

Psychiatrist's ad: "Two couches--no waiting."

I'm beginning to find out about myself, and I don't like it.

Psychiatry is the study of what people do that they should be ashamed of.

A psychiatrist watches everybody else when a pretty girl enters the room.

An over-zealous psychiatrist is one who only eats Southern Freud chicken.

A psychiatrist doesn't have to worry as long as other people do.

My analyst says if I don't pay my bill he'll let me go crazy.

My wife goes to a psychiatrist just so she can lie down and talk.

Psychiatry by mail: Tear off the top of your head and send it in.

I used to be the kind of guy that made coffee nervous.

In this world, you've got to be a little crazy, or else you'll go nuts.

Once I have a duplex personality, but now I have a split-level personality.

I went to an analyst in Miami. He didn't use a couch--he used a beach chair.

What bothers me is I've never met a happy psychiatrist.

A psychiatrist is a doctor who can't stand the sight of blood.

A chestnut is a guy who is crazy about chests.

Psychiatry is the troubled science.

I have a maple chair, but I hate it. The syrup sticks to my pants.

I joined the Campfire Girls--I was cold.

I won't go through analysis. I refuse to squeal on my parents.

The latest craze can be found in the insane asylum.

If you go off your rocker you land on a psychiatrist's couch.

You can get sent to the nut house for no reason at all.

Simile: as helpless as a psychiatrist without a couch.

My psychiatrist has a portable couch--for house calls.

I carry a compass to know whether I'm coming or going.

Like Whistler's mother standing up--he's off his rocker.

A psychistrist tries to find out what's kooking.

My analyst only listens to me when I don't make sense.

Psychiatry is a terrible waste of couches.

An analyst is a mental Peeping Tom.

My analyst is an ambivalence chaser.

A psychiatrist makes a living out of a complaint department.

A psychiatrist is a motive prophet.

Psychiatry is the art of analyzing ouches on couches.

A psychiatric examination is a check-up from the neck up.

My analyst is very strict--if you come late he makes you stand.

I'm as happy as if I were in my right mind.

Insanity is hereditary--parents get it from their children.

Like the Liberty Bell, he's half-cracked.

Mad money is the fee charged by a psychiatrist.

An analyst uses other people's heads to make money.

Psychoanalysis is a kind of panned parenthood.

Psychiatry is one business where the customer is always wrong.

Analysts have the same problems as anyone else, but with an accent.

Sign in a psychiatrist's waiting room: "Worry Now, Pay Later."

Psychiatrists find you cracked and leave you broke.

Insanity is different from love, but it's hard to tell the difference.

A neurotic prefers a psychiatrist's couch to a double bed.

He has a one-crack mind.

I only eat in restaurants where they serve soup to nuts.

Like a Hershey Bar--he's half nuts.

He's as sane as a lunatic's dream.

He's a psychoceramic--that's a crackpot.

The principal cause of insanity is indictments.

In Ireland psychiatrists use Murphy beds.

A psychiatrist is lucky: his patients never die and they never get well.

An analyst will listen to you for as long as you don't make sense.

Analysts never seem to find out anything good about anybody.

A psychiatrist is secure only as long as his patients aren't.

There's something wrong with my analyst--he understands me.

Analysts are psychological, some are more psycho than logical.

When two analysts get together, which one takes the couch?

Psychoanalysis is a sinecure that offers a cure for the insecure.

To entertain a neurotic all you have to do is sit down and listen.

A neurotic never puts off till tomorrow the worrying he can do today.

Psychoanalysis prepares you for the poverty in which it leaves you.

One cannibal went to a psychiatrist because he was fed up with people.

A psychiatrist's couch is where you land when you go off your rocker.

My analyst is so poor, instead of a couch he uses a sleeping bag.

In group therapy instead of couches they use bunk beds.

I'm learning to stand on my feet while lying on a couch.

My analyst is so busy he has an upper and a lower berth.

In just ten visits my analyst cured me of $500.

Show me a psychiatrist, and I'll show you a couch coach.

Your future is secure when they put you in a strait jacket.

In Hollywood, if you don't have an analyst people think you're crazy.

My analyst is very friendly--he lies down on the couch with you.

My analyst is so poor, instead of a couch he uses a cot.

I had a split personality, so my analyst charged me $50 each per visit.

Conversation when two analysts meet: "You're fine. How am I?"

For a shock treatment my psychiatrist sends his bills in advance.

Radio

A radio announcer is a person who works for the love of mike.

An announcer is a man who knows his N.B.C.s.

Radio teaches us the blessings of silence.

You remember radio--that's television with the picture tube blown.

Radio has never been accused of showing an old movie.

Neither radios nor women give you what you want when you want it.

Radio brings prefabricated din into our homes.

When an announcer feels old age creeping on he gets his voice lifted.

Radio gives a person the air without hurting his feelings.

A radio announcer gives you a headache, and then advertises aspirin.

Distance lends enchantment--even to the radio program.

I just installed a new loud speaker in my house. I got married again.

People who applaud movies talk back to their radios.

Radio advertising is an invisible message on a transparent screen.

I've just perfected a new invention: color radio.

I have a two-way transistor radio--it either plays or it doesn't.

Radio permits speakers to state without fear of contradiction.

What broadcasting needs is a cough medicine for radios.

Here is an unimportant announcement from our sponsor.

Now they have frozen radio dinners--for people who don't own a TV set.

A radio commentator has opinions on subjects he never heard of.

Radio commercial: jabber-tising.

Radio fallout is those damned transistors they play everywhere these days.

On radio and television it's the sponsor who makes the program impossible.

Now for the news that happened during our commercials.

I'm not saying she's ugly, but she has a perfect face for radio.

FM radio is the radio ecstatic.

Christmas Eve radio stations keep playing Silent Night until morning.

The only thing I can be sure of getting on my radio is dust.

Time out for a record and then back to our commercials.

A radio commercial is the signal to shut off the radio.

Nowadays the still, small voice is more likely to be a transistor radio.

A transistor is a small, noisy plastic case with a teen-ager attached.

Rip Van Winkle could sleep 20 years because his neighbors had no radio.

Radio static always knows just what program you prefer.

The radio is a repercussion instrument.

Radio advertising is persuasion by vibration.

You can't talk without a voice on radio--but you can sing without one.

The air is free, but not when you advertise over it.

Radio has succumbed to its first enemy: it has become static.

A lot of today's music is improved by bad reception on radio.

School

If the bees ever find out what I found out--the flowers are through.

In sixth grade they wanted me to count up to ten--from memory.

The leaves begin to turn the night before an exam.

We lived in a tent when I was a kid--so my head grew to a point.

He had an unfortunate accident in his childhood. He was born.

Sex is so popular with school kids. Is there an easier word to spell?

In elementary school, many a true word is spoken in guess.

Public schools are usually run by men, but overrun with women.

What you don't know doesn't hurt you, unless you're a dropout.

Don't become a dropout: a little learning is a dangerous thing.

Education teaches a man how to speak, not how long or how often.

The most widespread form of compulsory education is experience.

Adult education often begins with a teen-age marriage.

A college education doesn't make fools; it just develops them.

September is the month when most little boys develop class hatred.

I didn't really dislike school. It was the principal of the thing.

I know about Eskimos--they make pies.

I could never afford a telescope--that's why my eyes pop.

Professors are people who go to college and never get out.

I was in school so long the principal had to frame me to graduate.

College professors get what's left after the football coach is paid.

Know what my son is going to be when he graduates? An old man.

I was a poor student--but a whiz at recess.

Educating a born fool is a lot like fertilizing a stone.

You are never too old to learn--to make new mistakes.

Then one day I went to school. I couldn't get a table at the poolroom.

I was so thin the teacher kept marking me absent.

My neighborhood was tough. I had six notches on my pea shooter.

A college graduate is a person who had a chance to get an education.

The man who knows it all has lots to learn.

It's never too late to learn--and it's never too early either.

It's what a man learns after he knows it all that counts.

You're never too old to learn some new way to act like a fool.

The best way to haze freshmen is to make them study.

The proper study of mankind is man, but the most popular is woman.

The class yell of the school of experience is: "Ouch!"

In college I was a 3-letter man. The letters were: R-A-T.

The greatest college faculty is that of going without sleep.

Remember when the Board of Education was a hair brush?

All is fair in love and fraternity houses.

All some men get out of college is themselves.

Never let your studies interfere with your college education.

Teaching is the fine art of imparting knowledge without possessing it.

A self-taught man usually has a poor teacher and a worse student.

I'll never learn how to spell. The teacher keeps changing the words.

The more we go to school--the more we go to school.

The real college cheer is the check from home.

In football I was half-back--in my studies I was way back.

My son got the highest marks of any kid who flunked.

In school I won the Academy Award for playing hookey.

I still remember my college days--all four of them.

I joined a sorority. I had to. I was failing in anatomy.

Old teachers never die, they just grade away.

The kids in my school were so tough that the teachers played hookey.

One kid in my class was so tough he made the teacher stay after school.

I used to date a teacher who didn't have a principle.

One thing stopped me from going to college: high school.

College is a fountain of knowledge where all go to drink.

A college president never dies--he just loses his faculties.

Many a college boy's education is just pigskin deep.

A son in college means making allowances.

A college professor is a person who talks in other people's sleep.

My class voted me as the man most likely to go to seed.

A university is a football stadium surrounded by small buildings.

Education is almost as expensive as ignorance.

A report card is a poison pen letter written by a teacher.

The only thing I ever took up in school was space.

One year I even flunked recess.

The best aid to adult education is children.

Education pays everybody exept educators.

A girl's boarding school is an institution of higher yearning.

The school of experience is highly co-educational.

I won't graduate from college this year because I didn't go.

The only thing I really liked at college was the campus activity.

A college girl may be poor in history, but great on dates.

My son is majoring in pharmacy--he's always wanted to be a farmer.

I was a two-letter man in college. I wrote home twice a week.

The only thing I passed in college was the football.

My history teacher was so old, he taught from memory.

A kindergarten teacher has to know how to make the little things count.

At the school I went to there's a sign: (Your name) slept here.

I went pretty far as far as school goes--four blocks.

I started in school in the first grade. Years passed, but I didn't.

My teacher has a reading problem. He can't read my writing.

A son usually finishes college and his dad at about the same time.

It's a wise fraternity man that knows his own clothes.

It took my sister four years to get a sheepskin--and one day to get a mink.

Education is the concealment of ignorance.

A school is a mental institution.

Education is what's left over after you've forgotten the facts.

School is often just a part-time orphan asylum.

Education enables you to get into more expensive trouble.

School is the Child's Garden of Virus.

Education is the first step to something better.

You can't teach people anything they don't want to know.

Education is the battle against Nature.

It takes more than a sheepskin to keep the wolf away from the door.

Sex

Most girls are attracted to the simple things in life, like men.

The girl who stoops to conquer usually wears a low-cut dress.

Nudism is exposure with composure.

A woman with a past attracts men who hope history will repeat itself.

Eternal vigilance is the price of virginity.

Falsies: extra-padded attractions.

A man seldom robs a woman of her virginity without an accomplice.

Her baby is descended from a long line that she listened to.

A brainless beauty is often a toy forever.

At school she was voted the girl most likely to concede.

Assault: what every woman likes to be taken with a grain of.

Falsies: absentease.

Prostitutes' children: Brothel sprouts.

Falsie salesman: a Fuller bust man.

A lesbian is a mannish depressive with delusions of gender.

Drive-in movies: wall-to-wall car-petting.

A legal secretary is any girl over eighteen.

Some women can take a man to the cleaners as soon as they spot him.

Soft-soap makes many girls slip.

A May bride is one who may be pregnant.

A fellow once fought for her honor. Too bad she didn't.

That mink coat does a lot for her--but then, she did a lot for it.

She was just a local girl who everybody made good.

Protein: a call girl too young to vote.

Repeal: a stripteaser's encore.

Window dresser: a girl who doesn't pull down the shades.

Some girls get a lot out of a dress, and leave it out.

Stalemate: last season's girl friend.

The man who can read women like a book usually likes to read in bed.

Falsies: hidden persuaders.

A fellow asked her to be his mistress, and she reclined to do so.

If sex is overrated--where does everything else stand?

There's a new sexy doll--you turn her on--and she turns you on.

In college she was voted the most likely to succeed--with anybody.

Sex is a great problem to me. In fact, I find everything about it great.

Sex is evil--it makes men want to get married.

A beautiful woman who has yet to be made, has yet to be made.

Happy married couple: a husband out with another man's wife.

Proposal: a proposition that lost its nerve.

Shotgun wedding: a case of wife or death.

Vicious circle: a wedding ring.

Wanton women want not.

Blessed are the pure--for they shall inhibit the eath.

How do you tell the sex of a hormone? Take its genes off.

I could have an active, wholesome sex life if it weren't for my wife.

A mistress is a cutie on the Q.T.

These days a girl is known by the company that keeps her.

A person with a foot fetish gets a boot out of sex.

A pervert is a person who gets caught.

The Marquis de Sade was a big pain.

Some girls make friends quickly. With strangers it takes a little longer.

Show me a rapist, and I'll show you a stickup artist.

A peeping Tom is a private eye.

Shapely limbs help many a girl to branch out.

The best kind of girl is one who says stop only when she sends a telegram.

Show he a homosexual, and I'll show you a guy who loves his fellow man.

Show me a lesbian, and I'll show you who is girl-crazy.

Show me a transvestite, and I'll show you a case of mistaken identity.

A depressed person is a oyeur with failing eyesight.

Madam: someone for whom the belles toil.

Undercover agent: a girl spy.

One girl was picked up so often she began to grow handles.

It's usually a girl's geography that determines her history.

Nudists are people who go in for altogetherness.

Good clean fun: a couple taking a bath together.

Salesmanship: the difference between rape and rapture.

A person who makes obscene phone calls is a ding-a-ling freak.

Show me an exhibitionist, and I'll show you a man who is over-exposed.

She never sleeps with strangers. She always asks their name first.

My wife enjoys sex only on certain days--her birthday and mine.

It's easy to admire a good loser at a strip poker party.

To most modern writers, sex is a novel idea.

It's hard to keep a good girl down, but lots of fun trying.

Women are the kind of problem most men like to wrestle with.

An orgy is a kind of group therapy.

The best years of a girl's life are figured in man hours.

Girls who do right--get left.

A smart woman quits playing ball when she makes a good catch.

A well-proportioned girl is one with a narrow waist and a broad mind.

The difference between a wife and a mistress is night and day.

To most couples, curbing their emotions means parking.

Whether or not a girl can be had for a song depends on the man's pitch.

A wife made to order can't compare with a ready maid.

The difference between picnic and panic is twenty-eight days.

Sometimes when two's company, three's the result.

Slip cover: a maternity dress.

Husbands are like fires--they go out when unattended.

They say baseball is our national pastime--you'll never convince me.

Show me a procurer, and I'll show you a forni-caterer.

Support free enterprise--legalize prostitution.

Candy is dandy--but sex won't rot your teeth.

Sex is the formula by which one and one makes three.

To the poet, sex is love; to the psychiatrist, love is sex.

Sex is an intimate form of dancing.

Children never discuss sex in the presence of their elders.

Sex is the poor man's polo.

If sex is such a driving force, why is so much of it found parked?

Sex is a driving force that frequently runs out of gas.

Girls who like to show their knees, know all about the birds and bees.

Lie down. I think I love you.

I asked this girl--are you the opposite sex or am I?

A dirty book is seldom a dusty one.

Sex is the scream of life.

Nothing makes a man forget a passing fancy like something fancier.

When it comes to women, no man can be both logical and biological.

Politics makes strange bedfellows, and so does prostitution.

All is not sex that appeals.

The girl who loses her heart to a man loves to have him search for it.

Sex is a drive where there are just as many women drivers as men.

Adultery is a sport that was created by marriage.

In the war of the sexes, there are no conscientious objectors.

Sex proves that it is easier to get two bodies together than two souls.

Sex is the art of doing the wrong thing at the right time.

A girl's firm "No" is still the best oral contraceptive.

The art of sex is making advances.

Sex is a drive where there are too many reckless drivers.

Sex may never be fatal, but it has put an end to many a bachelor.

Children should be seen and not had.

A man who is hungry for love eats with his hands.

He who loves and runs away, may live to love another day.

I love the idea of there being two sexes, don't you?

A little foreplay now and then is why we have the married men.

Many a bathing suit has led a girl into deep water.

A man who likes to make out always has his hands full.

Sex is the mystery behind the mastery of woman over man.

An extramarital affair is often a game not worth the scandal.

One part of a domestic triangle is usually a curved leg.

When a husband is too good to be true, he probably isn't.

A sexy woman can make feminine capital out of masculine interest.

First it's boy meets girl, and then it's man cheats wife.

In the art of love it is more important to know when than how.

Sex is the most fun you can have without laughing.

Of two evils, choose the one with the better-looking legs.

A girl with a good figure can often shape her own destiny.

The 3 most popular things in life are a martini before and a nap afterwards.

A homosexual is a person who believes in vice versa.

The only unnatural sex act is that which you cannot perform.

One reason sex is so popular is that it's centrally located.

Shopping

I always lose my balance when my wife goes shopping.

My wife walks past shops window-wishing.

My wife's spending capacity is greater than my earning capacity.

My wife is trying to lick the recession single-handed.

When my wife goes shopping she comes home with everything except money.

Service while you wait is usually what the other fellow is getting.

My wife is very punctual. In fact, she buys everything on time.

I'm amazed at what my wife would rather have than money.

If you don't know what's up, you haven't been shopping lately.

It takes two to make a bargain, but just one to make money.

One store was so crowded, two women were trying on the same girdle.

Give my wife credit for anything and she'll take it.

Why does Christmas always come just when the stores are so crowded?

If only my car would go as fast as the installments fall due.

These days a bargain is anything that's only a little overpriced.

My wife's first question is: "How much is the down payment?"

Whatever I buy today is usually on sale tomorrow.

A luxury is something that costs $2 to make and $20 to sell.

Many people buy on time, but only a few pay that way.

I'm waiting to hear of the first woman to visit Paris on a non-shop flight.

A parking meter enables you to do two hours of shopping in one.

Economy is anything my wife wants to buy.

My wife loves a bargain but hates being told she's wearing one.

Men fight for what they want, and women attend bargain sales.

Present prices discourage buying at present prices.

A bargain is something you can't use at a price you can't refuse.

My wife will buy anything she thinks a store is losing money on.

A bargain is anything my wife buys and can't explain any other way.

My wife just took her shopping cart in for a 1,000 mile check-up.

The only voice I get in family shopping is the invoice.

My wife shops like a human dynamo--charges everything.

My wife thinks that charge accounts go further than money.

When my wife went window shopping she bought five windows.

Watching my wife shop you'd think whe was taking inventory of the store.

My wife went to the corner market. Bought two corners.

A woman is a creature that's always shopping.

Time is money, so when you go shopping take lots of time.

The most expensive vehicle to operate, per mile, is the shopping cart.

At the end of a shopping spree my wife is tired as well as spent.

The best time to buy a house is when you are selling.

The only thing my wife does on time is buy.

My wife'll buy anything marked down. Last week she bought an escalator.

Show Business

In show business, sex rears its ugly head in the shape of a beautiful body.

He's an agent now. He must know talent. He gave up acting.

I held the audience open-mouthed--they all yawned at the same time.

The way he reads clean lines is a dirty shame.

I often get stage fright--especially when I see an egg or a tomato.

A comic is a man who knows how to take a joke.

I no longer have an agent--I'm laying off direct.

The stripper was shy--she took her clothes off with one eye closed.

An opera house is a jukebox with a chandelier.

He's comedy relief--he relieves the picture of all its comedy.

One thing a musical comedy must have for a long run is good legs.

In show business, it's the box office that counts, not the applause.

It is never too late to visit another night club.

Some promising singers should promise to stop singing.

He's a mastoid of ceremonies--a pain in the neck.

What's worse than Thursday night on television? Thursday afternoon.

The critic was at the opening night incognito--he was awake.

Television slogan: The show must go off.

They gave the audience sandwiches; the play was from hunger.

The circus giant was only seven feet tall--he smoked as a kid.

Even his jokes about old jokes are old.

I knew Tom Thumb when he was a pinky.

He was one of the greatest actors ever--to clear his throat.

An original wit is a guy who hears the gag before you do.

Television has proved that sight has a definite odor.

She was so dumb they had to rehearse her two weeks for a pause.

She had everything a singer should have--and a good voice, too.

He was a modest actor--and he had plenty to be modest about.

I'm a stooge to no one man--I free lance.

The burlesque had to close due to a shortage of raw material.

He sings for charity--and he needs it.

Philadelphia is the Quaker City. They paid me off in oats.

Our band leader has a pen that will write under scale.

I had 'em in the aisles--heading for the exits.

Business is so bad they're selling loose cigarettes in the lobby.

Next week I appear in a fashionable line-up in Boston.

He's fast on the ad lib--all he has to do is hear it once.

A comedian is a person who knows a good gag when he steals one.

Television: looking at a movie through a dish of Jello.

Television: radio with eyestrain.

I had my ups and downs last night--I had an aisle seat in a movie.

My fan mail is growing. Today there were even a few from strangers.

In burlesque all girls look alike and all men like a look.

The midget was so small they rode him out of town on a nail.

The crowd was on edge. The seats were narrow.

She does a peek-a-boo act. The audience peeks, then boos.

The tickets were sky high and so were our seats.

My last tour was a great success. I outran every audience.

I would have watched television--but I'm on a diet.

Showgirl: more show than girl.

Wanted: understudy for a cannonball act. Must be willing to travel.

The show was so down to earth the critics buried it.

One stripper never does an encore--it sets off the sprinkler system.

One stripper was so ugly, the audience hollered: "Up in front!"

A discotheque is a place for people who want to be seen but not heard.

Don't applaud. When you applaud, you're not drinking.

Disc jockey: one who lives on spins and needles.

I know one TV star who rules his show with an iron head.

The show was full of surprises. I just wish it was full of talent.

My fan club can hold a mass meeting in a telephone booth.

If you think my act is monotonous, you should see my home life.

They ran out of film at one drive-in theater--nobody knew the difference.

I have a custom-made telephone. It doesn't ring, it applauds.

An actor is always me-deep in conversation.

A circus is two-and-a-half hours of opening acts.

Ad in "Variety": "Lion-tamer--looking for tamer lion."

The show had two strikes against it--the seats faced the stage.

The trouble with opera is that there is too much singing.

Never shoot pool with an actor--he's too darned sure of his cues.

They advertised a chorus of seventy--and they looked it.

Sin

Only the wages of sin have no deductions.

Misers are guilty of the sin of idle-dollar-try.

Every sin is the result of collaboration.

Providence is what we blame for our sins.

Sinning is the best part of repentance.

The wages of sin vary with the sinner.

The wages of sin is debt.

In a depression all wages go down except the wages of sin.

Two things never live up to their advertising claims: the circus and sin.

Men are not punished for their sins, but by them.

One man's sin is another man's singularity.

Some women are happiest when confessing the sins of other women.

Confession is good for the soul, but bad for the reputation.

Of two sins, choose the one you enjoy the most.

There may be no rest for the wicked, but there is often arrest.

Of two evils, choose the prettier.

The wages of sin are high--unless you know someone who'll do it for free.

Of two evils, pass up the first, and turn down the other.

The way of the transgressor is hard--to find out.

Today's adult movies must be sin to be appreciated.

Wild life isn't disappearing--it has just moved to the city.

A man usually forsakes sin after sin forsakes him.

Small Town

A small town is where...

You have to walk around a dog enjoying a nap on the sidewalk.

the newspaper prints the crossword puzzle on the front page.

there is no place to go that you shouldn't.

everyone knows which men beat their wives--and which ones need it.

everyone knows the troubles you've seen.

the phone book only has one page.

you can chat on the telephone even if you get a wrong number.

"Come Again" is painted on back of the "Welcome" sign.

the nine o'clock curfew wakes up most of the town.

the Sunday newspaper can be lifted with one hand.

there isn't much to be seen, but what you hear makes up for it.

a man is never too busy to tell you how busy he is.

absence makes the tongues go faster.

a flying rumor never has any trouble in making a landing.

a woman reaches for a chair when answering the telephone.

a person with a private-line telephone is considered anti-social.

people buy a newspaper to verify what they heard on the phone.

nothing happens every minute.

nothing ever happens, but what you hear makes up for it.

there are no rich policemen.

you don't need a credit card to get credit.

Henny remembers Barabara Walters as the little girl whose father owned "The Latin Quarter" club. The two share a moment with actor Kirk Douglas.

they use money instead of credit cards.

you wear your own clothes to formal parties.

the all-night restaurant closes at 4:30 p.m.

the postmaster knows more than the school master.

even a haircut changes the whole appearance of the community.

a fellow with a black eye doesn't have to explain--everyone knows.

if you don't know what's going on, nothing is.

you can get a week's rest in half the time.

the real news comes over the fence--not over the radio.

you don't have to keep an eye on your wife--neighbors do it for you.

they have to widen the streeets to put the white line in the middle.

when you use your electric razor, the street lights dim.

the news gets around before the newspaper does.

the only place open all night is a mailbox.

you can finish the Sunday papers at breakfast.

they aren't trying to raise money for an airport.

only the general store has a telephone.

the fire engine is mounted on a bicycle.

they have only one traffic light, which changes once a month.

they ring in the New Year at 7:00 p.m.

people go to church on Sunday to see who didn't.

the entire police department consists of one policeman.

an automatic dishwasher is not bought but married.

the town crier has only to whisper.

for excitement they watch an Alka-Seltzer fizz.

they have no hospital, only a First Aid kit.

for excitement they go to the bakery to smell the bread.

the ZIP code number is minus 2.

people go to the station just to make believe they are leaving.

for excitement they go to the store and try on gloves.

Medicare is known as Minicare.

if you go out for a night on the town it only takes a half hour.

you can't buy a bra without a prescription.

even the people who mind their own business know everything.

During a boxing match both fighters sat in the same corner.

We once held a beauty contest and a fellow won.

This town is so small it's only open two days a week.

The highlight of our cultural season was the arrival of a singing telegram.

Any town proud of its smog and its traffic jams isn't big enough yet.

My home town had dead-end one-way streets.

Smoking

More people are giving up smoking tomorrow than today.

If matches were made in heaven, where did the cigar-lighters come from?

One way to quit smoking is to carry wet matches.

I finally gave up smoking. It took a lot of will power. My wife's.

Never throw cigar butts in urinals. They get soggy and are hard to light.

Don't throw the filters away--that's the best part.

To stop smoking simply marry a girl who objects to it.

Modern widow's weeds are black-tipped cigarettes.

I always step on my cigarette butts so they won't burn the rug.

If you have matches but no cigarettes--make light of the situation.

I enjoy a quiet smoke, so I smoke cigars without bands.

This is a quarter cigar--someone else smoked the other three-quarters.

What this five-cent cigar needs is a good country.

I've seen smudge-pots that smelled better than this.

I'd walk a mile for a cigarette. But not blindfolded.

What this world needs is a good, fine-scent cigar.

Cigarette smoking is the Tobacco Road that runs into a dead end.

Tobacco is found in many Southern States and in some cigarettes.

It's better to smoke here on earth than in the hereafter.

Some men smoke between meals, others eat between smokes.

If you smoke your cigarettes shorter, you'll smoke them longer.

The greatest tobacco evil is the man who continually quits smoking.

My wife gave up smoking but she keeps on fuming.

Smoke and the world smokes with you, quit and you smoke alone.

As ye smoke, so shall ye reek.

Learning to smoke is almost as painful as trying to give it up.

What this country needs is an ashtray that looks like one.

To the man who smokes any piece of bric-a-brac looks like an ashtray.

No cigar is so bad that sooner or later it won't meet its match.

What this country needs is a good no-scent cigar.

What this country needs is a good five-cent-cigar extinguisher.

According to the tobacco ads, gentlemen prefer blends.

What this country needs is a cigarette with a built-in cough medicine.

What this country needs is a cigarette that will cure the smoking habit.

A woman is only a woman--but a good cigar is a smoke.

Then I became a chain smoker. I couldn't afford cigarettes.

You're heard of cigarette lighters that won't work? Mine won't go out.

Smoking not only shortens your life, it also shortens your cigarettes.

My wife is so neat she empties ashtrays even before they're used.

Where there's smoke--there's my wife--cooking.

The family that smokes together, chokes together.

My wife smokes like Chicago after the fire.

Smokers are people who, the more they fume, the less they fret.

I'm a chain smoker--I'm chained to smoking.

My wife's a pot smoker. Have you ever seen a pot smoking?

Snobs

Many a man would be a snob--if he had the clothes to go with it.

He's one of the Bore Hundred.

It takes a snob to buy a status-fying home.

The exclusiveness of some families is a good thing for their neighbors.

Most snobs are only flakes off the upper crust.

The only thing he ever did for a living was inherit.

His family tree could stand a lot of trimming.

The best part of some family trees is underground.

A snob is a person who was born with his face lifted.

A snob's eyes look down on others while his nose turns up.

Snobs are in favor of equality, but only with the right people.

A snob talks as if he had begotten his own ancestors.

A snob lives in public as the rich do, and in private as the poor do.

Mostly snobs suffer from I-strain.

Their old butler is serving their third degeneration.

A snob is proof that an empty head and a stuffed shirt can go together.

A snob thinks it's his duty to be snooty.

When a snob grows old, he spends his life in solitary refinement.

A superior person won't look down on you; an inferior person can't.

Why does the man with an inferiority complex always feel so superior?

Superior men seldom feel superior, and inferior men seldom feel inferior.

She should go to a plastic surgeon to have her nose lowered.

She's as stuck-up as a billboard.

A snob tries to go from the cash register to the social register.

She belongs to the uppish classes.

A snob returns from a European trip brag and baggage.

A snob is a guy who wears a riding habit to pitch horseshoes.

She's as overbearing as a woman giving birth to quintuplets.

Some people would feel snubbed if an epidemic overlooked them.

He comes from the shady side of his family tree.

His family tree was started by grafting.

She's so snooty, she has alligator bags under her eyes.

He's proof that stuffed shirts come in all sizes.

I know a couple that just moved to Snuburbia.

A snob is full of rectitude, platitude, and high-hatitude.

He deliberately broke his leg skiing. The cast is his status symbol!

She won't even eat ladyfingers unless they're manicured.

She won't eat a hot dog unless it's registered in the Kennel Club.

She keeps her nose in the air--that's to avoid smelling herself.

What a neighborhood! Even Chicken Delight has an unlisted number.

The greatest pleasure of a snob is to be asked everywhere and go nowhere.

He even knows the right wine to go with a TV dinner.

A snob only wants to know the people who don't want to know him.

Too much of the uplift in this country is confined to noses.

Speakers

A finished speaker seldom is.

Some speakers electrify an audience--others gas it.

Too many after-dinner speakers are merely after dinner.

All work and no plagiarism makes a dull speech.

The recipe for a good speech includes some shortening.

Many dry speeches are all wet.

I hate those speakers who appeal to the emotions by beating the eardrums.

Some speakers are as gabby as a barber.

Some men can speak for an hour without a note--and without a point.

When all's said and done, too many people keep on saying and doing.

Free speech is a right--not a continuous obligation.

What we need is more free speech that's worth listening to.

Speech should be free, considering how little of it is worth anything.

He needs no introduction--what he needs is a conclusion.

A speech is like a wheel--the longer the spoke, the greater the tire.

Some people know very little, but they know it fluently.

If your mind goes blank--be sure to turn off the sound.

Some people only listen when they're talking.

Many a man won't shut his trap until he has his foot in it.

Most of us know how to say nothing--few of us know when.

A good line is the shortest distance between dates.

You can't tell whether a man is a finished speaker until he sits down.

The best test of a sermon is depth--not length.

An after dinner speaker is the man who starts the bull rolling.

Eloquence has been defined as "logic on fire."

The female of the speeches is deadlier than the male.

I can't stand speakers who babble over with enthusiasm.

Some people would be enormously improved by laryngitis.

It is very difficult to finish your speech before you stop talking.

A lecturer is a person who makes talk money.

Dry speeches never satisfy a thirst for knowledge.

A filibuster is a long speech, about nothing, by an authority on the subject.

A speaker often makes you feel dumb at one end and numb at the other.

Dry lectures never satisfy a thirst for knowledge.

The first rule of public speaking is to speak up, the second is to sit down.

An impromptu speech is seldom worth the paper it is written on.

The three "Bs" of public speaking are: be brief, be interesting, be gone.

Always leave your audience before your audience leaves you.

The worst speech makers are those with an addiction to diction.

God gave eloquence to some--brains to others.

Little boys who talk too much usually grow up to be public speakers.

The only way to stay awake during an after dinner speech is to give it.

If you don't strike oil in an hour, stop boring.

Like a ship, some speakers toot loudest when they're in a fog.

Listening to some speakers makes you wonder who writes their immaterial.

Orators cover indefinite ideas with infinite words.

When some speakers end their talks, there is a great awakening.

I just introduce the speakers, I can't guarantee them.

You have great speaking ability. You never let up.

As a speaker, he's the greatest blow on earth.

To be a good speaker--just stop talking.

He knows how to speak for himself--and enough for twenty others.

Speeches are like babies; easy to conceive but hard to deliver.

If you don't know what to talk about--talk about three minutes.

Sports

Interest your children in bowling--get them off the streets, into the alleys.

The only fishing through the ice I ever do is for cherries.

I hunted bears--but only bagged my pants.

I learned to ski in just ten sittings.

Unfortunately fish seem to go on vacation the same time we do.

In olden days, boxing wasn't as modern as it is today.

I've been skating for hours on end. Should I take lessons?

My favorite outdoor sport is helping a woman into a cab.

Spade your garden early, when the worms won't be such a temptation.

I tried to learn to ski, but by the time I could stand, I couldn't sit.

What a team! Even their breath is offensive.

We went fishing. Had a few bites and plenty of nips.

They invited me to play water polo--I can't even ride a horse.

A swimming pool is a crowd of people with water in it.

Maybe a fish goes home and lies about the size of the bait he stole.

Fights are not like weddings. In a fight you don't know who'll win.

Indoor sports are all right if they go home at a reasonable hour.

I met a fisherman who hadn't had a bite all day--so I bit him.

I lost a big wad--that's the last time I bet chewing gum.

He was the cream of fighters--and he got whipped.

The way most fishermen catch fish is by the tale.

Polo is golf with fertilizer.

I put on my ski suit--that's Esquire for long underwear.

It was a clean fight. The manager threw in the towel every round.

My luck! When the fish don't bite the mosquitoes do.

She follows the sports and vice versa.

A boxer is a fellow who wakes up and finds himself rich.

Some men don't fish, they just drown worms.

What killed six-day bicycle racing was the five-day week.

I used to be a lifeguard--in a Turkish bath steam room.

To keep fish from smelling--cut off their noses.

In college I was string changer on the Yo-Yo squad.

It's football season when girls whistle at men in sweaters.

To communicate with a fish--drop him a line.

I sat on the bench so long I became very calloused.

Unfortunately to be looked upon as a good sport, you have to lose.

My sister caught a fish--now he's my brother-in-law.

Tennis professionals are usually satisfied with net profits.

I used to play hockey, but then I ran out of things to hock.

If the fish are biting today--it's only each other.

Boxing is a form of tap dancing with gloves on.

The Boxing Commission is a kind of punch board.

More big fish have been caught with words than with a hook.

Bowling is the game of marbles for grown-ups.

Croquet is chess with sweat.

Croquet is the polo of senility.

Fencing is a game of chess accomplished on foot.

Show me a boxing ring, and I'll show you a punch bowl.

The art of fishing is sitting still until you don't catch anything.

A go-cart is transportation for a mad moment.

Hialeah is French for "Hello, suckers!"

I go fishing because my wife won't let me drink at home.

Hockey is a form of mayhem on ice.

A pugilist is a boxer with an education.

A rabid fan is a guy who boos a television set.

It takes a sports expert to write the best alibis for being wrong.

It's a crime to catch a fish in some lakes, and a miracle in others.

A professional wrestler is a muscle-bound comedian acting like an athlete.

Wrestling is the art of gripping, grappling, and griping.

They also serve who only stand and wait--unless they're playing tennis.

Football and golf are fine sports, but they can't hold a scandal to baseball.

Wrestling is the sport of clings.

In wrestling, the participants groan almost as much as the customers.

When better predictions are made, sports writers won't make them.

Usually a resort's best fishing is found in its literature.

In football, the players do the running, and the spectators do the kicking.

The trouble with football is they have too many committee meetings.

When better records are made, somebody will break them.

What do they mean when they way "the stands were filled to capacity?"

Perhaps there is too much bawl in baseball.

A basketball player is a guy interested in plugging loop holes.

The position I played on my college football team was drawback.

Without basketball where would the high school dances be held?

A football player is a prominent figure in the passing parade.

I don't ski. I'm headed downhill fast enough as it is.

Athlete's foot is a fungus game.

A rolling football gathers no score.

The skin that many a young man loves to touch is the pig skin.

Two halves make a hole, and the fullback goes through.

A sky diver is soar with the world.

Bowling is a sport that should be right down your alley.

He was a colorful fighter--black and blue all over.

I shadow box every day. Today I won, after only ten minutes.

You can't keep a good golfer downtown.

Two can live as cheaply as one can play golf.

The course of true golf never did run smooth.

After the fight I was smiling from ear to ear--no teeth.

They handed me a cup after the fight--to keep my teeth in.

A boxer is a man who makes money hand over fist.

When a golfer misses his drive he expresses himself to a tee.

All is fair in love and golf.

Birds of leather sock together.

We were lucky when we went bear hunting. We didn't find any.

I like to hunt mules--I get a big kick out of it.

I never hunted bear, but I've gone fishing in my shorts.

My brother is a swimming instructor. He gives drowning lessons.

Tennis professionals are satisfied with net profits.

Too much attention to the pigskin doesn't help the sheepskin.

Golf is an ideal diversion, but a ruinous disease.

Show me a swimming instructor, and I'll show you a hold-up man.

The pool was so crowded I had to dive five times before I hit water.

One swim club is so exclusive, even the tide can't get in.

In hunting season the wise hunter disguises himself as a deer.

Any American boy can be a basketball star if he grows up, up, up.

She was only an athlete's daughter, but she was willing to play ball.

Of all sports, basketball attracts the highest type of youth.

The boxing ring is no place for a slowpoke.

A successful prize fighter always considers the rights of others.

Some girls go in for swimming, while others know every dive in town.

Fishing is my favorite form of loafing.

Everyone admires a good loser--except his wife.

To be a fisherman all you need is patience and a worm.

Some players are good losers, while others don't pretend.

All men are divided into three classes: fish, fishermen, and bait.

Every athletic team has a coach and Charley horses to pull it.

Fish may be bought if they can't be caught.

My favorite winter sport is looking at last summer's snapshots.

Some people catch fish--I just feed them.

An athlete is as young as he feels, but rarely as important.

There are better fish stories in the sea than ever came out of it.

One of the most popular winter sports is taking a plane to Florida.

The best weather for fishing is the weather when they are caught.

Many a girl thinks she is fond of sports until she marries one.

To catch a fish you've got to worm your way into its confidence.

Skiing is best when you have lots of white snow and Blue Cross.

In a world without fish there would be a lot less lying.

Football, not baseball, is our national pass time.

A ski jump is a leap made by a person on his way to the hospital.

What I enjoy most about table tennis is stepping on the ball.

There's nothing like your first horseback ride to make you feel better off.

Stingy

I'm not staying he's stingy, but. . .

as a freeloader, he's known from host to host.

he does have a burglar alarm on his garbage can.

he makes every dollar go as far as possible--and every girl, too.

he won't even spend the time of day.

of all the near-relatives in the family, he's the closest.

if he ever found a box of corn plasters, he'd start wearing tight shoes.

he puts boric acid on his grapefruit to get a free eyewash.

the reason he's so clean is that he's been sponging for years.

he's so small, if he ever sat on a dollar, 95 cents would show.

he does his Christmas shopping surly.

he thinks the world owes him a giving.

he only picks up a check if its' made out to him.

he never takes anything but a sponge bath.

he tosses quarter tips around like manhole covers.

at the Last Supper he would have asked for separate checks.

he is saving all his toys for his second childhood.

his money talks with a stutter.

he has a physical handicap--he's hard-of-spending.

after shaking your hand he counts his fingers.

he always licks his eye glasses after eating grapefruit.

before counting his money he gets drunk so he'll see double.

even his 8 by 10 photos are only 7 by 9.

he always counts his money in front of a mirror so he won't cheat.

for supper he sits out on the porch and bites his lips.

even if he was in a canoe he wouldn't tip.

for an icepack he only uses one cube.

he keeps a moth as a pet because it only eats holes.

he keeps his piggy bank in a safe deposit box.

he always takes long steps to save on shoe leather.

he even washes his paper plates.

he learned to read Braille so he can read in the dark.

he married a skinny girl so he could get a small wedding ring.

he always wears mittens so money won't slip through his fingers.

he bought his daughter a doll house with a mortgage on it.

he shot his parents so he could go to an orphan's picnic.

he shakes hands with only one finger.

he called up his girl friend to find out which night she was free.

he's waiting for the Encyclopedia Britannica to come out in paperback.

he only goes to drive-in movies in the daytime.

he never enjoys dessert in a restaurant; it's too close to the check.

he only rides the bus during rush hours to get his clothes pressed.

he re-threads his old shoelaces.

he decided to become a divorce lawyer--so he can get a free woman.

he quit playing golf when he lost his ball.

he even stops his watch to save time.

he's tighter than the top olive in the bottle.

it's a sure sign of summer when he throws away his Christmas tree.

he got his money the hoard way.

he's satisfied to let the rest of the world go buy.

in a nightclub, he always sits with his back to the check.

he'd skin a flea for its hide and tallow.

he drinks with impunity--in fact, with anyone who'll buy.

he's so tight, when he winks, his kneecaps move.

he takes corners on two wheels to save his tires.

when he goes on a week's vacation, all he spends is 7 days.

he's first to put his hand in his pocket--and keep it there.

he hasn't ever cut much ice because he's a real cheapskate.

he's one guy who knows how to hold his liquor.

he's always living within his relatives' means.

he throws money around like a man without arms.

the only thing he ever gave away was a secret.

his pockets always outlast the rest of his suit.

every time he shaves he goes on a date to powder himself.

he's the kind of guy who drinks on an empty pocket.

he once gave a penny to a blind man--he needed a pencil.

anyone can borrow his lawn mower--it has a coin slot on it.

he wouldn't even buy happiness if he had to pay a luxury tax on it.

after a blood test he demanded his blood sample back.

when he pays you a compliment, he asks for a receipt.

he orders asparagus and leaves the waiter the tips.

when everyone else gives three cheers he gives two.

he won't even let you borrow trouble.

he had a brass band at his wedding--he put it on his bride's finger.

to save money on his honeymoon--he went on it alone.

his motto is: "Money doesn't grow on sprees."

the way he avoids picking up a check--you have to hand it to him.

he's so tight, he even refuses to perspire freely.

he'd give you the sleeve out of his vest.

he has a greater love for specie than the species.

money flows from him like drops of blood.

he uses the same calendar, year after year.

he believes that charity begins at home--and should stay there.

he won't even tip his hat.

he takes his kid's glasses off when they're not looking at anything.

he's the kind of guy who takes things for gratis.

you can always find him with his best friend--his bankroll.

he has all of his clothes tailored with one-way pockets.

he weighs 185 pounds--155 pounds without his money belt.

he got married in his own backyard so his chickens could get the rice.

he dry cleans Kleenex.

he goes to a drugstore and buys one Kleenex.

he fed his cat salted peanuts so it would drink water instead of milk.

he remarried his wife so he wouldn't have to pay any more alimony.

the only time he puts his hands in his pockets is on very cold days.

the only thing he ever spends on a girl is passion.

last night he took his date out to see a fire.

he takes his electric razor to the office to recharge it.

he would never even pass the buck.

he wouldn't even spend Christmas.

the only thing he ever paid was a compliment.

the only thing he ever took out was his teeth.

he thinks he's treating when he pays his own check.

he took his kids out of school because they had to pay attention.

he won't even give his wife an argument.

when he feels sick he goes to the stationery store and reads get-well cards.

he not only pinches pennies, he pets them.

he not only pinches pennies, he pinches them from children.

the only work he's ever done is to freeload.

he is always forgetting, but never for giving.

he takes for granted that taking's for granted.

he gave his kids violin lessons so they wouldn't have to get haircuts.

he left everything he had to an orphanage--four children.

he's so tight that you can hear him squeak as he goes by.

he wouldn't offer to buy a round of drinks at an A.A. meeting.

His kids don't have his love of money. They don't know what it is.

He knows how to take it easy. Giving is what he finds hard.

The height of folly is to live poor so you can die rich.

Stinginess is just practicing economy before you have to.

Stinginess generally limits its contributions to good advice.

Many a man who gives till it hurts is extremely sensitive to pain.

The closer a man is, the more distant his friends are.

A miser is known by the money he keeps.

A miser is a poor wretch who has nothing but money.

My dentist is so tight that he refused to treat a tooth.

He's got cost-rophobia--that's the fear of parting with money.

Money is the last thing I think of--before going to bed.

My boss is a dollar-a-year man--that's all he ever spends.

I'm a carefree guy--I don't care as long as it's free.

I'm not particular how people treat me--just so long as they do.

I go out with my girl Dutch treat--we dance check to check.

I came to work an hour early and the boss charged me rent.

He's a man of rare gifts--it's rare when he gives one.

I'm a man who gives no quarter--any waiter can testify to that.

Some day a check is going to reach out and grab him.

A cheap date is a guy who walks you to a drive-in.

In December, I start dreaming of a tight Christmas.

I'm a two-fisted spender--both tightly closed.

Stocks

I'd lose more in the stock market if my wife spent less in the supermarket.

I had a bad week. My stocks went down and my weight went up.

Government bonds give you back some of the money you paid in taxes.

A stockbroker is a man who plans how you should spend your money.

The bulls and bears aren't dangerous on Wall Street--it's the bum steers.

Many an innocent lamb is drowned in a stock pool.

I've been burned in the stock market by picking up a hot tip.

Some of the most insecure things in the world are called "securities."

A friend in need is a friend who has been playing the stock market.

I'm a pessimist because of the stocks an optimist sold me.

An ulcer is the extra dividend you get while playing the stock market.

People who play the market are often led astray by false profits.

In stocks a dividend is a certain per cent, per annum, perhaps.

The best time to buy stocks and bonds is in the past.

Wall Street is made up of 3 types of investors: bulls, bears, and asses.

A broker is seldom original, but great with quotations.

Some men operate in the stock market--but most are operated on.

There's many a slip between the stock and the tip.

A broker is a man who runs your fortune into a shoestring.

The only way to beat Wall Street is to beat it.

Even my blue chips are turning green.

Some stocks split--mine just crumble.

I'm doing well in the market this week--my broker is on vacation.

He's called a "Broker" because after you see him, you are.

The money I'm investing in the market today is in fruits and vegetables.

I own several blocks of Penny Stock. Unfortunately I bought it at $5.00.

Never do business with a stock broker who has a blue chip on his shoulder.

I think my broker specializes in stock losses.

I made a killing in the Stock Market. I shot my broker.

I had a seat on the curb but the street cleaner swept me off.

I just wish my blood pressure would go down the way my stock does.

New rules at the Stock Exchange--all the seats have to have seat belts.

I dropped a lot of money at the market today--my bag split.

What's the latest dope on Wall Street? My brother.

The only liquid assets I have are two bottles of muscatel.

I see where 7-Up is down to 3 and a half.

Wall Street is where the day always begins with good buys.

Styles

Today's styles show a woman's good taste--and a lot more.

Style goes out of fashion as soon as most people have one.

Today's bathing suits let a woman slink or swim.

Style is the tax on vanity imposed by the clothing industry.

Every woman who wears a hat has a price on her head.

According to Vogue, next year women will be wearing their legs longer.

I'm curious about where my wife didn't get her new bikini.

Bikini bathing suit: two dots and a dash.

The way I like my wife to dress for me is--fast.

My wife has a generous girdle--it keeps giving and giving.

The best camouflage for bow legs is a plunging neckline.

Today a woman believes in love, honor and display.

My wife's new evening dress is more gone than gown.

After seeing her in slacks I stopped calling my wife "the little woman."

Suspenders are the oldest form of social security.

On Easter you see a lot of women in new hat-rocities.

A woman shows a lot of style if her style shows a lot of woman.

A woman should wear a gown that brings out the bust in her.

Today little girls believe that they should be seen.

Some women look good in slacks, but not the bulk of them.

The trick seems to be to squeeze the most out of a bikini.

To be in style a woman should get along with the bare necessities of life.

The trouble with women's fashions is that you finally get used to them.

Strapless gown: when a woman won't shoulder the responsibility.

My wife will spend $25 on a slip and then be annoyed if it shows.

A girdle holds a girl in when she's going out.

A girdle is another thing that gives 'til it hurts.

Today's skirts are tight, but the women can't kick.

It's high time for the teen-age skirt.

Today's dresses are cut to see level.

Give some women an inch and they'll wear it for a dress.

My wife paid $200 for a gown--but her heart isn't in it.

They call them "unmentionables" because they're nothing to speak of.

when a woman selects an evening gown today she goes practically all out.

A woman who is Vogue on the outside is often vague on the inside.

Today's woman wears so little farmers could hire her to shock their grain.

My daughter wears too much of not enough.

This season peek-a-bosom blouses are in.

Today's teen-agers dress like they are fleeing from a burning building.

Women dress to be seen in the best places.

I like those styles that show more of a lot of woman than a lot of style.

Today women dress as if every day is the dawn of a nude day.

My daughter looks as if her clothes were thrown on her with a pitchfork.

Women over sixty aren't just dressed--they're upholstered.

Today's teen-ager goes to the beach to try to outstrip the other girls.

As I understand it, today's woman should dress like an un-made bed.

My wife dressed like a lady--Lady Godiva.

Success

The secret of success is a secret to most of us.

I'd be quite a success if it weren't for taxes.

The easiest way to get to the top is to go to the bottom of things.

How can you climb to success by remaining on the level?

Ever notice that three-fourths of "grit" is "git"?

Success is the difference between doing good and making good.

Sometimes it's harder to be a success than to become one.

Success gives some people big heads, and others big headaches.

You can't get a square deal in life by going around in circles.

Success is being able to afford what you are spending.

A success is a failure with a fresh coat of paint.

You're successful to the degree to which other people envy you.

Success comes before work only in the dictionary.

All that stands between me and the top of the ladder is the ladder.

Success is the end of hope.

Success is getting up just once more than you fall.

The road to success is paved with good inventions.

A successful man starts at the bottom and wakes up.

Women are rarely as successful as men--they have no wives to advise them.

I have the rare gift of instant decision--that's heading me for bankruptcy.

Success is the ability to get along with some people and ahead of others.

Success can turn a man's head and wring his neck at the same time.

A successful woman is one who finds a successful man.

Success gives a man a big head--also a big headache.

Success is the reward of everyone who looks for trouble.

Success is self-expression at a profit.

I tried for a corner on the market--now I have a market on the corner.

I only lack three things to get to the top: talent, ambition, and initiative.

The road to success is always under construction.

Success is the art of making your mistakes when no one is looking.

If at first you don't succeed--you're running about average.

The secret of success: never let down and never let up.

I know a fellow who climbed the ladder of success wrong by wrong.

Nothing recedes like success.

You can't leave footprints in the sands of time by sitting down.

None of the secrets of success will work unless you do.

Starting from scratch isn't so bad--it's starting without it that's tough.

Triumph is just "umph" added to "try."

Behind most successful men is a public relations man.

When success turns a person's head, he's facing failure.

To be successful don't rust on your laurels.

People sitting on top of the world usually arrived there standing up.

None of the secrets of success will work unless you do.

There's plenty of room at the top, but not much company.

Don't put things off--put them over.

Marriage is usually a howling success after the baby is born.

Success doesn't always go to the head--at times it goes to the mouth.

If hard work is the key to success, I'd rather pick the lock.

Success that goes to a man's head usually pays a very short visit.

You don't have to stay awake nights to succeed--just stay awake days.

A boat that isn't being rocked isn't moving.

Advice on becoming a success: don't take any advice.

The man who is on the ball can roll right along in this life.

Behind every successful man is his golf pro.

Success is determined by determination.

Don't miss the silver lining because you're expecting gold.

You can't climb the ladder of success with cold feet.

Success is still operated on the self-service plan.

Most people quit looking for work when they find a job.

The law of success: more bone in the back and less in the head.

It's no disgrace for a man to fall--to lie there and grunt is.

You can't be a howling success by simply howling.

If you can't win, make the one ahead of you break the record.

Some people are born good and others make good.

The road to success is filled with wives pushing their husbands along.

For success you need luck and pluck--luck in finding someone to pluck.

Anyway, there's a lot of good company at the bottom of the ladder.

Tact

Tact is the ability to arrive at conclusions without expressing them.

Tact is the knack of making a point without making an enemy.

Tact is the ability to change a porcupine into a possum.

Tact is the ability to describe others as they see themselves.

Giving a person a shot in the arm without letting him feel the needle.

Hammering a point home without hitting the other guy on the head.

Putting your best foot forward without stepping on anyone's toes.

The ability to shut your mouth before someone else does.

The art of knowing how far one may go too far.

Tact is the unsaid part of what you think.

Tact is lying about others as you would have them lie about you.

Thinking twice before saying nothing.

Bringing home the bacon without spilling the beans.

You're tactful if you can keep a civil tongue in your cheek.

Juggling a hot potato long enough for it to become a cold issue.

Remember, you can't bend a nail by hitting it squarely on the head.

Tact is social lying.

Some people are tactful; others tell the truth.

Tactless people suffer from chronic indiscretion.

Tact is the art of letting someone else have your way.

A tactful person never heard that old joke before.

Tact is the art of dressing the bare facts and draping the naked truth.

When people lie about a matter of act, it's generally a matter of tact.

People with tact have less to retract.

Tact is not opening your mouth wide enough to put your foot in.

The art of saying the right thing while thinking the wrong thing.

The ability to see others as they see themselves.

Tact is praising married life but remaining single.

The ability to cut someone's throat without their noticing it.

Tact is when you're sure you're right, but still ask your wife.

Talking

To get a word in after you're married, marry a woman who stutters.

I don't like people to talk while I'm interrupting.

A gum chewer's mouth goes without saying.

Most after dinner speakers are men. Women can't wait that long.

When all is said and done--too many people just keep on talking.

My wife is outspoken--but not by many.

Back talk is more honest than behind-the-back talk.

First we teach a child to talk, then we spank him for not keeping quiet.

The mayonnaise said to the refrigerator, "Close the door, I'm dressing."

Libel is the kind of talk that's not cheap.

I acquired a huge vocabulary by marrying it.

A woman may be taken for granted, but she never goes without saying.

A word to the wise interrupts a monologue.

A man of few words generally keeps them mighty busy.

My wife is miserable when she has no troubles to speak of.

Another of life's problems is how to keep ignorant people from talking.

Watching a three-ring circus is like listening to one woman talk.

Close a woman's mouth and she'll talk through her nose.

My wife believes in free speech--she is certainly free enough with hers.

There is a distinction between free speech and cheap talk.

My wife is breathtaking. Every hour she stops talking and takes a breath.

After all is said and done, more is said than done.

My wife has a chronic speech impediment--palpitation of the tongue.

My wife never puts off till tomorrow what she can say today.

To say the right thing at the right time, keep still most of the time.

My wife has a voice that's very hard to extinguish over the telephone.

What this country needs is not more fast readers, but less fast talkers.

It takes my boss an hour to tell you he's a man of few words.

Talk is cheap, but not when money does the talking.

I got a gliberal education listening to my mother-in-law.

When women speak of love, how they love to speak!

People with double chins speak twice as much.

Money talks, but it doesn't always speak when spoken to.

Where my wife is concerned, one word leads to another ten thousand.

Telling all you know is as bad as believing all you hear.

You can count on my mother-in-law to respond to any wordy cause.

My mother-in-law would be enormously improved by laryngitis.

The two main sins of conversation are talkativeness and silence.

People who shoot off their mouths never seem to run out of ammunition.

At the end of the day I'm so tired I can hardly keep my mouth open.

My wife's tongue has become part of her autonomous nervous system.

Some people's talk is small talk no matter what the subject is.

Taxes

A taxpayer is a person who has the government on his payroll.

Considering our taxes it can hardly be called, "Cheap Politics."

Taxes may be staggering, but they never go down.

One thing that keeps a man from holding his own is the I.R.S.

Eventually we'll all make our living by collecting taxes from each other.

Aftar paying my taxes, I'm income-pooped!

After paying my taxes I feel that all my success I owe to Uncle Sam.

The tax collector is a man looking for untold wealth.

Any man who doesn't complain about taxes is either very rich or very poor.

April 15th has come and gone--and so has my money.

A tax on liquor is the only one which provides its own anesthetic.

With my latest raise, I can now afford to pay last year's taxes.

Want to avoid paying income tax? Don't work.

The I.R.S. must love poor people--it's creating so many of them.

About the time a man is cured of swearing, it's income tax time again.

An honest taxpayer is one who makes the supreme sacrifice.

Instant tax: Instant poverty.

With today's taxes, you work like a dog to live like a dog.

The only difference between death and taxes is: death is often painless.

Everything I have I owe--to the I.R.S.

Now they have a tax on funerals--I'll die before I'll pay that!

After paying my taxes all I have left is a deficit.

Taxes are what you have to pay for doing well.

I'm putting all my money in taxes--the only thing sure to go up.

I pay income tax like a stripper--I take off as much as the law allows.

It's hard to believe that America was founded to avoid taxes.

Nobody hits his taxes when they're down.

Taxes defy the law of gravitation.

Why not call them income tax "blankety-blanks"?

Not only are the tax forms shorter this year--but so is my income.

I have no trouble filing my income tax--but I have trouble paying it.

I just send my income to Washington--who can afford taxes?

Great simile: She looks as good as an Income Tax refund.

One thing I found out--you can't pay your income tax with trading stamps.

The I.R.S. has made more liars out of the American people than golf has.

The I.R.S. was very nice to me this year--they let me keep my mother.

I can't seem to support a wife and the government on my income.

Today's take-home pay is hardly worth the trip.

Many an income tax report is muffled.

Death and taxes are inevitable, but death isn't a repeater.

What I'd like to see in Congress is a taxpayers' bloc.

Nobody ever proposes a bonus--or a rebate--for the taxpayer.

The general sure to survive a war is General Taxation.

The three R's of the I.R.S.: This is ours, that is ours, everything is ours.

When your ship finally does come in--the government docks it.

A dime is a dollar with all the taxes taken out.

Two classes of people don't like to pay taxes: men and women.

The way taxes are today, you may as well marry for love.

The I.R.S. knows what to give the man who has everything--an audit.

Earning money would be a pleasure--if it wasn't so taxing.

Every child is as good as gold--at least at income tax time.

After paying your income tax you know how a cow feels after milking.

The government should be glad the taxpayers have what it takes.

Congress passes bills--the taxpayers pay them.

You've got to hand it to the I.R.S.--they'll get it anyway.

A tax cut is the kindest cut of all.

If it were only as easy for the people to raise taxes as it is for Congress.

The greatest invention of the age would be a computerized taxpayer.

Save your pennies, the dollars go to the I.R.S.

If crime could be taxed, there would be no need for other taxes.

The I.R.S. not only believes what it is told, but twice as much.

There's no such thing as a small taxpayer.

There are no atheists in the waiting room of the I.R.S.

Taxation without representation was tyranny, but it was a lot cheaper.

Providence giveth and the income tax taketh away.

Time, tide and the tax collector wait for no man.

April 15th is when the government spring-cleans your wallet.

The income tax form is the only blank that's loaded.

Income tax forms are generally filed, but more often chiseled.

Taxes are a form of Capitol punishment.

Build a better mousetrap and the I.R.S. will beat a path to your door.

April 15th: when millions of Americans test their powers of deduction.

Television

On television the happy ending is always preceded by a bad commercial.

Well folks, I finally got a TV program--I cut it out of a newspaper.

Television has made a semi-circle out of the family circle.

Television has not only replaced radio, but homework, too.

On television the jokes last longer than the comics.

Television helps you meet new people--especially repairmen.

The evil that men do lives after them--especially when they are TV reruns.

It's a family show--more families are started during that show.

Television stimulates conversation, but only when the set breaks down.

We've got pay TV at our house--I just got the bill from the repairman.

Giant screen television makes a bad program much worse.

TV is in its infancy--which is why we have to change it so often.

Television does away with a lot of useless conversation.

If television programs don't improve, I may go back to listening to my wife.

The more you see of television, the more you like it less.

Television's crime shows are often worse than the crimes they portray.

I'm in favor of pay television. We should get paid to watch some shows.

Television goes in for movies that are not worth going out to see.

Television show for nudists: "Who Shed That?"

Television is still in its infancy. People keep changing channels.

Television quiz show: reward for everyone but the audience.

Television will never replace the old fashioned keyhole.

A good TV mystery is one where it's hard to detect the sponsor.

We now interrupt the commercial to bring you a television program.

Television proves that things are as bad as they sound.

TV spectacular: the bill you get from the repairman.

Whatever is not worth saying is sung as a television commercial.

Television is where old movies go to die.

Just watching westerns on television has given me saddle sores.

A television commercial is the Pause That Depresses.

Television is summer stock in an iron lung.

Seeing is believing, but not when you're looking at a TV commercial.

Television: vidiot's delight.

Television gives you nothing to do when you're not doing anything.

TV commercials wouldn't be so bad if they weren't so often.

Television is where the law of the jingle prevails.

To get on television a girl must know somebody or have some body.

"The good die young" does not refer to television jokes.

Television proves your nose was right in its opinion of radio.

Have you noticed that TV families never watch television?

The only thing we can definitely get on our TV set is dust.

Our TV repairman is so fast, he fixed my set before he could say $75.

I'm now putting a kid through college--my TV repairman's son.

TV cowboy shows unfortunately stick to their guns.

If your minds don't run in the same channel--get two TV sets.

To talk to friends who own TV sets, you have to go through channels.

Television's broadening influence comes more from sit than set.

Television gives you a dim view of life.

Television opens many doors--mostly on refrigerators.

Television is a kind of smog with knobs.

My TV set gives me great pleasure. It keeps my wife quiet all evening.

Before television nobody knew what stomach trouble looked like.

Television is the triumph of machinery over people.

TV is true to life--you can rarely get what you want when you want it.

Television has become the longest amateur night in history.

Television is where all the little movies go when they are bad.

My television set has only two controls: my wife and my child.

I was never on television, but I was on radar twice on the Freeway.

I met my repairman at the ballpark. His TV set must be broken, too.

Television is wonderful. We should all be proud to go blind watching it.

Before you retire, take a week off and watch daytime television.

I never believed in ghosts, then I bought my new television set.

We all have to go sometime--usually during commercials.

The trouble with portable television is you can take it with you.

No one ever got sore eyes from listening to radio.

Television commercials are the last refuge of optimism in a world of gloom.

One quick way to get a doctor is to turn on the TV set.

The trouble with the late show is that it's not late enough.

Television is eyestrain with knobs.

There's a lot of money to be made in television--ask any repairman.

The good things on television last night were the vase and the clock.

Television's biggest problem is killing time between commercials.

Like your wife, television is home and it's ree.

Television is the greatest aid to sleep since darkness.

Television commercials are not so bad, but, oh, so often!

Time

Time heals all things--except a leaky radiator.

Take time at railroad crossings--or take eternity.

Time is the only money that cannot be counterfeited.

Time flies but during working hours it bucks head winds.

The two kinds of time are standard and wristwatch.

Perfect timing: turn the hot and cold faucets on together.

Every time I ask what time it is I get a different answer.

An alarm clock is a device to scare the daylights out of you.

Time may be a great healer, but it's no beauty specialist.

An alarm clock enables a man to rise in the world.

A clock-watcher usually remains one of the hands.

No sooner does a watch stop than it ceases to mark time.

An alarm clock is a non-alcoholic eye opener.

The only thing that comes to him who waits is whiskers.

An alarm clock is a device to wake adults who have no babies.

Just when you think tomorrow will never come, it's yesterday.

You can't make footprints in the sands of time sitting down.

Time is the arbitrary division of eternity.

Every time history repeats itself the price goes up.

Time is the stuff between paydays.

The calendar is what a speaker goes by if he forgets his watch.

Time is a great artist but women don't like its line work.

In two days, tomorrow will be yesterday.

My clock runs well--it does an hour in forty-five minutes.

Lost time is never found.

I threw the clock out the window so I could see time fly.

The best way to save daylight is to use it.

Eight hours for sleep, eight for work, and eight to spend the money.

Time wounds all heels.

Time remains the champion flyer of them all.

Kissing doesn't shorten life--it makes the time pass quicker.

I spent a year in Philadelphia, one Sunday.

A woman on time is one in nine.

A committee is a body that keeps minutes and wastes hours.

I wonder how much time we lose by being on time?

The greatest reformer of them all is Father Time.

Times are not as bad as they seem--they couldn't be.

Now is the time for all good men to come to.

If you kill time you'll eventually mourn the corpse.

Time is not gallant--it tells on a woman.

Time is money, except when it's on your own time.

There is no time like the present--for those who like to worry.

Time flies with love--and love flies with time.

Time is money--especially overtime.

Time flies because there are so many people trying to kill it.

Time waits for no man--it is too busy waiting for woman.

Travel

A short road is a road on which you can't find anybody to ask where you are.

I took one of those "all-expense tours" and that's just what it was.

To feel at home, stay at home.

Travel brings out anything in a man--especially sea travel.

Half a loaf is better than no vacation at all.

Travel broadens people--it also flattens them.

Seasickness is when you travel across the ocean by rail.

Things are so tough in Miami, even the holdup-men are taking I.O.U.'s.

A map is a piece of paper to help you get lost.

This season, in California, they use anti-freeze for sun tan lotion.

I came to see her off, and she certainly was.

A traveler is a person who returns with brag and baggage.

Show me a travel folder, and I'll show you a trip tease.

The English drive on the left side of the road--just like in California.

Distance lends enchantment--but not when you're out of gas.

Our flight was so rough, they poured the food directly into the airsick bag.

Travel broadens people, but not during the rush hours on the subway.

I made myself understood in Paris--I pointed to the labels.

New York is a fine place to visit if you're flying over it in a plane.

Travel brings something to your life you never had before: poverty!

In France, Playboy Magazine is referred to as the Ladies' Home Journal.

I learned French in six easy liaisons.

When I looked at my passport photo I realized I needed the trip.

It's so cold in Alaska that the Eskimos go to Siberia for the winter.

I've seen more strange places than a Swedish cameraman.

Travel develops a man's mind, especially his imagination.

The best travel slogan is: Let yourself go.

Travel is educational--it teaches you how to spend money in a hurry.

Travel is a pleasure, and space travel is out of this world.

You can't take it with you, but don't try to travel without it.

Sign in travel agent's window: Why don't you go away?

The best place on a ship for a hang-over is the rail.

A tourist first travels to learn, and then learns to travel.

My mother really travels. She's been in Paris more than April.

Tourists are alike: they all want to go places where there are no tourists.

I have a set of matched luggage--two shopping bags from the supermarket.

I came to see her off, and she certainly was.

Travel broadens one, so do too many desserts.

In Alaska, many are cold, but few are frozen.

The one crop in Europe that is harvested green is the tourist crop.

Europe is great! If you ever go there don't miss it!

I'd like to go where the hand of man has never set foot.

Truth

Figures don't lie, but girdles condense the truth.

Not a true word is spoken through false teeth.

A half-truth is seldom the better half.

Truth is stranger than fiction--and also more decent.

Statistics may be made to prove aything--even the truth.

A legend is a lie that has attained the dignity of age.

The truth never hurts unless it ought to.

If you stop telling lies about me, I'll stop telling the truth about you.

Truth is stranger than fiction.

Your mirror doesn't lie to you--why should I?

The truth will ouch.

Honest people tell the truth, tactless people tell the whole truth.

Always tell the truth--if you want to make trouble.

A gentleman would never tell the naked truth in the presence of ladies.

Never tell the truth to people who don't deserve it.

I don't mind the lies told about me; what worries me is the truth.

The trouble with stretching the truth is that it's apt to snap back.

The truth is mighty and will prevail, but it's mighty hard to find it.

Truth is merely a lazy expedient of the imagination.

Truth is even stranger than fish stories.

The pure and simple truth is rarely pure and never simple.

Truth may be stranger than fiction but it will never sell as well.

Truth is stranger than fiction, but not so popular.

Rumors are never equal to the truth.

A good mirror doesn't lie; a reflection on us all.

Some people are just too modest to speak the naked truth.

Weather

It was so hot, a coyote was chasing a rabbit--and they were both walking.

It was so cold, I had to use an icepick to take off my clothes.

Weather forecasting is witchcraft by bureaucracy.

Cold? When I opened my closet my spring coat was wearing my overcoat.

The weather is today's climate.

If a girl sneezes, she's catching cold; if she yawns, she's getting cold.

Climate is permanent weather.

It was so cold in Alaska, the Eskimos went to Siberia for the winter.

I can make it rain anytime. All I do is wash my car.

Many are cold, but few are frozen.

"Unsettled" covers a multitude of weather possibilities.

It was so cold, the candle froze and we couldn't blow it out.

To keep the barometer from falling--use a big nail.

I was freezing to death, but I didn't care--I look good in blue.

Weather report: Strong winds, followed by high skirts, followed by me.

It was so cold, I was wearing my toupee upside down.

They ought to develop a clearing-house for the weather.

Cold? I was wearing long underwear under my Bermuda shorts.

What a sizzler! The thermometer is up in the Hades.

The early bird catches a cold.

Rheumatism was nature's first effort to establish a weather bureau.

It was so cold, we even welcomed a hotfoot.

The weatherman is a seer who is always right, except for his timing.

Cold? My color television set turned blue.

New York has a secret weapon against snow--July.

There are five kinds of weather: spring, summer, fall, winter, and unusual.

Cold? We had to put alcohol in the whiskey to keep it from freezing.

If it weren't for the sun, the rain would never be mist.

It was so cold, my wife wore a mink girdle.

Kids like snow, but adults prefer rain because it's self-shoveling.

It was so cold, my grandfather's tooth was chattering.

April showers bring May flowers, unless you're an amateur gardener.

Cold? Even the icicles were frozen stiff.

Snow is beautiful--when you're watching the other fellow shovel it.

Cold? I wore my pants with the cuffs inside.

No matter how bad the weather is, it's always better than none.

Cold? I bought an electric blanket with long sleeves.

The man who makes hay while the sun shines ends up with sunstroke.

In Florida they're selling frozen orange juice right off the trees.

When the weather lacks dryness you first feel it in your sinus.

It was so cold in my house, even the janitor was banging on the pipes.

It never rains but it pours, especially on someone without an umbrella.

I was born in the winter, a penguin brought me instead of a stork.

Bad weather always looks worse through a window.

It was so cold, the hens were laying eggs from a standing position.

The weather in Florida isn't unusual; it's unbelievable.

Nothing is as cold as a woman who has been refused a mink coat.

It was so cold I was looking for a girl with a high fever for a roommate.

If you save up for a rainy day in Florida, you're considered a traitor.

It was a perfect marriage--he was cold and she was frigid.

It was so hot, the cows were giving evaporated milk.

It was so hot we had to open the window to see the fire escape.

My wife likes it cold--without the goose-pimples she's have no figure at all.

I've been sleeping with the air-conditioner under my pillow.

I can't understand why it's still raining--the weekend is over.

My wife is very neat. When it rains we have wall-to-wall newspapers.

The wind was so strong, it blew out three fuses.

We really don't need calendars--when it rains it's Sunday.

I blew into town yesterday--strong wind.

Rain makes the flowers grow, and taxis disappear.

A weatherman is a man who can look into a girl's eye and tell whether.

You only enjoy walking in the rain if you don't have to.

In getting a suntan, ignorance is blister.

The weather has been so changeable lately, I don't know what to hock.

It was so hot in the shade that I decided to stay in the sun.

Wives

My wife was in the Olympics. She was a javelin catcher.

I just discovered a new birth control device. My wife takes off her makeup.

My wife's meals are putting color in my face--purple.

When our home burned down, it was the first time the food was hot.

The only time I find my wife entertaining is when I come home unexpectedly.

I asked her for her hand and it's been in my pocket ever since.

I wouldn't object to my wife having the last word--if she'd only get to it.

I stopped believing in dreams when I married one.

Women are good losers, especially when it comes to husbands.

My wife may not be a magician, but she can turn anything into an argument.

The hand that socks the husband rules the checkbook.

Don't speak of your private ailment in public; she might hear you.

The only thing my wife doesn't know is why she married me.

I know we're going to be happy. She adores me and so do I.

Every wife leads a double life--her husband's and her own.

She finally got him--hook, line and stinker.

My wife just won the title of Miss Charge Account.

My wife looks her best in the same old thing--the dark.

I learned about women the hard way--I married one.

A word to the wife is sucfficient, provided that word is "yes."

When my wife goes up in the air she always lands on me.

If at first you don't succeed, cry, cry again.

I never kept any secrets from my wife, even when I tried.

I saved her from drowning, and she married me. That's gratitude?

He who marries a chicken gets henpecked.

I told my wife who the boss is. I said: "You're the boss."

She's lonesome for me, especially when I'm not home.

There's one habit I'd like to break my wife of--breathing.

Just when I make both ends meet, my wife moves the ends.

If your wife doesn't treat you as she should--be thankful.

For years my wife and I have had words--hers--always.

I wish my wife would learn to complain in monosyllables.

Here's a profound thought: women make the best wives.

Try praising your wife, even if at first it frightens her.

A wise husband talks in his wife's sleep.

Every time I argue with my wife, words flail me.

It only takes one to make an argument--if she's your wife.

A wife is a former sweetheart.

A wife is a dish jockey.

A wife is often the gun you didn't know was loaded.

An onion, or a husband, can make any woman weep.

My wife can be sweet--when she wants.

I have the best wife in the country. Sometimes I wish she'd stay there.

He has an impediment in his speech--his wife.

I lost my voice on our wedding day.

Midwife: the second wife of a man who marries three times.

Many a man lives by the sweat of his frau.

The ideal wife grows dearer, but not more expensive.

I have a way with my wife, but it's seldom my own.

My wife never throws a fit--unless I'm around to catch it.

A horse is usually a horse; but a wife can also be a nag.

If there is anything my wife doesn't know, she imagines it.

I always meet misfortune like a man; I blame it on my wife.

The only time my wife stops talking is when her mother starts.

His wife loves him for what he is--rich.

When my wife was pregnant she asked me to bear with her.

My wife runs up expenses so fast it leaves me breathless.

Before we were married she was my secretary; now she's the treasurer.

My wife is the salt of the earth--I just wish I could shake her.

My wife's not a cook--she's an arsonist.

I should've known how jealous my wife is--she had male bridesmaids.

We've been married for ten years, and I love her still.

I'm leaving my wife because of another woman--her mother.

I carry pictures of our children--and a sound track of my wife.

There's nothing wrong with my wife that a miracle won't cure.

Wives are people who feel that they don't dance enough.

It's better to have your wife with you than after you.

My wife is like a fisherman: she thinks the best ones got away.

It's easier to procure a wife than to cure one.

Half the world doesn't konw how his better half lives.

A nag never seems to have enough horse sense to bridle her tongue.

When a wife reigns, she often storms.

The President met my wife--and declared my home a disaster area.

A wife's strong will always dominates over her husband's weak won't.

My wife lost her glasses. She spent twenty minutes nagging a coat rack.

My wife isn't talking to me--and I'm in no mood to interrupt her.

Every morning I wake up with this nagging headache--my wife.

Wives don't get ulcers--they're just carriers.

Wife-swapping is the suburbs' answer to Bingo.

I would never buy an encyclopedia. My wife knows everything.

I'll never forget our wedding. I've tried to but my wife won't let me.

I can't ask for a better wife--but I'd sure like to.

Talk about henpecked! He's still taking orders from his first wife.

My wife doesn't treat me the way she should--and I'm thankful!

My wife missed her nap today. She slept right through it.

My wife hasn't been feeling well. Something she agreed with is eating her.

A word to the wife is sufficient--to start a fight.

My wife's so extravagant, last week she tipped at a toll booth.

When it comes to housekeeping, my wife likes to do nothing better.

Some wives can cook, but don't. My wife can't cook, but does.

My wife has no minor voices.

I'm the third man she's led to the halter.

I'm happy when my wife is in bed, safe and soundless.

My wife can dish it out, but she can't cook it.

My wife is very gifted--I have the bills to prove it.

My wife's upkeep will be my downfall.

She can bring more bills into the house than a Congressman.

Without my wife I'd never be what I am today--broke.

Sex in marriage isn't everything, but it comes awfully close.

I married my wife for better or for worse, but not for banksuptcy.

My wife is beginning to understand me, which really has me worried.

This is our third anniversary. The third week in a row we haven't had sex.

Work

It's better to wear out than to rust out.

All work and no play makes jack for your psychiatrist.

Work is the only thing that keeps some men from a job.

No man goes before his time--unless the boss has left early.

The reason I work so hard is that I'm too nervous to steal.

Our maid's idea of work is to sweep the room with a glance.

Be careful that you don't garden from daybreak to back-break.

I've been working myself to death to buy labor-saving devices.

An assistant is a fellow who can't get off.

Ideas won't work unless you do.

Some people get results--others get consequences.

I've handled some pretty big jobs. I used to house-break elephants.

Nothing makes a man work like being "debt propelled."

I believe in putting off work until Labor Day.

I'm interested in the higher things in life--like wages.

In the Spring a young man's fancy lightly turns from thoughts of work.

The average American works himself to death trying to get ready to live.

I've always felt that work is a form of nervousness.

Work may be a tonic, but I haven't found it a habit-forming drug.

A working girl is one who quit her job to get married.

It takes hard work to make an easy living.

I like the job; it's the work I hate.

Today, if you want to relax you really have to work at it.

When it comes to work, there are many who will stop at nothing.

Who says nothing is impossible? I've been doing nothing for years.

Work is all right if it doesn't take up too much of your spare time.

I never worked a day in my life. I'm a night watchman.

I was a white collar worker until the collar got dirty.

I may get to work late, but I make up for it by leaving early.

I won't let my wife work--I'm afraid to stay home alone.

The only thing you can get without working is hungry.

It takes me an hour to get to work--after I get there.

I don't like work even when someone else does it.

You can work yourself to death by burying yourself in your work.

Men who lead double lives never do the work of two.

Hard work never hurt anyone who hired someone else to do it.

There's nothing like hard work--thank heavens!

I work like a horse, but only when my boss rides me.

Worry kills more people than work, because more people worry than work.

Work is the easiest way man has ever invented to escape boredom.

Fellows who roll up their sleeves seldom lose their shirts.

Work is good for you--it's labor that kills.

My greatest pleasure in life is having lots to do, and not doing it.

Like every man of sense and good feeling, I hate work.

Two can live as cheaply as one--if both work.

All work and no play makes Jack a big tax bill.

Busy souls have no time to be busybodies.

Almost any system of government will work if the people will.

If you are too busy to laugh, you are too busy.